W9-BTR-887

THE PSYCHOLOGY OF THE INTERNET

THE PSYCHOLOGY
OF THE INTERNET

PATRICIA WALLACE

CAMBRIDGE
UNIVERSITY PRESS

PUBLISHED BY THE PRESS SYNDICATE OF THE UNIVERSITY OF CAMBRIDGE
The Pitt Building, Trumpington Street, Cambridge, United Kingdom

CAMBRIDGE UNIVERSITY PRESS
The Edinburgh Building, Cambridge CB2 2RU, UK
40 West 20th Street, New York, NY 10011–4211, USA
10 Stamford Road, Oakleigh, VIC 3166, Australia
Ruiz de Alarcón 13, 28014 Madrid, Spain
Dock House, The Waterfront, Cape Town 8001, South Africa

http://www.cambridge.org

First published 1999
First paperback printing 2001

Printed in the United States of America

Typefaces Stone Serif 9.25/13 pt and Futura   *System* Quark XPress™   [HT]

A catalogue record for this book is available from the British Library

Library of Congress Cataloguing-in-Publication Data

Wallace, Patricia M.
    The psychology of the Internet/Patricia M. Wallace
        p. cm.
    Includes biographical references
    ISBN   0 521 63204 3   (hardcover)
    ISBN   0 521 79709 8   (paperback)
        I. Communication – Psychological aspects. 2. Internet (Computer network) –
    Psychological aspects. 3. Computer networks – Psychological aspects. I. Title.
    BF637.C45W26   1999
    025.04′01′9 – dc21   99-12696

ISBN   0 521 63204 3   hardback
ISBN   0 521 79709 8   paperback

For Julian and Callie, my *real life* family.

CONTENTS

1 THE INTERNET IN A PSYCHOLOGICAL CONTEXT   1
   Environments of the Internet: A Taxonomy   4
   Language on the Net   9
   Empowering Internet Users   12

**2 YOUR ONLINE PERSONA: THE PSYCHOLOGY OF
   IMPRESSION FORMATION**   14
   Warm and Cold Impressions   15
   The Chilly Internet   15
   The Socioemotional Thaw   18
   Impression Formation Shortcuts   19
   Person Types and Categories   21
   Beyond Age and Gender   24
   Social Cognition and Categories   25
   The Rhythms of Impression Formation   26
   Online, Onstage: Impression Management
      on the Internet   28
   Online Self-Descriptions   30
   The Home Page Advantage   31
   Focus on Self   34
   Making that Keyboard Work Harder   36

3 ONLINE MASKS AND MASQUERADES   38
   The Origins of Role Play   40
   Leakage on the Internet   41
   Role Play Danger Areas   44
   Identity Experiments in the Internet Laboratory   47

The Dupes in the Experiment   49
Detecting Deceit, Offline and On   50
Deceit and Suspicion: Dance Partners   51
Pros and Cons of the Internet's Identity Lab   53

4 GROUP DYNAMICS IN CYBERSPACE   55
"Groupness"   55
Conformity   59
Conforming on the Net   62
The Sign on the Door   64
The Arched Brow   66
In Search of the Leviathan   69
Experimenting with the Leviathan On a Social MUD   71
Group Polarization   73
Polarization on the Net   76
Finding Others of Like Mind   79
Virtual Work Groups   80
The Biased Dicussion in Online Workgroups   81
Minority Opinions in Online Workgroups   82
Workgroups and Electronic Brainstorming   83
Developing Trust in Virtual Teams   84

5 INTERGROUP CONFLICT AND COOPERATION   88
The Robbers Cave Experiments   89
Intergroup Rivalries on the Internet Games   91
Player Types and Motivations   96
Ingroups on the Internet   99
"Expert-ism"   101
Global Villagers: Are We a Group?   103
Internet Group Power   105

**6 FLAMING AND FIGHTING: THE PSYCHOLOGY OF
AGGRESSION ON THE NET**   110
Born to Fight?   111
Frustration and Aggression   112
The World Wide Wait   113
The Hair Trigger   116
Retaliation   117
In the Eye of the Beholder: When Is a Flame a Flame?   119
Lab and Field Studies of Flaming   120
Reproaches   122

Over-Retaliation 123
Anonymity and Physical Distance 124
The #$@@!!!& Software 127
Catharsis: Is Letting Off Steam Good for You? 129
Aggression: Internet Style 130

7 **LIKING AND LOVING ON THE NET: THE PSYCHOLOGY OF INTERPERSONAL ATTRACTION** 133
Who Makes Friends Online? 134
The Nature of Online Relationships 135
The Magnet of Physical Attractiveness 136
Attractiveness in the Dark 138
Proximity: Who's Next Door on the Net? 139
Birds of a Feather, Flocking on the Internet 141
Complementary Relationships 143
The "You Like Me, I Like You, You Like Me More" Spiral 144
When the Spiral Spins Down 145
Humor 147
Self-Disclosure 150
Enhancing Real Life Romance on the Internet 151
Virtual Passion 152
Roses on the Net 155

8 **PSYCHOLOGICAL ASPECTS OF INTERNET PORNOGRAPHY** 157
Sensationalizing Cyberporn 157
But What Is Really Out There? 159
Psychological Aspects of Pornography 161
Aggressive and Violent Pornography 163
Views From the Internet 165
Checking IDs 167
How Much Should We Worry? 169

9 **THE INTERNET AS A TIME SINK** 171
Locus of Control 173
Section 2 175
The Online Auction 177
The Internet's Addictive Properties 178
What Is So Compelling About the Internet? 181
The Psychology of Addiction in Synchronous
  Psychological Spaces 182

Life at the Palace   185
Newbie Disease?   186
Naming the Affliction: Addiction? Overuse?
   Self-Indulgence?   188

10 ALTRUISM ON THE NET: THE PSYCHOLOGY OF HELPING   190
Random Acts of Kindness: Internet Style   190
By the Numbers   192
Let Someone Else Take Care of It   194
Numbers on the Net   195
Who Helps Whom?   198
People Like Us   200
Asking For Help on the Net   201
The Internet's Support Networks   204
Support For Stigmatized Groups   205
How May I Help You?   206

11 GENDER ISSUES ON THE NET   208
Male and Female: Not Opposite Sexes   208
Gender and Language   210
Language and Power   211
Interaction Styles   212
The Leap to Cyberspace: Are We Typing
   in Pink and Blue?   214
Adapting to the Male Majority   217
Stereotypes and Perceptions   218
The New Battlefield for the War Between the Sexes   219
Women-Only and Men-Only Groups   222
Gender IDs in the Games   224
A Hostile World for Women   225
Legal Aspects of Online Harassment and Threats   227
The Mr.Bungle Affair   230
Gender Issues on the Frontier   232

12 NURTURING LIFE ON THE INTERNET   233
Technological Determinism Revisited   234
A Perfect Place For Conspiracies   236
The Metadiscussion   237
Anonymity and Accountability   239
The Tragedy of the Electronic Commons   242

Trust and Grassroots E-Commerce   244
Encouraging Critical Thinking   245
Providing Guidance   246
Rewards on the Internet   249
Psychology of the Internet: The Next Generation   251

Index   257

PREFACE TO THE PAPERBACK EDITION

"WHAT HATH GOD WROUGHT" were the words transmitted in 1844 to officially inaugurate the telegraph line running from the Supreme Court chamber in Washington to a platform 15 miles outside of Baltimore. Today's Internet generates some of the same debates that the "Victorian Internet" did more than a century and a half ago, in which the promise and perils of an astonishingly capable network are linked to the ways in which we behave when we use it. The goal of telegraph inventors was to transmit intelligence instantaneously across any distance, but for better or worse, the technology quickly became involved in all kinds of human activities, from clandestine romances to stock manipulation schemes.[1] So it is with the Internet.

This book, *The Psychology of the Internet,* examines how we behave when we act and interact online, and why the characteristics of the medium can affect our behavior in surprising and sometimes troubling ways. After the first publication in 1999, the Y2K doomsayers were proven wrong, and for the most part, the world's computer infrastructure survived the transition easily. Technically, the Internet had very little trouble with the cutover, but much has happened recently that highlights the growing importance of the psychological aspects of this Internet environment.

The explosive growth in the number of people online continued, and by mid-2000 estimates topped 350 million. The breathtaking growth was not only in the number of users, however. It was in the expansion of the net's role and capabilities, driven especially by commercial interests and innovations in Internet technologies. These three factors – the growth in

---

[1] Standage, T. (1998). *The Victorian Internet.* New York: Berkley Books.

numbers, the rise of e-commerce, and the avalanche in netcentric technologies – are combining to transform the Internet environment and its effects on human behavior. We are confronting significant new issues as a result, and though some of them have been around for a long time, the change in scope, scale and speed has catapulted them to the headlines and affected the way people behave when they log on.

One important example involves heightened concerns about privacy, an issue that has been at or near the top of the list for Internet users. The Victorians were also concerned about privacy and used innumerable ciphers to protect messages transmitted via telegraph. For Internet users, though, the scope of the privacy issue goes well beyond encryption.

ONLINE CUSTOMER PROFILING AND PRIVACY

The dramatic rise in commercial activity on the net, combined with some remarkable innovations in Internet technologies, has generated considerable discussion and thought about privacy. Software is widely available to allow Web site hosts to gather information about site visitors and track their behavior – even if they don't buy anything and provide their name, credit card number, and billing address. The growing stockpile of electronic data about the way humans behave online can, in principle, be explored with data mining techniques to provide what corporations hope will become useful psychographic profiles.

Corporations defend the practice of online customer profiling, citing the value of tailored marketing to both company and consumer. A corporation that knows more about you when you drop into the Web site can dynamically present advertisements, coupons, discounts, and other kinds of promotions, focusing on products and services in which you'd be more interested. For the consumer, the use of profiling could reduce the flood of commercial messages, especially about products of little interest, and present special bargains. Targeted marketing did not arrive with the Internet, of course, but the new capabilities have vastly expanded possibilities for profiling, and for collecting and reselling very detailed information about individuals that they might have preferred to keep private.

Doubleclick's troubles illustrate how technology-enabled leaps in the scale and scope of targeted marketing heightened everyone's awareness of Internet-related privacy issues. The online advertising company places invisible images measuring just one square pixel on the sites of its business partners, and each time a person visits any of those sites, Doubleclick's software code leaves a cookie on the visitor's hard drive, often without the person's knowledge or permission. This technique allows the company to collect information about people *across* Web sites, not just from the behavior they displayed when they visited a single site. Doubleclick acquired Abacus Direct, a national marketing database with details of mail-order catalog purchases from 88 million households. They planned to combine the data contained in it with the information from the online profiling activities, a merger that arguably would have created the most detailed database in existence about the activities of individual consumers. The company dropped the plan in 2000 after a storm of protest and a significant drop in its stock price.

Amazon.com experienced another wave of online consumer protest when they began testing "dynamic pricing." It is very easy to change product prices on the net, and an online retailer can program various algorithms to adjust prices based on any number of factors, from customers' zip codes to time of day. Amazon, however, has an enormous stockpile of information about the buying habits of their 23 million customers and can potentially use their demographic and psychographic profiles to assess factors like ability to pay, loyalty, or level of interest in specific products, and charge accordingly. One customer found he could get a lower price from Amazon for a particular DVD when he stripped his own computer of the cookies that identified him as an Amazon customer. He shared his outrage about such practices on the net, and the company immediately backed off. As I discuss in Chapter 5, Internet-based community protests and group power can be a formidable force.

"Spyware" presents yet another opportunity for collecting information about behavior surreptitiously and using it in ways that are very troubling to consumers. This category covers programs installed on hard drives without the individual's knowledge, often through downloads or through installation of purchased products, that can use the person's Internet connection to "phone home" and send information from the person's computer to the company's Web site. A father in Seal Beach, California, for example, discovered one on his laptop. His daughters had been using educational software on the machine and when he attempted to log on to the net through his business firewall, he learned that a program on his laptop was attempting to transmit data to the software vendor's Web site. Though corporate executives insisted the programs were innocuous, the potential for invasion of privacy is considerable.

Although many people enjoy the convenience and individual attention that may come with profiling and other forms of data collection, others are appalled by the growing power of technology to collect sensitive data that can be so easily disseminated or used in unexpected ways. People are especially concerned when attempts are made to collect data without their knowledge or permission, when companies resell their data without their knowledge, or when companies violate their own privacy policies. Mary J. Culnan and Pamela K. Armstrong at Georgetown University argue that corporations are missing a valuable opportunity by not managing customer privacy issues strategically. In their analysis of survey data, they found that customers were more willing to disclose personal information and have that data used to create marketing profiles when their privacy concerns were explicitly addressed by fair procedures.[2] Unfortunately, the lure of these new technologies and the potential for competitive advantage appear to be so compelling that many companies are blinded to their negative effects on consumer trust.

WORKPLACE SURVEILLANCE

The power that digital networks offer to corporations to profile their customers can also be applied to employees. The American Management Association conducts surveys of major U.S. firms each year about the extent of workplace surveillance, and from 1997 to 2000, the percent of companies who reported that they store and review computer files more than doubled, from 13.7% to 30.8%. Email monitoring rose even more rapidly during this period, from 14.9% to 38.1%. In 2000, the AMA added a new question to gauge how much corporations are monitoring Internet connections. More than half the companies (54.1%) reported that they did some form of surveillance of Internet use.[3]

Corporations cite several reasons for deploying surveillance systems, including the need for general performance reviews. Increasingly, concerns about legal issues lead employers to monitor their employees because companies have been held liable for allowing hostile workplace environments to persist. As I discuss in many places in this book, the

---

[2] Culnan, M.J., and Armstrong, P.K. (1999). Information privacy concerns, procedural fairness, and impersonal trust: An empirical investigation. *Organization Science,* 10(1), 104–115.

[3] American Management Association (2000). 2000 AMA Survey: Workplace Monitoring & Surveillance. Retrieved September 29, 2000, from the World Wide Web: http://www.amanet.org/research/pdfs/monitr_surv.pdf

Internet environment encourages disinhibition, as people interact with one another via their computer screens and keyboards and are more insulated from the direct consequences of their behavior. At Dow Chemical, for example, more than fifty employees were fired because they used email in inappropriate ways, especially to transmit sexually explicit materials.

In her *Guide to E-Mail and the Internet in the Workplace,* Internet law attorney Susan Gindin cautions corporate executives to ensure that their company has a comprehensive Internet use policy in place. It should cover acceptable use, ethics, disciplinary procedures, expectations about monitoring and privacy, and a host of other issues that have surfaced as the Internet became a common feature on employees' desktop computers.[4] Most corporations now have policies in place that address the use of email and other network resources, but the psychological aspects of the email environment are difficult to control – even with corporate edicts. Those fired employees would probably not have used interoffice mail to send glossy photographs around, but email is different.

Email and other forms of Internet-based communication also become tangled with legal issues because messages are usually archived and can be used as evidence in subsequent litigation. People continue to use it in very informal ways, despite the growing mound of cases in which email contains the most revealing admissions.

Another reason organizations are increasingly choosing to monitor Internet use concerns productivity. Personal email and net surfing can be very time consuming, and the attraction of new Internet-related technologies can be extremely high. Now, employees can use their high-bandwidth connections to check their portfolios and trade stocks, compare prices with shopping bots, gamble, compete in hot auctions, and communicate via instant messages with distant relatives. Some reports suggest employees spend an average of five to ten hours per week on personal Internet use.

From a psychological standpoint, the effects of this rapidly growing workplace surveillance are not clear. The software to monitor Internet use is widely available now and very easy to implement, so it is not surprising that so many companies have deployed it. Yet it remains to be seen whether the pros outweigh the cons. Generally speaking, people do not like to be electronically monitored and many have filed suits about inva-

---

[4] Gindin, S.E. (1999). *Guide to E-Mail and the Internet in the Workplace.* Corporate Practice Series. Washington, DC: Bureau of National Affairs, Inc.

sion of privacy. Some believe that their use of the fast Internet connection at work to shop or research travel bargains constitutes a positive job benefit. In a tight labor market, a strict policy about Internet use combined with monitoring may turn away potentially valuable employees.

While online profiling and surreptitious data collection endanger trust between businesses and their customers, electronic workplace surveillance may do the same thing between employers and their employees. Privacy may become the civil rights issue of the twenty-first century because of the explosion in netcentric technologies that make online data collection so simple, and its use so tempting. Privacy is not the only issue that gathered so much steam this year, however. The Internet played a major role in another year 2000 clash between commerce and online human behavior. At its center was a software program called Napster.

INTELLECTUAL PROPERTY, NAPSTER, AND PEER-TO-PEER SHARING

The net has always been a place in which intellectual property rights were very challenging to enforce. As I discuss in Chapter 12, the Internet distributes power to individuals and diminishes the power of authorities to control what happens. Software, music, even whole books have been traded and passed around in chat rooms and over email and discussion forums on the Internet for a long time. However, recently developed Internet technologies have vastly increased the scope and scale of this activity and its usability for average computer users. Napster, for example, attracted some 22 million users in a few months and became a household word. Its teenage inventor – Shawn Fanning – found himself in the middle of a tense debate about the nature of intellectual property in the age of the Internet.

Napster is software that people download from the net for free that allows them to swap digital music files stored on each other's computers. Users can search a central database to find where particular titles can be found and then connect to one of the locations to retrieve the file. This distributed musical library maintained on individuals' hard drives around the globe contains both copyrighted and uncopyrighted materials. Exchanging these files became so popular, especially among college students, that Internet traffic jams became common and some universities barred or restricted its use to protect the networks.

Fanning and his infant company are involved in rounds of lawsuits and countersuits with the Record Industry Association of America (RIAA) and artists such as Lars Ulrich of the rock group Metallica, which may take years to unfold. Napster is not charged with copyright infringement, but with contributory infringement, because the company launched technology that makes it easy for users to infringe. In mid-2000, a U.S. District Court judge ruled in favor of the RIAA and ordered that Napster shut down access to copyrighted material within two days. Just nine hours before the order was supposed to go into effect, an appeals court ruled that the company should be allowed to continue operating. As of this writing, Napster is still up and running.

From a psychological perspective, the Napster episode raises several key issues about the evolving relationship between the Internet and our own behavior. One issue is obviously about intellectual property and copyright laws in the digital age. Clearly, the new technology makes it easier for people to enjoy music at their convenience, without buying a CD. They could do this before, of course, by listening to the radio, taping their favorite songs, swapping MP3 files in chat rooms, exchanging CDs with friends, and other methods. The difference now is scope and scale, and its threats to the economic model of the recording industry and the reward structure for artists. While many people insist that the millions who swap copyrighted music through Napster are guilty of stealing, just as if they shoplifted a CD from a store, others believe that existing laws about sharing such property among individuals are vague. Napster attorney David Boies argues that noncommercial consumer copying has been recognized as fair use by the courts, but the scale of copying and sharing through Napster is clearly unprecedented.

Many Napster users do think they are breaking the law when they take one of the copyrighted songs from a fellow user, but they seem relatively untroubled by any ethical or moral concerns over their behavior – partly because they do not see much harm. From years of psychological research on moral reasoning, it is clear that people definitely consider the extent of harm that comes from a particular act, along with the intentions of the actor, when they make moral judgments. Napster users are also convinced they could never be caught. We are left with a vague law that technological innovation and widespread Internet access have made very easy to evade and that appears to carry scant moral muscle to encourage compliance. A recent article in *US News and World Report* about the Napster debate, for example, carried the headline "The Empire Strikes Back," suggesting an alignment of the anti-Napster forces with the evil empire from *Star Wars* and the pro-Napster forces with Luke Skywalker and the rebels.

Napster is just one of the services that facilitate peer-to-peer, distributed information sharing on the net. Several others are already available that have the potential for even more dramatic confrontations with current business models and existing laws protecting intellectual property. Gnutella is a particularly interesting example because it raises other issues about online behavior and group dynamics.

Unlike Napster, Gnutella is not a company and has no central servers or databases. It is a software protocol that creates a decentralized network of peer-to-peer relationships. A session starts with a connection between two peers, then fans out to other peers like a chain letter. A query for a particular file would trigger searches on each of the connected peers until the file is found or a time limit is reached. Also, unlike Napster, the source code for Gnutella applications is widely shared.

Gnutella will generate even more issues involving intellectual property because there is no central database, and thus no entity – like Napster – that could be sued or organized into a fee-collecting enterprise. It also provides means to mask the identity of a peer that generates a query, making users feel even more anonymous online than they feel when using Napster. Gnutella, however, is not a technically efficient way to locate and transmit files, and its use could lead to a tragedy of the bandwidth commons even more than Napster does.

Some research on Gnutella traffic sheds light on the way the system affects group dynamics and demonstrates that the characteristics of this peer-to-peer network encourage considerable free-riding. Eytan Adar and Bernardo A. Huberman of Xerox Palo Alto Research Center examined traffic patterns among more than 31,000 peers over a twenty-four hour period in 2000, during which more than 4 million files were shared.[5] They found that consumers far outnumber providers. More than two-thirds of the peers shared no files at all during this period. A very small number (about 1% of the sample) did most of the providing on this network, responding to about 50% of the queries. To succeed, a large peer-to-peer information sharing network like this would need to have considerable voluntary contribution, in terms of files (and information) and bandwidth. The providers, after all, must sacrifice some speed on their own connections and computers in order to share. However, this study suggests that the perceived anonymity associated with a network like Gnutella may create more free riding than cooperation.

[5] Adar, E., and Huberman, B.A. (2000). Free riding on Gnutella. Internet Ecologies Area, Xerox PARC. Retrieved September 29, 2000, from the World Wide Web: http://www.parc.xerox.com/istl/groups/iea/papers/gnutella/index.html

Anonymity, as you will see in this book, is a key ingredient of the Internet environment for human interaction, and it affects our behavior in predictable ways. Sometimes it unleashes a surprising level of intimacy and self-disclosure, but it can also protect people from the consequences of their actions.

Napster, Gnutella, and their clones raise concerns about copyrights in the digital age and how a society can promote a healthy growth in intellectual and artistic capital. When technology changes the game rules and products are so easily disseminated with no middleman and no royalty payments, will creativity be stifled? These new technologies also raise difficult questions about how to protect a valuable and shared resource. Large-scale environmental movements have made much progress through education, even when enforcement is problematic, partly because they rely on group pressure as well as moral awareness. A homeowner watering her lawn during a drought may never be fined by the county, but she would receive some harsh looks from her neighbors – an even more effective method of ensuring compliance.

THE WEBCAM PHENOMENON

Netcentric innovations threaten our privacy and our conceptions of intellectual property, but they also provide a means to voluntarily abandon both, if we choose. Since the first publication of *The Psychology of the Internet,* the Webcam phenomenon took off with lightning speed and became an international craze, and it shows again how the Internet can support an extraordinary range of human activity and motivations. For a very small amount of money, people can now become producers of their own life dramas and broadcast them on a twenty-four hour basis to the entire world. They can mount a small camera in any room – or all rooms – of their homes, connect the cameras to a computer, and maintain an always-on Internet connection. Visitors to these Webcam sites can refresh the image every few seconds to see what is happening. Databases of Webcam sites now contain thousands of entries, from the practical to the pornographic.

Many Webcam sites are functional and utilitarian, showing traffic patterns at busy intersections or progress on construction sites. However, psychological issues arise when we ask why people would want to create a site that broadcasts their own day-to-day activities from cameras in their homes and why anyone would want to watch. The creators report motives of profit, if they can sell subscriptions or advertising, or simply a need for attention and a desire to reach out to a global audience.

A large number of these sites are launched by women, individually or in groups, and one of the earliest – jennicam – was created by Jennifer Ringley. The camera watches as she combs her hair, dresses, works at her computer, pays bills, and sleeps. On the surface, it would not seem to be something that would attract many viewers, but it receives millions of hits a week. Viewers can open a small window on their computer screens that refreshes with the latest image every fifteen minutes, and they can subscribe for $15 to step up the refresh rate to once a minute. On the site, visitors can read the journal entries by Jennifer herself, complete with liberal use of smiley faces:) and news of her latest boyfriend. She is eager to add new features to her site, including streaming video, a technology that will allow visitors to see live action and not just a succession of snapshots.

The Webcam can be an extension of the home page described in Chapter 2, in which people focus on their own identities and explore ways to manage their online impressions. Webcams, however, are also real-time so the creators are unable to think through their self-presentation and tinker with it in the same way they would when designing a home page. Exhibitionism is one ingredient for many Webcam creators, and some freely admit and cherish this aspect of their Internet activity. The desire for attention, to be noticed, is another driving motivation, though the attention is certainly not always positive. Most women creators, for example, become the target of harassment and hate mail. In Chapter 6, I discuss the nature of online aggression and why the Internet environment can escalate it.

Why do people visit Webcam sites, become involved in the lives of the creators, and join their fan clubs? One email received by New York City freelance writer Gabrielle, creator of the GabGab Webcam site that features her own apartment and editorials, showed clearly that the visitors often don't know themselves: "I just came across this whole web cam thing. I find it interesting despite the lack of ... well everything. I can't turn it off. Why do you think that is?"

One explanation is that the visitors have an opportunity, not just to observe the endless life details of another human being from a safe distance, but to watch that person's life move along without any editorial reviews or constraints, any time of day or night. Anything can happen on live Web cams, and visitors hope for that big surprise. The stars of the Web cam sites usually share more intimacies of their lives through online journals, chats, and discussion forums, so the viewers become more involved and even interact with the person they watch on screen. These differences take voyeurism a step further than the way it unfolds on soap operas or even on the wildly popular "reality TV" show *Survivor*.

Gabrielle helps people start up their own Webcam sites for profit or other reasons, and the technology is now easily available and inexpensive. The Webcam phenomenon demonstrates that the privacy issues raised by the growing power of Internet technologies are complicated ones that from the standpoint of human behavior may seem contradictory. Central to the concerns, however, are control and choice. Chapter 9 explores the way the Internet offers people who have a strong internal locus of control many options for exercising it. Increasingly, it also provides an expanding variety of tools that can diminish people's ability to control.

SHIFTING PATTERNS OF INTERNET USE

As e-commerce expanded and more netcentric technologies rolled out, the way people use the Internet and what they use it for have changed. Much of what we know about patterns of use has come from self-selected samples, such as the people who choose to complete the annual World Wide Web surveys conducted by the Graphics, Visualization, and Usability Lab at Georgia Tech. Conclusions from such surveys must be tentative because of sampling biases. For example, people who are very involved in the Internet are more likely to run across such Web-based surveys, so their behavior and attitudes would be overrepresented. Recently, Norman H. Nie and Lutz Erbring of the Stanford Institute for the Quantitative Study of Society made an important contribution to our understanding of Internet use in the United States by conducting a survey with a randomly selected sample of households.[6] Each selected household was equipped with a WebTV settop box and given free Internet access and email accounts. The survey results are based only on the responses from people who had Internet access independent of their WebTV equipment.

A key finding was that email was overwhelmingly the most widespread activity among Internet users, with more than 90% reporting that

[6] Nie, N. H., and Erbring, L. (2000). Internet and society: A preliminary report. Stanford Institute for the Quantitative Study of Society. Retrieved June 1, 2000, from the World Wide Web: http://www.stanford.edu/group/siqss/Press_Release/Preliminary_Report.pdf

they used the technology. People are exchanging emails with their coworkers, friends, and family members, and also with businesses, educational institutions, teachers, government representatives, former classmates, long lost relatives, and total strangers. After this book was first published, I received emails from all over the world from people who offered many examples of how the net affects their behavior. Clearly, the widespread use of email via the Internet demonstrates that communication is a central feature of this technology, though it was not in its infancy. There appears to be no phrase analogous to "WHAT HATH GOD WROUGHT" for the history books to document the net's inaugural use for human communication. Instead, an early demonstration of ARPANET in 1972 focused on resource sharing and its use to access computer applications across a network, such as meteorological models, chess games, and the software program called ELIZA that simulates a therapist. Michael S. Hart, one of the net's early users, described the bleak communication environment in an email to Janet Abbate, author of *Inventing the Internet:* "You have to realize how FEW people were on the Net before the '80s... There just weren't enough to support a conversation on any but the most geeky or the most general topics ... It was boring, unless you could "see" down the cables to the rest of the world ... and into the future."[7]

Email remains primarily text-based and asynchronous, and as you will see in this book, those characteristics have important effects on human interaction and impression formation. The "send" button is much easier to use than an envelope, stamp, and trip to a mailbox, but email is very easily misdelivered, forwarded to unintended recipients, or copied and quoted out of context. The communication style remains mostly informal and conversational, despite the flurry of litigation in which emails thought to be private were actually archived, resurrected, or monitored in some other fashion. Increasingly, tools are available to track the origin of emails even when the sender takes measures to remain anonymous. Joan Feldman, president of a computer forensic company in Seattle, reported that it was rather easy to track down people who were posting messages critical of their companies through alias email accounts. She simply called the Internet Service Provider and asked for the real name of the person who used that account.

Email traffic now outpaces phone traffic, and even when a phone call or face-to-face encounter is possible, many people choose email to com-

---

[7] Abbate, J. (1999). *Inventing the Internet.* Cambridge, MA: The MIT Press.

municate. This indicates that email is not just a poor cousin to other forms of communication with greater media richness that is used only when others are unavailable. Despite its drawbacks, it has significant advantages and has become a preferred method of communication for many people. I often send a letter when contacting a colleague I've never met in person, but often I receive no reply. Then I send the same thing via email and receive a reply within a couple of hours, with apologies for missing the snail mail that could remain unread for weeks.

Other findings from the Nie and Erbring study indicate that people are taking advantage of many of the growing services on the Internet and using them for a wide variety of activities. Most use the net to obtain general information about products and services, to read, to engage in hobbies, and to explore travel options. While more than a third had purchased something online, the actual volume of online transactions between business and consumers is still quite small. More than a third of the sample said they used their Internet access for entertainment, by playing games such as chess, cards, or role-plays.

The new financial services are becoming especially popular, with more than a quarter of the sample using the net to check stock prices. Smaller numbers were using the net for online banking (12%) and trading stocks (7%), but these services are relatively new and are likely to grow quickly. Overall, the average Internet user engaged in more than seven different activities.

The study also pointed to ways in which our use of time is changing as a result of the Internet. For example, the more hours people spend on the Internet each week, the less they use the mass media – especially TV. Also, increased Internet use cuts into time spent on outside activities and talking with friends and family by phone. Earlier, some research suggested that more Internet use could be leading to increased levels of social isolation, in which people might be substituting weaker ties with virtual acquaintances for the stronger ties of family and friends (see Chapter 9). However, more research is needed on this because it is not clear whether people are replacing phone contact with email or other forms of electronic communication, particularly if they have just one phone line.

Another time-related issue involves the increasingly fuzzy boundary between work and nonwork. With Internet access to email and corporate networks from home, hotels, shopping malls, airports, and beach cafes, people appear to be extending work to time slots that were ordinarily exempt in the past. For example, Nie and Erbring found that

15% of the respondents who were employed full or part time reported an increase in the amount of time they spent working at home. The general increase in connectedness, through cell phones, voice mail, pagers, and wireless devices adds more ways in which we can continue working outside the office, regardless of whether we are officially called "teleworkers."

Another significant trend involving the way netcentric technologies are changing how we use time involves wireless text-messaging via handheld devices. These services are exploding in Europe and Japan, especially among the young, and their growth rate came as a surprise to nearly everyone. Though Internet access, information, financial services, games, and other applications are available, most of the use is for interpersonal communication.

With a properly equipped cellular phone, an individual can use the keypad to type in a short text message and send it to a single individual or a predefined group. In Japan, the DoCoMo cell phones with Internet access are emerging as the biggest consumer boom since the Walkman. Schoolchildren use their phones to send each other messages during long, boring subway rides or send messages home to inquire about dinner. Thomas L. Friedman, *NY Times* Foreign Affairs Correspondent, described watching one of the schoolgirls use her phone on a train: "Her thumb moved around the keyboard with the lightning dexterity of a Midori playing a violin concerto."[8]

In Europe, short text messaging services are growing in popularity as well, and businesspeople use them as an unobtrusive way to communicate with others when they are sitting in meetings or conference presentations and have time to spare. This is one reason why the services are likely to continue to gain popularity. There are many moments during a day, away from a desktop computer, that could be productively, or at least amusingly, filled with a quick bit of interpersonal communication that would not disrupt others in the way that cell phone conversations do.

From a psychological standpoint, these services create a new Internet-based environment for human interaction that will have its own characteristics and will influence the way we behave when we use them. A phone call already has a defined set of norms associated with it, and increasingly, so does email. The norms that evolve are affected by the nature of the communication medium and by the tendency toward group conformity, as you will see in Chapter 5. These wireless

[8] Friedman, T.L. (2000). Brave new world. *The New York Times*, September 22, 2000. Retrieved September 22, 2000, from the World Wide Web: http://www.nytimes.com/2000/09/22/opinion/22FRIE.html

services have very small screen real estate so they must be brief and to the point. They also may involve lower expectations about response because the message seems much more ephemeral and time-dependent than email.

Patterns of use, evolving group norms, and advanced capabilities continue to interact and influence how people behave when they are online. Jenny Preece of the University of Maryland, Baltimore County, argues that successful online interactions, especially for the online communities she studies, require both usability and sociability.[9] Usability refers to the characteristics of the technical environment and the way it interfaces with human behavior. Sociability refers to the features of this environment that support and influence social interaction, such as policies about online behavior or norms that surface over time.

As netcentric technologies expand into and invent new avenues of human communication, experiments intended to advance both usability and sociability continue. For example, DoCoMo cell phones include a special key that transmits a beating heart, which means "I can't wait." Instant Messenger has many features to give users better control over their communication, especially to help users create communities of "buddies" who list one another and communicate regularly in this way. For example, a user can block all messages from nonbuddies and can play special sounds when certain buddies log on.

Within online communities organized around some commercial theme, the sponsors have developed many innovative efforts to improve sociability. One example is e-pinions, which is an online consumer advisory group that has an elaborate rating and reward system. Members can view the opinions of other members about various products and then rate each review. Members who submit reviews can also join an "e-royalty" program in which they earn a few cents each time another member reads their opinion about a product. The site also uses a "Web of Trust" in which members can indicate how much they trust the opinions of other members. The software presents a personalized list of recommendations to each member, sorted by this "trust" factor. Many sites have adopted strategies like this that encourage community members to help enforce and promote group norms by commenting on one another's behavior. Amazon.com, for example, lets anonymous visitors submit book reviews, but also encourages visitors to rate the usefulness of each review.

[9] Preece, J. (2000). *Online Communities: Designing Usability and Supporting Sociability.* New York: John Wiley and Sons.

KEEPING THE BALANCE

The Internet remains a complex concept to most people, and we hold many conflicting and contradictory viewpoints about its role in society, its potential for revolutionary change in commerce, and its impact on our behavior. We have spent untold millions wiring schools to ensure students have access, and then we began to learn that too much computer and Internet time could hinder learning. We delight in connecting to others through email and chat and then wonder whether important ties to family and friends are becoming weaker. We herald the new net-centric technologies that offer so many personalized services, from book recommendations to online portfolio analysis. Then we wonder what we gave up, in terms of privacy and control, to obtain them.

Our notions about heroes and villains in the digital age are challenged as well. Napster certainly raised some high-profile ethical issues, and many more are on the horizon. A boy in New Jersey, described by those who know him as a loner and an outsider, started playing around with some investments, and at fifteen he learned how to manipulate prices by his comments in Internet chat rooms. In the fall of 2000, he was fined $273,000 by the SEC, but his broad smile and his friends' favorable comments suggest he had no regrets or ethical qualms. His father described him as a "good student" and complained that the SEC picked on a kid.

The Internet has also captured the attention of economists, such as Alice Rivlin and Alan S. Blinder at the Brookings Institution. From 1973, which is about the time the personal computer was invented, to 1997, growth in productivity in the United States actually slowed down. This was a mysterious puzzle, the so-called "productivity paradox" since the prevailing wisdom suggested that growing investments in information technology during these years should have accelerated productivity growth because applications of technology generally have this effect. Many explanations have been offered, including higher energy costs and deteriorating skills of the average worker, but no agreement has been reached.

Perhaps it is a coincidence that productivity growth began to accelerate in 1997, about the same time the Internet began winding through the economy of the United States and other developed countries. Nevertheless, there are compelling reasons to think we may be on the verge of a sustained period of productivity growth, one that started with and will be sustained by the Internet. While business-to-consumer transactions may not become a large factor in this equation, business-to-business e-commerce is just in its infancy and has enormous potential.[10] Of course, others argue that the surge will come to an end despite the Internet's contribution; time will tell.

We have much to learn about human behavior and the Internet, whether we are dealing with family, friends, coworkers, or people in a different company with whom we are trying to conduct some of the business-to-business e-business that has so much promise for the economic future. In this book, I draw on decades of research in psychology, communications, business, information science, and many other fields to define the issues and lay the groundwork for understanding the net as a special environment for human interaction. New netcentric technologies will continue to emerge, the dot coms have certainly landed on Internet shores, and issues the Victorians did not have to confront will rise up to challenge our old business models, value systems, and beliefs. But human beings still have the responsibility to navigate through this turbulent period and know enough about the psychology of the Internet to guide it wisely from awkward adolescence to young adulthood.

ACKNOWLEDGMENTS

I want to thank the many people – too numerous to name – who helped bring this book to life with their intellectual contributions, creative ideas, commentary, editing skills, and support. Many colleagues at universities, corporations, government agencies, and private organizations shared their insights and research results, and their contributions were especially valuable because the work in this area is going on in so many disciplines and settings. Students around the world have been enormously helpful, responding via email and instant messages to questions and demonstrating how easily they adapt to the netcentric era. I also want to thank the good people at Cambridge University Press in New York and the UK for their support, especially Julia Hough, a senior editor at the Press, who played a key role in the development of this book with excellent ideas and advice. Finally, a special thanks to all the Internet users who volunteer their time and talent to nurture the net through its formative years.

Patricia Wallace
Center for Talented Youth
The Johns Hopkins University
Baltimore, Maryland
November, 2000

[10] Blinder, A.S. (2000). The Internet and the new economy. The Brookings Institution, Policy Brief no. 60, June, 2000.

THE INTERNET IN A PSYCHOLOGICAL CONTEXT

From almost total obscurity, the Internet swiftly leapt into our lives. Once an arcane communication medium for academics and researchers, it now sustains almost any human activity you can imagine, from shopping to sex, from research to rebellion. We use it to keep in touch with friends and coworkers, search for bargains, conduct research, exchange information, meet strangers, hatch conspiracies, and even – as I recently learned – talk to animals. Koko, the mountain gorilla who has been learning American Sign Language from Penny Patterson for more than 20 years, has now participated in live Internet chats. People from all over the world logged into the chat room to ask questions and hear Koko's views on motherhood, pets, food preferences, friendship, love, and the future. She was not in the best mood, having just had a tiff with her mate, Ndume, and she shared her annoyance with the crowd by referring to him derisively as *toilet,* which is her word for bad.[1]

The Internet explosion happened so rapidly that we have not had much time to step back from the medium and look at it more systematically, as a new environment that can have potent effects on our behavior. It is a place where we humans are acting and interacting rather strangely at times. Sometimes its effects seem to be quite positive, but sometimes, we do things online that we might never do in any other environment, and that we regret later. At the same time, it is an environment that we, as Internet users, can affect and mold – provided we have some inkling of how, and why, it can change our perceptions and behavior.

---

[1] *An Internet Chat with Koko the Gorilla* (1998). [Online]. Available: http://www.geocities.com/RainForest/Vines/4451/KokoLiveChat.html1 [1998, May 20]. The chat was held on America Online in honor of Earth Day, and Patterson served as translator while an assistant typed Koko's remarks on the keyboard.

Based only on newspaper headlines, someone who has never ventured online might begin to think the Internet is overpopulated by people with psychological disorders, bizarre ideas, and questionable motives, and that normal folk had better tread very cautiously. Yet, decades of research on human behavior in many different settings show us how minor tweaks in the environment can cause those "normal" people to behave differently, and sometimes the effects are quite striking. Although we might think of ourselves as kind-hearted, cool-headed, assertive, or generous, we routinely underestimate the power of the situation on our behavior. People who rate themselves a 10 on cool-headedness can lose their cool in certain situations. Someone who scores high on kindliness and who ordinarily behaves courteously toward people in person might lash out aggressively in a heated Internet flame war (an online argument that gets really nasty). Psychological research reminds us that the environment in which humans are behaving can and does affect the way they behave. Under the right circumstances, almost everyone will do things that they themselves consider quite uncharacteristic.

As human environments go, the Internet is relatively new, and we can learn much about how it affects us by looking closely at what is going on from a psychological perspective. Research about actual online behavior is still sparse, although it is quickly attracting the attention of scientists in many disciplines. Nevertheless, we need not start from scratch; we know a great deal about the factors that affect our behavior in other settings, and we can draw meaningful parallels. When we watch a flame war break out in an otherwise sedate discussion group, for example, we can turn to a long history of psychological research on aggression to better understand what is happening, and why. When we hear of a chat room romance, we can turn to studies of interpersonal attraction to comprehend why such relationships might be intoxicating.

In *Psychology of the Internet*, we begin, in chapter 2, with the online persona, delving into classic research on impression formation and impression management. These processes unfold differently in cyberspace because the cues you use to form impressions, and the tools you use to create your own, are quite different than they are in real life. (In this book, I use *real life* to refer to anything and everything that is not on the net.) Next, in chapter 3, we explore a particularly important feature of the Internet in the context of our online personas – its ability to support elaborate role plays and identity experiments. Because of the environment, we can make some remarkable alterations to our persona – including swapping gender or choosing a new date of birth.

The next two chapters look at group dynamics on the Internet, and show how many psychological phenomena involving groups play out differently online. Examples include conformity, group polarization, brainstorming, group conflict, and group cooperation. These studies are especially important as we move more and more workgroups to the online world and tacitly assume they will be more productive than their real life counterparts.

One of the first surprises for researchers investigating online behavior was how disinhibited people sometimes became, and how their tempers seemed to flare more easily as they interacted with others. Chapter 6 looks at the psychology of aggression as it unfolds on the net, searching for the roots of those harsh emails, acerbic flame wars, and other forms of contentious online behavior. A second surprise was that the Internet environment is also very supportive of friendships and romances, perhaps for some of the same reasons. Chapter 7 examines the nature of interpersonal attraction in the online world.

Government attempts to regulate Internet content – especially pornography – have met much resistance from Internet users. Chapter 8 reviews the kinds of pornography on the net, how it differs from sexually explicit materials distributed through other channels, and what its psychological effects on Internet users might be.

In chapter 9, we explore the Internet as a time sink, examining why certain features of the environment are psychologically so compelling that some people seem barely able to log off. Preliminary research suggests that greater Internet use is associated with increases in loneliness and depression, and also reductions in family communication and social involvement. These are warning signs that too much of even a good thing might not be beneficial, especially as we invest heavily to wire every home, classroom, and business.

Many corners of the Internet are filled with people who are willing to invest considerable time to help others in need. Chapter 10 examines altruism on the net, and especially looks at the enormous network of support groups that flourishes online. The Internet is particularly well-suited to certain kinds of support groups, such as those involving members who feel stigmatized by society and who are reluctant to share their concerns with people in their community, or even their own families. Online, they can talk quite intimately with caring others who share their problem without risking real-life censure.

Although the demographics of the Internet are changing fast, the environment began as overwhelmingly male. This has left its legacy, and chapter 11 examines how gender roles, stereotypes, and conflicts unfold online. For women, certain corners of the Internet can be hostile places, and it will take time for this to change.

Finally, in chapter 12, we look at ways in which we, as Internet users, can help mold and shape this environment for the better. This is not television, a technology we can only affect through our passive viewing habits or occasional fan letters. Relying on knowledge of the many psychological phenomena that influence our behavior online, we can develop strategies to shape our own behavior and influence others with whom we interact on the net. I also take out the crystal ball and try to predict the psychological effects of emerging technological developments on the Internet.

Studies of online behavior have been complicated by the fact that *online* can mean many things from a psychological perspective. Though a computer and keyboard are usually involved as the mediator of your online experience, there are numerous ways you can explore the Internet, present yourself, and interact with other people. It is a potpourri of experiences, and we need a special kind of taxonomy – one that divides up the known virtual world into better-defined spaces that share features from a psychological perspective. This taxonomy has less to do with technology than with the way certain features of the Internet world affect our behavior.

ENVIRONMENTS OF THE INTERNET: A TAXONOMY

The Internet is not just one environment, but several. Although there is much overlap between and variation within environment types, they differ on certain fundamental characteristics that seem to affect the way we behave when we experience them.

The first is the *World Wide Web*, when it is used as a kind of library/magazine rack/yellow pages, and also as a self-publisher. Though the cataloging system leaves much to be desired and Internet users complain bitterly about navigation problems, most people say they can find what they were looking for at least half the time. This may be because they know where they are going and wisely wrote down (or bookmarked) the address, because a simple keyword search can bring up hundreds of thousands of hits. Guessing can also be frustrating. (The U.S. president, for example, may not be pleased to hear that a net surfer who takes a chance on www.whitehouse.com instead of www.whitehouse.gov will land in a pornography site.) The fact that the Web offers everyone vanity press services at very cheap rates is another feature of the Internet that has potential psychological impact.

Electronic mail *(email)* has become a vitally important Internet environment for net users, who now consider it to be side by side with the Web as an indispensable technology. People use it to communicate with friends, family, and business colleagues. It is widespread in colleges and universities, government agencies, corporations, and homes. I began seeing email addresses on business cards several years ago, and now the practice is the norm. Although few elementary or secondary schools offer email accounts to their charges, the students themselves often have access at home or through one of the Web sites that offers free email accounts, paid for by the advertising you must watch when you log in. An item on the humorous test called "You know you are addicted to the Internet when..." is, "You get up to go to the bathroom at 3 A.M. and stop to check your email on the way back to bed."

Another distinctive space on the Internet is the *asynchronous discussion forum*. These are the ongoing conferences in which participants start topics (or *threads*), post replies to each other, and read what others have said. They are asynchronous in the sense that you can catch up on the discussion and contribute your thoughts at any time of day or night, so the conference's rhythms can be very slow. A discussion of a single topic might go on for days or weeks. The forum could also be very erratic, with several topics under discussion at the same time and other topics completely ignored. In these groups, you become part of a discussion among people with similar interests, regardless of their geographic location; you may know the participants in real life, or you may have never met any of them.

Because this book is about psychology more than technology, I group the asynchronous discussion forums together as a distinct environment, even though you might be using your Web browser, email software, or some other tool to participate. There are, however, a few forum flavors that have slightly different psychological dimensions. One is the mailing list, which is a special kind of email address with an automated feature that remails all the messages it receives to everyone who is subscribed to the forum. For example, if you are interested in genealogy, you might want to subscribe to one of the hundreds of mailing lists devoted to the subject, such as GENTIPS-L, in which participants share tips about how to research their ancestors.[2] Once you subscribe, all messages posted to the main GENTIPS-L email address will land in your inbox as well, and anything you send will reach all the other subscribers.

Another flavor of asynchronous discussion forums is the collection of conferences known as *newsgroups* on a distributed bulletin board system called Usenet. This is one of the oldest Internet niches, and the forums span every conceivable human interest – from the scholarly to the salacious. A loose hierarchical naming structure was established in a somewhat futile effort to stay organized. Some examples are sci.space in the science hierarchy, which focuses on space research, soc.culture.british in the social issues hierarchy, and rec.arts.tv.soaps under recreation. The alt (alternative) hierarchy is wide open, and any net user can create a newsgroup under this heading. Examples include alt.backrubs, alt.conspiracies, alt.evil, alt.flame, and alt.sex. Though many thoughtful discussions occur in the newsgroups, Usenet has a reputation for being a stronghold in the Internet's "wild west". For this reason, many moderators of the more serious discussion forums prefer to stay out of Usenet and choose mailing lists or other types of asynchronous forums.

Before the Internet became a household word, hundreds of local bulletin board systems emerged to offer asynchronous discussion forums to subscribers with computers and modems in their geographic areas. The WELL in the San Francisco Bay area, MiniTel in France, and ECHO in New York are some of the better known examples, and their members discuss local as well as global issues. Many Web sites also host asynchronous discussion forums in which visitors can participate in a conference related to the Web site's contents. Also, the same companies that offer free email boxes might give you the software tools to create your own discussion forum, on your personal Web page.

The *synchronous chats* are the fourth environment on the Internet. When people are online at the same time, they can enter chat rooms to engage in a kind of real-time conversation with the others in the room. They type out their brief messages and read the contributions of the others as they scroll up the screen. Chat rooms have emerged in numerous forms on different platforms, and they are used for myriad purposes. Faculty teaching students through distance education, for example, sometimes use a chat room as an inexpensive way to hold "virtual office

---

[2] In this example, you would send email to gentips-1@rootsweb.com. To subscribe, send the following to gentips-L-request@rootsweb.com, leave the subject line blank, and type "subscribe" in the body of the message (without the quotes).

hours" for their geographically dispersed students who could never drop by in person. Although some rooms open up for a short time and then disappear, many have been in existence for years. Conversations go on 24 hours a day, 365 days a year, and the "regulars," bearing well-known nicknames, frequent the places.

America Online is a stronghold of chat rooms accessible to its subscribers. Also all Internet users with the right software can reach the hosts that are part of the worldwide Internet Relay Chat, or IRC. At any hour of the day, thousands of rooms bearing names such as hottub, chatzone, brazil, francais, or cybersex are open for business, and people from all over the world are in them. Some are jam-packed with hundreds of people, while others lean toward the cozy and quiet with just a few visitors. People can open multiple "chat windows" simultaneously and join many different conversations if their attention spans permit. It is not uncommon for a chatter to be logged into a busy room, but also "whispering" in a different window with a buddy in the room.

A fifth environment is the *MUD,* an acronym that once stood for multiuser dungeons because the early ones were based on the adventure game, Dungeons and Dragons. These are text-based "virtual reality" environments that mix several ingredients together to create a stronger feeling of place and community among the users. These users are usually called *players* because of the environment's gaming origins. For example, you move from place to place inside a MUD by typing "go north" or "go down," and when you enter a room on a MUD a vivid description of the location appears on your screen. Players create their own description, and they can build their own rooms. With a little effort, creativity, and programming skill, they can create jeweled boxes with locks and keys, secret notes that only certain players can read, telescopes to spy on other rooms, and time bombs that tick and explode. Communication possibilities are also extensive. Depending on the MUD, their synchronous choices could include regular chatting, paging, whispering, yelling, or emoting. Many MUDs also offer asynchronous discussion forums and inter-player email.

I use the term *MUD* in this book to refer to all the text-based virtual reality environments that have these kinds of features, though purists distinguish MUDs from similar species, such as the MOO (MUD, Object-Oriented) or MUSH (Multiuser Shared Hallucination). From a psychological standpoint, these environments share much in common and their differences have more to do with whether they lean toward the social MUD, which is more like synchronous chatting, or the adventure MUD, in which players slay monsters and evildoers, including one another. Educational and professional MUDs have also been launched, such as Media MOO, an online community for media researchers.[3]

Technological advances made the Internet-based graphical multiuser worlds possible a few years ago, and these I group together as a sixth type of online environment, called *metaworlds* for lack of any consensus about terminology. Though still small, participation is growing rapidly because these highly imaginative worlds can be some of the most vivid and absorbing on the net. With specialized software, the computer screen comes alive with vistas, castles, taverns, and also other people who appear inside the movie set as avatars – their graphical personas. These metaworlds are the multimedia descendants of the MUDs, but the addition of visual imagery and appropriate sound effects adds considerable psychological impact. Although MUDs and chat rooms can support limited sound effects, the metaworlds are moving way out in front in that arena. Not everyone agrees they are superior, however; many prefer the freedom MUDs offer to exercise the imagination.

A distinct seventh category that incorporates live Internet-based *interactive video and voice* is already out there, and many of the psychological factors that affect how we behave online now may change dramatically when these features become widely available. Soon those distant Internet buddies will be able to see your face and hear your voice; it remains to be seen how people will react to that particular technological advance. In some settings it may be very welcome. For example, as you will see in this book, online workgroups suffer some disadvantages because of the current limitations of the medium. The addition of sight and sound would reduce some of these disadvantages. In other groups, however, it might kill some of the magic that makes the Internet so enchanting and liberating.

Weaving through all seven of these general categories and mediating their psychological effects are certain features that affect our behavior in any setting, including online. A crucial one is the degree of anonymity, and this can vary dramatically, depending on where you are on the net and what you are doing. If you are replying to email from friends and colleagues or using the net for work-related purposes, you would not be anonymous and you would no doubt sign your name. However, if you enter other kinds of Internet environments, such as the entertainment-

---

[3] Bruckman, A. (1999). MediaMOO: A Professional Community for Media Researchers. [Online] Available: http://www.cc.gatech.edu/fac/Amy.Bruckman/MediaMOO/ [1999, March 11].

oriented MUDs or one of the many Internet-based support groups, you might use a nickname instead and conceal your true identity. Research suggests that the degree of anonymity affects our behavior in important ways and leads to disinhibition – a lowering of the normal social constraints on behavior. It is not an all or nothing variable, especially on the Internet, but we feel more or less anonymous in different Internet locales, and this affects the way we act.

Another example of a mediating variable is the presence or absence of some local authority, such as a group moderator, who has the power to resolve disputes, enforce policies, and kick wrongdoers out. Adding an armed sheriff to a lawless town had predictable effects on the frontiers, and it isn't that different on the Internet.

Perhaps the most important mediator of behavior in these different Internet environments is the purpose of the people who visit or inhabit them. Though I like the "global village" metaphor, the Internet is not really like that most of the time. With respect to human interaction, it is more like a huge collection of distinct neighborhoods where people with common interests can share information, work together, tell stories, joke around, debate politics, help each other out, or play games. Geography may have little bearing on the way these neighborhoods form, but purpose does, and it has a strong influence on our behavior. People can belong to multiple neighborhoods and they change their behavior as they click from one to the next, just as you would when you move from a business meeting to a beach.

LANGUAGE ON THE NET

Written language is the Internet's bread and butter, so you will see many examples throughout *Psychology of the Internet* of how people online use language deliberately, playfully, and sometimes intemperately to express themselves. A recent addition to the Web, called *The Dialectizer*, humorously underscores how important language is in the online environment. You can enter text in normal English and have it instantly "dialectized" to Redneck, Jive, Cockney, and several others, with a click of the mouse. I experimented with JFK's famous line and received the Redneck version: "Ask not whut yer country kin does fo' yo', ax whut yo' kin does fo' yer country."[4]

---

[4] Stoddard, S. (1998). The dialectizer. [Online]. Available: http://www.rinkworks. com/dialect/ [1998, October 31].

Linguists have demonstrated that the way we use language is closely related to the social context, and this is what they mean by the term *register*. Your style of speech changes when you speak on the phone, talk to a child, brief your boss, write in your diary, or compose a political speech. Linguists have studied many different register variations and found that language use in specific social contexts is heavily influenced by social norms and conventions, and also by the medium. They have also analyzed the registers of two categories in the taxonomy: the synchronous chat and the asynchronous discussion forum.

The online chat is a relative newcomer to the communication scene, and it mixes features of face-to-face conversation and phone talk because it is synchronous. However, people have to type to use it and the medium has some special influences. Christopher Werry analyzed logs from many chat sessions, trying to identify some of the properties of this highly unusual register. The following transcript was part of his study:[5]

```
(<anya> catch you all in about 10 mins:)
<Keels> booooooo
<ariadne> k e e l s !!! you in and out today?
<bubi> keels, don't scare me !!!
<Keels> you mean youre
<Shaquille> ariadne - what the hell is your problem?
<Keels> who are you bubi
<Alvin> bubi: What does your friend want to do in
Australia...work
<Alvin> Shaquile: You're the problem.
<ariadne> shaq: i have no problem … you were the
"asshole"
<bubi> al, he wants to live and work, i guess
<Alvin> bubi: depends what sort of qualifications,
experience, intentions, area
<Shaquille> Alvin-spell the name right!!!!!!
<Alvin> GRRR
<Keels> has anybody seen a pomme called daco?
```

5 Werry, C. C. (1996). Linguistic and interactional features of Internet relay chat. In S. C. Herring (Ed.), *Computer-mediated communication: Linguistic, social and cross-cultural perspectives* (pp. 47–63). Amsterdam: John Benjamins Publishing Company.

If you have never been involved in an Internet chat, this log must look rather ridiculous. On the surface, it seems as though communication among people is barely occurring at all and that most of the utterances are a jumbled mass of disconnected insults and meaningless grunts. Yet, experienced chatters learn how to follow the threads as though they are in a room in which several conversations are going on at the same time. They might participate fully in one and just eavesdrop on the others. Dissecting out the threads is made a little easier by the fact that the messages scroll slowly and remain on the screen for a while.

The chat medium affects the register in several ways, pushing it toward a highly economical use of language in which we struggle hard to emulate a face-to-face conversation. Acronyms like lol (laughing out loud) and rofl (rolling on the floor laughing) abound, and anything that *can* be abbreviated *will* be. This includes common words like pls (please), cya (see you), u r (you are), and thx (thanks), as well as nicknames. To help chatters keep up with the threads, they often preface their message with the name of the person they are addressing. Emoticons and other linguistic forms that convey emotion are also widely used in chat rooms. Werry suggests that the chatters are evolving innovative linguistic strategies as they create a register for conversation and adapt to the constraints of the medium.

On the asynchronous discussion forums, another form of electronic language appears that seems to have a register of its own. Milena Collot and Nancy Belmore analyzed more than 2000 messages taken from discussion groups that covered a range of topics such as current events, film and music, sports, and science fiction.[6] They used specialized software and some tedious hand-coding as they searched for linguistic features – past tenses, pronouns, participial clauses, prepositions, and others. The same coding strategies had been used in the past to analyze samples of several other forms of speech and writing, so they were able to do some useful comparisons.[7]

---

[6] Collot, M. and Belmore, N. (1996). Electronic language: A new variety of English. In S. C. Herring (Ed.), *Computer-mediated communication: Linguistic, social and cross-cultural perspectives* (pp. 13–28). Amsterdam: John Benjamins Publishing Company.

[7] These researchers very wisely chose to build on the extensive linguistic work by Douglas Biber, and use the same coding strategies. He analyzed enormous volumes of personal letters, academic prose, official documents, speech transcripts, news broadcasts, adventure fiction, face-to-face conversations, and many other kinds of speech and writing, so these researchers were able to perform direct comparisons to his data on those registers. For more information about Biber's approach, see Biber, D. (1998). *Variation across speech and writing*. New York, NY: Cambridge University Press.

One intriguing finding was that this sample of electronic language turned out to be somewhat similar to the public interview style of speech. We may be looking at the effects of the Internet soap box, rather than just a discussion going on inside a group. When people respond to a post and debate various points, they appear to be talking to a single individual but they know they have a wider audience, as though they are sitting in front of a camera and Barbara Walters is tossing out questions. Yet unlike a TV interview, there is no one to interrupt them, so they can express their opinions with some very long-winded and detailed messages.

Speaking of language, our use of it when we refer to Internet-related things is decidedly imprecise. For example, unless there is a clear reason to make a distinction, I use *Internet* and *net* interchangeably in this book. Purists might argue that the term *net* is actually broader than just *Internet* because it includes proprietary services (like America Online's member areas) that may not be accessible to all Internet users. But then, not all the services on the Internet are accessible to all Internet users either, so I see no reason to exclude research that explores behavior in these proprietary online services. My emphasis is on the psychological aspects of the environment, and these are often similar in networks that are not actually connected to the Internet.

EMPOWERING INTERNET USERS

My first goal for this book is to explore the psychological impact of the online world on our behavior, and show how the medium itself can influence the way we act in surprising ways. The second goal is to suggest ways we can all use this knowledge to improve the psychological climate of the Internet. This is still a young technology, and most of us are pretty "young" in our use of it. We are rather naive about how much some of its features can affect the way we act, and blunders are common. I hardly know anyone, for example, who doesn't have a horror story to tell about how someone grossly misinterpreted something they wrote in an email. But we can do better.

The Internet is not simply a technology thrust upon us, one that we can choose to use as is or avoid altogether. We *can* do only that, but we have more power to influence this environment than we ever had for television or telephone because we are the creators, producers, and users at the same time. For the mature, set-in-its-ways, broadcasting medium of television, for example, our activism is now expressed mainly by whether we turn the set on and what we watch if we do. We can write letters to TV moguls, legislators, or newspaper editors, but this is so impotent compared to what we can do on the Internet – a technology still in its youth.

Karl Marx provoked a debate about the power of technological innovation to drive social change when he pointed out, "The hand-mill gives you society with the feudal lord; the steam-mill, society with the industrial capitalist." His point was that certain new technologies have incredible power to shape human behavior and social structures. In 1967, economist-historian Robert L. Heilbroner revisited the issue of technological determinism. It is, he wrote, "peculiarly a problem of certain historical epochs ... in which the forces of technical change have been unleashed, but when the agencies for the control or guidance of technology are still rudimentary."[8] We may be right smack in the middle of one of those historical epochs right now, and the last thing we want is for some "agency" to come along to "control and guide" the Internet. That leaves us – the millions of users who share the online world – and we have a responsibility to do our best.

---

[8] Heilbroner, R. L. (1967). Do machines make history? *Technology and Culture, 8,* 335–345.

YOUR ONLINE PERSONA

THE PSYCHOLOGY OF IMPRESSION FORMATION

Consultants eager to help us create the right impression abound, whether the goal is to impress a personnel officer, get elected to public office, make a sale over the telephone, or get a date. The tips they offer might include "Show confidence with a strong handshake" for a job interview, or "Show interest with good eye contact" for the potential dating partner. The verbal and nonverbal nuances associated with our real-life personas – appropriate for each individual on different occasions with different audiences – have been explored in great depth in popular magazine articles, and also in psychological research.

Most of us enter cyberspace, however, giving little thought to the online persona – how we come across to the people with whom we interact online. Many times those people are already known to us because they are friends, family members, or business associates, and they will interpret whatever we project through email, discussion groups, or personal Web pages within the context of the familiar real-life personas. If we sound harsh or abrupt in an email, they may temper any conclusions based on what they already know about us. Increasingly, however, the online persona is playing a larger role in first impressions as people rely on email, Web sites, and discussion forums more for the first contact, and the phone call, letter, or face-to-face meetings less. For some Internet relationships, communication starts on the net and later develops in other environments. For others, the entire relationship never strays away from the net, not even with a phone call, so the online persona is the whole story.

I recall receiving an email many years ago from a distant colleague I had never met in person that highlighted how clumsy we can be at constructing an online persona. It was 13 screen pages long and closed with one of those automated signatures containing the sender's name, a string of letters announcing his many degrees and certifications, a list of academic affiliations, and a lofty quotation surrounded by asterisks. I was tempted to click *delete* immediately, but then I thought, he is struggling with his online persona, just as we all are, and without the aid of the image consultants. I don't know how to address a stranger online, how to make the impression I want to make, and I might be making similar blunders. I printed it out and read his missive.

WARM AND COLD IMPRESSIONS

First impressions are notoriously susceptible to misperception. Soon after World War II, Solomon Asch did a simple but provocative study on first impressions and found that people tend to leap to conclusions with blinding speed and few cues to guide them.[9] He first described a man as "intelligent, skillful, industrious, warm, determined, practical, and cautious." The people who heard this brief description had no trouble painting in the rest of the personality. They assumed he was also honest, good-natured, wise, popular, sociable, and imaginative – an all-around good fellow. In retrospect, I could imagine a friendly cat burglar with the same traits that Asch listed, but the subjects apparently could not.

Asch wondered how small changes in the list of traits might affect the impression the man was making, so in variations of the same experiment he read the list again to other groups, substituting *cold, polite,* or *blunt* for the single word *warm.* Neither polite nor blunt changed the impression very much, but when the man turned cold, he was transformed into a very unlikable fellow. He became an unpopular, disagreeable, cheapskate. The change in his psychological temperature was the step in the recipe that turned Dr. Jeckyll into Mr. Hyde.

Warm and *cold* say a great deal about our dispositions and influence how others will react to us in social settings. They are heavily weighted central traits when people are forming a first impression. You may be considered brilliant and industrious, but these will pale next to your warmth or coldness.

THE CHILLY INTERNET

The cues people use to form some impression of your warmth are mainly nonverbal. Your facial expressions can be a giveaway: a scowl is all your

[9] Asch, S. E. (1946). Forming impressions of personality. *Journal of Abnormal and Social Psychology, 41,* 258–290.

observers need to take your measure. Your vocal patterns, body posture, gestures, and eye contact will also tip the scales toward one end of the warm/cold continuum. Folding your arms and looking away will lead to a cold impression, while moving a little closer when your partner speaks will make you seem warmer. Research on nonverbal communication and its role in impression formation is very extensive, and there is no question that your words – what you actually say – take a back seat to other cues when observers are drawing conclusions about warmth and coldness.

In many corners of the Internet, your typed words take center stage and observers have little more than ASCII characters to take your temperature. Much of the early research on socioemotional expression online, the kind that leads to impressions of a person's warmth or coldness, showed that we all seem cooler, more task-oriented, and more irascible than we might in person. In the 1970s, Starr Roxanne Hiltz and Murray Turoff conducted one of the first studies to compare the way people express themselves in computer-mediated and face-to-face meetings, and their results did not bode well for this youthful medium.[10] They analyzed utterances in the two settings and found that the face-to-face groups expressed more agreement with one another. The simple "uh-huhs" that a person uses to show understanding and agreement with the speaker were far less common in the online meeting. This isn't too surprising – it would seem odd to type an utterance like that, but perfectly natural to say it. What was more surprising was that the computer-mediated groups made more remarks to express *disagreement* and fewer remarks that might relieve a tense situation. It sounds like they were getting on each others' nerves and acting in ways that made it worse rather than better. Those differences would easily account for the chilly impressions.

Many people have at least a passing acquaintance with the Myers Briggs Type Inventory (MBTI) personality test. Rodney Fuller, a researcher at Bellcore who investigates human-computer interfaces, used a similar but shorter test derived from the MBTI[11] to learn more about online impression formation, and found that mistakes about warmth and cold-

---

[10] Their extensive studies appear in one of the earliest books on computer-mediated communication: Hiltz, S. R., and Turoff, M. (1978). *The network nation: Human communication via computer.* Cambridge, MA: The MIT Press. These researchers used a standard system to analyze what people were saying, or typing, developed earlier by Robert Bales. It included categories such as "shows solidarity," "releases tension," "agrees," "gives suggestion," "gives opinion," "asks for orientation," "disagrees," and "shows antagonism." [R. F. Bales (1950). A set of categories for the analysis of small group interaction. *American Sociological Review, 15,* 257–263.]

[11] Keirsey, D., and Bates, M. (1978). *Please understand me.* Del Mar, CA: Prometheus Nemesis Book Company.

ness were common. He asked people to identify someone they had never met in person, but with whom they communicated on the Internet, to take this brief test – but not with their own answers. He told them to put themselves into the shoes of their email partner and answer the questions as they thought the other person might. The colleagues, or targets, also completed the test, but they answered for themselves.[12] As a control, people who knew one another face-to-face also completed the test, with one member of each pair playing the role of the other.

How well could the role players guess how their colleagues would answer the questions? The ones who had the advantage of face-to-face contact did reasonably well, but the email-only partners showed some intriguing misperceptions. They thought their partners preferred the logical and analytical "thinking" approach far more than they actually did, and they underestimated the possibility that many of them would prefer a more people-oriented "feeling" approach. The targets' need for structure and order, at the expense of spontaneity, was also overestimated by the role players who only knew them through the wires.

Together, these two studies show that what we type is not quite what we would say in person, and others react to this subtle alteration in our behavior. We don't just *appear* a little cooler, testier, and disagreeable because of the limitations of the medium. Online, we appear to be less inclined to *perform* those little civilities common to social interactions. Predictably, people react to our cooler, more task-oriented impression and respond in kind. Unless we realize what is happening, an escalating cycle begins. The online group members *could* have typed simple phrases to express more agreement and to release tension if they had realized the importance of such utterances to the impression they were making and to the group's functioning. They could have softened their typed verbal disagreements, with "Oh, not sure I quite agree with that," as they might have done in person. Though their emotional intelligence might have been high in real life, it was less acute online.

In the 1970s when this technology was very new, we were struggling just to get our point across and get something done. Over the years, though, our lingering doubts about the harsh, cold-fish impression we seemed to be making online have led to some imaginative experiments. Intuitively, people began to appreciate the need to make adjustments in the way they conveyed feeling.

[12] Fuller, R. (1996). Human-computer-human interaction: How computers affect interpersonal communication. In D. L. Day, and D. K. Kovacs (Eds). *Computers, communication and mental models*. London: Taylor & Francis.

THE SOCIOEMOTIONAL THAW

The drive to get more socioemotional mileage out of the keyboard so we can create a human impression online started gathering momentum even in the 1970s. As people began using email and online discussion forums more regularly, they acquired more skill at expressing themselves. About a decade after Hiltz and Turoff finished their study, Ronald Rice and Gail Love looked at socioemotional content in a sample of postings on one of CompuServe's nationwide bulletin boards, using the same category scheme.[13] They found that almost 30% of the messages fell into the socioemotional category, with a surprising 18% in the "shows solidarity" group. People were getting over the early struggles with the new interface and trying to do more than just "get the job done." We adaptable humans are still learning how to thaw the chilly Internet, using whatever tools we can find. Few of us really want to be thought cold, and for good reason, as Asch's studies demonstrated.

Out of this vacuum came the creation of emoticons – those playful combinations of punctuation marks designed to show some facial expression – to add warmth to online communication. In an adolescent way, lying on our sides, we can smile :-), frown :-(, wink ;), and stick our tongues out :P.[14] In Project H, for example, in which researchers are trying to develop a codebook to analyze material from newsgroups and other online discussion forums, 13.4% of a sample of 3,000 posts contained at least one of these graphic accents to enhance the socioemotional content of the message.[15]

Linguistic "softeners" atypical of memos or written letters also began appearing online. These are the little expressions we use to add some hesitation or uncertainty to the way we present our views so we will not seem too abrupt and dogmatic. Vocally, we can lift the pitch at the end of a sentence so even a disagreement will sound more like a question. The familiar "y'know" and "like" make any utterance less decisive and bold. Coming from a teenage girl, the remark "Y'know, well, I don't really like *like* him," is orders of magnitude more complex and subtle

---

[13] Rice, R. E., and Love, G. (1987). Electronic emotion: Socioemotional content in a computer-mediated communication network. *Communication Research, 14,* 85–108.

[14] An amusing one designed to express naive caring was @@@@@@@@@:-) (Marge Simpson).

[15] Witmer, D. F., and Katzman, S. L. (1997, March). On-line smiles: Does gender make a difference in the use of graphic accents? *Journal of Computer-Mediated Communication* [Online], 2(4). Available: http://jcmc.mscc.huji.ac.il/vol2/issue4/witmer1.html [1998, May 20].

compared to its unsoftened version, "I don't like him." Online, abbreviations such as IMHO (in my humble opinion), BTW (by the way), and FWIW (for what it's worth) became part of the lexicon, widely used to ease the brusqueness of a typed message.

Outside of the email world, some environments on the Internet contain even more explicit tools to add socioemotional expressiveness to the online persona, tools that are especially valuable in the socially oriented locales. The synchronous online chats and MUDs offer at least one command people can use to act or emote rather than just speak, and the text that appears on the screen can be clearly distinguished from a phrase meant to be spoken. On a MUD, for example, the players use different commands to create an interaction with speaking, shouting, and acting:

```
Silas says "I never get any respect."
*Silas lowers his head and stares at the floor sadly.
MythMaster shouts "Don't be such a baby!"
*Silas grins at Myth.
```

In some of the graphical metaworlds where participants appear as avatars, you can click on "happy" to make your graphical persona do an upbeat be-bop dance, or "angry" to make the avatar flail its arms and wave its fists. Some worlds let you choose a sound, such as clapping or a rousing chorus of "Amen," to send over the wires to everyone in the same virtual room. Though still primitive and blunt, these technological tools are the result of the ineluctable drive to thaw the Internet's icy landscape with nonverbal cues, so we can express ourselves in warmer, more socioemotional ways.

IMPRESSION FORMATION SHORTCUTS

Our social thermometers give us a quick take on a stranger's warmth or coldness, and we only need a bit more information to form that first impression. Barraged by sensory information and rushed for time, we take shortcuts and rely on just a few cues. Once we have those, we think we have that person nailed and can move onto other matters. Social psychologists Susan Fiske and Shelley Taylor coined the term *cognitive miser* to describe our interest in conserving energy and reducing cognitive load.[16] It would be too time-consuming to collect comprehensive infor-

[16] Fiske, S. T., and Taylor, S. E. (1991). *Social cognition.* New York: McGraw-Hill.

mation to form unique impressions of everyone we meet, so we overuse certain cues that serve as rules of thumb. The impression of a person's warmth or coldness is one example. It dominates the picture as soon as we know anything at all about it and our conclusions about other personal characteristics flow from it.

On the Internet, one of the first things people see is your email address, and the information it conveys can also contribute to your impression. Consider these fictitious but typical examples:

```
tufdude888@aol.com
jtravis@vs2.harvard.edu
FoxyLady@flash.net
75664.8843@compuserve.com
rgoldman6@microsoft.com
```

You might question tufdude's objectivity on women's rights, for example, and you might be inclined to listen more carefully to rgoldman's views on the future of the Internet than to FoxyLady's. The Harvard address of jtravis might carry some weight in the absence of any other information about the sender.

Most people with Internet accounts have not spent much time considering the impression their email addresses make. The domain name to the right of the @ is usually acquired by default. Those connected with colleges and universities get whatever they are assigned, though most will end with the name of the institution followed by the *edu* top-level domain name. That ending instantly identifies you as a member of an academic community, though your actual role is concealed. (jtravis might be a freshman, or on the kitchen staff at Harvard). *Edu* is a little tag that separates its owner from the world of capitalism, where addresses end in *com* (for commercial). Other endings announce your connection to government *(gov)*, nonprofit organizations *(org)*, or particular countries. As Internet usage exploded, the U.S.-dominated naming scheme based on organizational affiliation gave way to nationalism. Australian email addresses, for example, end in *au*.

People who purchase an account from a provider have more choices, but this consumer decision is usually based on costs and services, rather than the name itself. A major video rental chain called Erols began offering very inexpensive Internet access, and consumers seemed unconcerned that their email address (username@erols.com) would project a certain image. It is the electronic equivalent of wearing a tee-shirt emblazoned with a company brand name, day and night. The technology got away from us on this, but the Internet Service Providers love the free advertising.

When a choice of user name (to the left of the @ is possible, some people select a frivolous name like tufdude and regret it later. A friend of mine picked LoveChik as a joke when she first got her account, thinking she would never use it for more than fun and games. But as her editorial and desktop publishing business expanded, she began using the account to exchange files with clients around the country. They always asked about the name, and she found herself tediously apologizing and making excuses for it.

PERSON TYPES AND CATEGORIES

Our cognitive miserliness emerges in the tendency to use categories and stereotypes to form impressions about people, regardless of the person's own behavior. Asch's early approach emphasized the use of cues that people themselves provide, but researchers have found that the impression you make is also the result of your observers' preconceived biases and stereotypes. We are all, in a sense, "naive scientists" who develop our own theories of human behavior based on our experiences with other people, our culture, the media, and our family traditions. We choose the speediest route we can to form an impression, even if it leads to some misperceptions and mistakes. Often, that route means pigeonholing an individual based on the person's apparent similarity to a social category that already has, in our minds, personality attributes associated with it.

Age and gender are two categories that top the list. If I say that you are about to meet a 64-year-old woman, you already have some impression of her personality, even though I never said a single word about what she thinks or how she acts. Marilynn Brewer at UCLA showed how powerful these two categories can be when people are forming first impressions about personality.[17] She collected 140 facial photographs of Caucasian men and women of all ages and asked her subjects to sort the photos into separate stacks that contained pictures of people they thought were similar in character. The piles nearly always contained people of the same gender and approximate age. Nevertheless, when the

---

[17] Brewer, M. (1988). A dual process model of impression formation. In T. K. Srull, and R. S. Wyer Jr. (Eds.), *Advances in social cognition, Volume I. A dual process model of impression formation*. Hillsdale, NJ: Lawrence Erlbaum Associates, Publishers.

subjects were asked to provide verbal labels for their stacks, they rarely used age or gender as part of the description. Instead, they came up with vivid personality labels:

"serious professionals with I-dare-you-to-challenge-my-opinion attitudes"
"white collar workers who are uptight about their jobs"
"Barbara Walters-types, gossipers, nosey, yet sly and slightly snobbish"
"people who are persistent talkers and don't pay attention to their listeners"

On the Internet, gender is more easily deciphered than age simply because so many people sign their messages, or use nicknames that suggest male or female. As I'll discuss in a later chapter, gender can be an especially important cue online when your acquaintances know little else about you, and this aspect of the Internet raises a number of issues about gender roles. In a professional discussion group participants rarely inquire about age, but in the social niches, the pressure to divulge age, and also gender if it isn't obvious, is relentless. We seem almost paralyzed in a social interaction until we know these two simple facts. Such interrogation would be rude in other settings, and mostly unnecessary anyway, but on the Internet it is not unusual.

The gender question is handled through a strategic probe called MORFing on one online system. The acronym stands for *Male OR Female?* In chat rooms, a participant with a gender-neutral nickname who joins a group as a stranger can expect two questions very early in the conversation: "How old are you?" and "Are you male or female?" These direct questions are usually asked just this baldly, though sometimes the probe may be a bit more subtle. A chatting partner might ask if you are a student, and if so, whether college or high school. The goal of these probes is to get two essential pieces of social information: your age and gender.

On the text-based MUDs, participants can choose to describe themselves as male, female, plural, or neuter. Newcomers are assigned the neuter gender, but players can then use a special command to set it to whatever they like. Once set, the players' descriptions include the appropriate pronouns.

Pavel Curtis, a legendary figure in the MUD world and architect of the socially oriented MUD called LambdaMOO, observes that a player's gender is one of the most important variables affecting the way other players interact with you. Players are largely male, but there is some cross-dressing and gender-swapping, mainly by men posing as female characters. Curtis, a Xerox researcher, notes that those who choose gender neutral pronouns are pressured to reveal their true gender, and sometimes even "prove" they are what they say they are. Like other Internet users, MUD players find it disorienting to interact with someone whose gender is unknown. Partly because female players are in the minority, they may be harassed or get special treatment on the MUD:

> *"One [MUD player] reported seeing two newcomers arrive at the same time, one male-presenting and one female-presenting. The other players in the room struck up conversations with the putative female and offered to show her around but completely ignored the putative male, who was left to his own devices."[18]*

On the Web's visually rich metaworlds, where visitors can select one of many avatars provided by the software to represent themselves in interactions, any truth about age and gender could be distorted by the visual image. Ironically, these environments can be even more disorienting for impression formation than the Internet's text-based worlds, because your visual appearance has a strong impact on how others in the world react to you.

At the entrance gate to Alpha World, I observed a milling crowd of fish-eyed aliens. With gray, scaly skin and no secondary sexual characteristics, they stumbled jerkily around like the re-animated corpses in *Night of the Living Dead*. Eager to escape this barren landscape, I clicked on the gate and entered a dazzling planet with fountains, pools, expanses of colorful marble surfaces, Corinthian columns, and a throng of imaginatively dressed and talkative people. Their brief utterances (typed into a chat window) appeared over their heads along with their nicknames, and the little paragraph followed them about like a balloon on a string. I watched for a few minutes, and soon my screen filled up with the face of a dark-skinned man resembling Tonto, the Lone Ranger's trusty sidekick, dressed in primitive leathers. He said, "Don't keep looking like that." "Like what?" I typed. He told me to press the *Home key* on my keyboard and watch.

AlphaWorld's interface is first person; you appear to be viewing the world through your own eyes but can't see your own character. When you turn or move, the scene moves with you. My mentor's suggestion to

---

[18] Curtis, P. (1997). Mudding: Social phenomena in text-based virtual realities. In S. Kiesler (Ed.), *Culture of the Internet* (pp. 121–142). Mahwah, NJ: Lawrence Erlbaum Associates, Publishers. An early version is also available online at http://www.oise.on.ca/~jnolan/muds/about_muds/pavel.html [1998, May 20].

press the Home key changed it to third-person view. I saw that my avatar was the fish-eyed alien, not the disembodied presence I assumed. Dismayed by my hideous appearance, I clicked Avatar on the menu, and randomly picked "Kelly" from a list of uninformative first names. In a microsecond, I was transformed into a copper-haired babe in purple leotards, and others began waving. One avatar asked my age, and when I replied, the next balloon read, "Yeah, and I'm 102."

Just as in a face-to-face setting, the nonverbal cues are more important to impression formation that mere words, even when all of us know – intellectually – that an avatar is as fake as an Elvis Presley Halloween mask. Ignoring my words, he gravitated toward the impression the avatar made rather than what I said, and also his own stereotypes about the demographics of Alpha World inhabitants.

BEYOND AGE AND GENDER

In the social neighborhoods of the Internet the pressure to reveal age and gender is high because these two features are so fundamental to the initial impression. Nationality and race are also salient characteristics. Questions about location, from which you can infer national origin, are quite common. "Where are u?" is a frequent opening gambit in synchronous social conversations because the Internet's global reach makes the answers surprising. However, people do not probe others about race with the same kind of direct boldness they inquire about age, gender, or location. Strangely, social Internet users do not want to create a racially prejudiced impression, but the norms of this environment carry no sanctions against queries that might divulge other kinds of prejudices.

Besides the central traits we rely on so heavily, we all have constructed many more categories over our years of experience with other human beings. Although they rarely have obvious verbal labels, they might reflect such category groupings as fascists, space cadets, valley girls, geeks, scam artists, pointy-headed professors, wild-eyed terrorists, generous philanthropists, gullible believers, or ambitious manipulators. It takes more cognitive energy to place someone into any of these categories because we need more than the quick scan of age, sex, race, and warmth/coldness to do it. Nevertheless, it takes less energy than patiently reserving judgment until we can collect enough information to form an impression of a unique individual without relying on our social categories.

Posters on Usenet inadvertently provide their audience with some useful clues to help readers drop them into one of these more detailed categories. When a message is posted to a group such as alt.psychology.personality, the sender might cross-post it to others, perhaps alt.conspiracy and alt.paranormal. Despite endless advisories against this deluge, senders continue to include all their favorite groups in their audience, and readers will learn something from these group affiliations. In the United States, that is like mailing a letter to your senator explaining your views on a budget amendment, noting that you are sending the copies of the letter to the National Rifle Association, the American Veterans of Foreign Wars, and conservative talk show host Rush Limbaugh. None of the receivers is left in the dark about your political leanings.

SOCIAL COGNITION AND CATEGORIES

At any moment in time, some of your social categories are more accessible than others, and you will be more likely to use the ones closest to the surface to form an impression of a newcomer. This effect is known as *priming*. If you just read a story about a cult's use of the Internet for recruitment, for example, the person-type of "treacherous enticer" would be primed and much more accessible from the standpoint of social cognition. Suppose after reading the article, you logged on to one of your favorite synchronous chat rooms and encountered a new person, Trajyk, who made some ambiguous remarks:

```
<Trajyk> I've had some tough times in my life
<solo> heh, heh, what difficult times were those Traj?
<Trajyk> much sadness, much disappointment
<solo> are you happy now?
<Trajyk> I've found real, true friends:)
<solo> here?
<Trajyk> No, in our little community of friends
<Trajyk> Are you lonely, solo?
```

Category priming can happen naturally in the Internet's discussion forums because you proactively go to one of its hundreds of thousands of distinctive neighborhoods when you log in. The Internet consists of countless subcommunities, each with its own norms and category-priming potential. Some bring our work-related categories to the surface, such as a mailing list for dentists or a specialized MUD for journalists. Others, like the riveting multiuser hack-and-slash adventure games, are highly competitive and task-oriented. And of course, the many social corners of the Internet are evolving their own set of expectations.

The online auction house called eBay.com, for example, hosts discussion forums for its registered users on their special interests – whether that happens to be rare coins, antiques, books, or Beanie Babies. When you start reading the posts in your favorite forum the category you associate with people who hang out there is already primed. It is right on top of your cognitive memory stack. You will be the miser, conserving your cognitive energy, by relying on your person-type for stamp collectors or rare book lovers to get some impression of new posters. The same shortcut occurs when you visit a new Internet group to see what is going on. If you drop into the Usenet newsgroup alt.alien.visitors, you might be primed to find "paranormal devotees," "weirdo freaks," "open-minded critics of modern science," "anti-government firebrands," or whatever category you use to characterize people who talk alien visitation.

On MUDs, the vivid room descriptions that you read the moment you enter each one serve an additional priming function. A room called Sensual Respites on LambdaMOO, for example, exudes images of sophisticated sexuality, reminiscent of a trendy singles bar in upscale Soho, while the informal and relaxed Living Room encourages a more family atmosphere. Just the rooms' text descriptions can influence your impressions of the people you meet.

As cognitive misers, we are reluctant to rethink the impressions we form of others. Once we slap a label from our category collection on someone, we are not prone to peel it off or alter it much. That first impression is so critical because of this human resistance to admit mistakes, and the desire to leave the label in place leads to *confirmation bias*. Not only do we ignore evidence that might contradict our original impressions; we actively search for information to confirm them. Our desire to validate that first impression is a potent force that guides how we collect and assess new information about another person. The open mind we demand of jurors at the start of a trial is a tall order, one that few could fill. Once we form some impression we selectively pick up confirming evidence. In long Internet messages, it is usually not difficult to find snippets to support our first impression and to ignore the rest.

THE RHYTHMS OF IMPRESSION FORMATION

In a face-to-face interaction, it is easy to get the business of forming an impression of another person over with quickly. Online, however, the rhythms of impression formation show some roller coaster variations, and the medium has much to do with this. It is always slower than face-to-face, and much choppier. The pacing is like the belabored ascents and thrilling descents on Disney World's Space Mountain ride.[19]

When a stranger addresses you in a chat room, for example, and you type a reply immediately, your remark may appear on everyone else's screen within a second or two, or it may take a full minute. Long transmission delays and a large number of users may lead the stranger to think you're a hesitant or uninterested conversationalist. If nothing appears within 2 or 3 minutes, the stranger's query is electronically dead and buried. It scrolls off the communal screen and the chatting session moves on to other matters. As I mentioned in the last chapter, the lag in chat sessions and the need to type your replies affect the register, and though people strive for a "conversational" tone the pace is slower than one on the phone or in person. The "bursty" nature of transmission makes it impossible to use ordinary rhythm norms associated with these other settings.

We do try to borrow some of the rhythmic and social conventions we're accustomed to, especially those from the telephone. A person might start a synchronous chat by saying "hi" or "hello," and anticipate some response within a short period of time, and then expect the usual conversational turn-taking. To end the discussion, one might type "nice talking to you," or an abbreviation like *bbl* (be back later). On the phone, the same general rules apply, though any breaks in pacing like those typical in chat sessions would be devastating to the exchange. Try waiting just 3 seconds before saying "hello" when you answer a ringing phone, or avoid using vocal fillers like "uh huh" when your phone partner pauses for a moment. You will probably hear, "Hello? Are you still there?"

The rhythms in email and the asynchronous discussion forums are much slower than the chat sessions, and communications researcher Joseph Walther suggests that this feature might make people seem colder than they would in a face-to-face interaction, at least initially. Much of the early research comparing impression formation online and in person involved short-term interactions, so-called zero-history groups, in which strangers worked together for brief periods. The people may simply not have had enough time to form more than an amorphous impression of their invisible partners. With the lean communication channels available online and the slow and choppy pacing, a well-developed impression of an individuated other may take longer, even using all our shortcuts, but it will probably emerge.

[19] This famous roller coaster is inside a cavernous building and, except for a few dim stars and distant control panels, is entirely in the dark.

Walther demonstrated how these rhythms work with an asynchronous discussion forum and an unusually long experiment. Groups of three people each were asked to develop policy recommendations on several different issues, by means of either face-to-face meetings or online discussion forums. Whenever a group completed a task, the members rated the personality characteristics of the others in their group. Unlike most such scales, this one included a "don't know" check box so the people wouldn't just check the noncommittal middle box when their impressions were weak. After the first task, the face-to-face group members had already developed strong impressions of one another, but the computer-mediated groups had not. By the end of the third task, though, the people who knew each other online developed much stronger impressions of one another, almost as vivid as those who were meeting face-to-face.[20]

ONLINE, ONSTAGE: IMPRESSION MANAGEMENT ON THE INTERNET

Managing your own impression on the Internet is like navigating white water with two-by-fours for oars. Your impression management toolkit is strangely devoid of the tools most familiar to you, and new ones appear that you may not know how to use. In a text-based environment, you can't project your high status the way you could in visual mode – with impeccable grooming or a gold watch. Your commanding voice is silenced. Your contagious smile and raised eyebrow are invisible. Unless you bring up your own graphical Web site and direct others to it, the main tool you have to manage the impression others form about you is the QWERTY keyboard. Compared to cosmetics, clothing, hair styles, and all the other accoutrements that swallow our paychecks, the keyboard can be an unfamiliar and awkward impression-making device. Nevertheless, the drive to manage our impressions in any social setting is strong, and Internet users are extraordinarily creative.

Erving Goffman, the father of impression management theory, believed that everyone uses tactics to present themselves in whatever light they think appropriate for the context. Your motives are key. You might want to be liked by your audience, to dominate them, to throw yourself on their mercy, or to have them fear or respect you, and you will choose tactics for your self-presentation that you hope will accom-

---

[20] Walther, J. B. (1993). Impression development in computer-mediated interaction. *Western Journal of Communication, 57,* 381–398.

plish your goal. You also want to be very careful about being perceived as a manipulative social chameleon who fakes an impression for social gain. We spend a lot of time and effort managing and refining the impression we want to make, but we certainly don't want others to know how hard we work at this. Goffman calls it "an information game – a potentially infinite cycle of concealment, discovery, false revelation, and rediscovery."[21]

As I mentioned earlier, if you explore Internet niches in which nicknames are commonly used, the one you choose for yourself becomes part of how you manage your impression. In the Internet's synchronous chat rooms, MUDs, and metaworlds, for example, participants choose their nicknames – or *nicks* – with great care and come to think they "own" that name, at least in that corner of cyberspace. Each time you type a line and contribute it to the conversation, your nick appears in brackets, so it becomes an attribute linked to every utterance you make.

For more than a year, Haya Bechar-Israeli at the Hebrew University of Jerusalem studied nicknames chosen by the regular visitors to #NICE-CAFE, #IRCbar, #Truthdare, and #30plus, all on Internet Relay Chat.[22] He probed their reasons for selecting a particular nick, and gradually developed a taxonomy of nickname types. The largest group (45%) chose nicknames that related to themselves in some way (<shydude>, <pilot>, <handsom>, <dutchman>), and another 8% just used their real names. Only 6% chose nicks that referred to figures in fairytales, films, or literature. Even in the anonymous IRC world, at least half the people were creating self-presentations that were not too far afield from their true identities, or at least their idealized selves.

Bechar-Israeli also found that people rarely change their nicks, even though it is very easy to do. They establish an online persona and work on the self-presentation of that identity rather than jumping from online skin to skin. Reactions to a nickname "thief" are strong and immediate. Online friends who noticed that someone had usurped Bechar-Israeli's nick while he was absent immediately informed him and pressured the thief to choose a different name. The thief complied. Pavel Curtis tells of a player called ZigZag on LambdaMOO who even complained to him when other players chose similar names such as ZigZag!

---

[21] Goffman, E. (1959). *The presentation of self in everyday life*. Garden City, NY: Doubleday.

[22] Bechar-Israeli, H. (1996). From <Bonehead> to <cLoNehEAd>: Nicknames, play, and identity on Internet relay chat. *Journal of Computer-Mediated Communication* [Online], *1*(2). Available: http://jcmc.mscc.huji.ac.il/vol1/issue2/bechar.html [1998, May 20].

or just Zig.[23] People own little in the virtual world but they appear to treasure the property they do possess.

ONLINE SELF-DESCRIPTIONS

On the Internet, opportunities to manage your impression with a written self-description, something like an informal and brief biography, are not uncommon. In online college classes, for example, faculty typically ask students to introduce themselves in the computer conference during the first week of class. They do this partly to make sure the students are connected and are learning the ins and outs of the software, but they also want the students to become acquainted with one another. For many of them, this is a first experience at online self-presentation, but patterns emerge quickly even without any specific instructions from the teacher. The style that the first two or three students use often becomes the norm. In some classes, each introduction might be only one or two sentences with little more than major and class. In others, it becomes much longer and richer, with hobbies, family life, hopes for the future, and fears about taking a course on the Internet.

When you subscribe to a mailing list, the moderator often asks you to introduce yourself to the group by an automated return message that also contains the list's purpose, discussion topics, and general instructions. Again, many people are new at this self-presentation mode and in this context they have no model to follow. They just joined and have not yet seen anyone else's introductions, or even had much chance to see what others are discussing. The result is a bizarre mixture of first impressions that range from the brief and highly professional to the heart-rending personal confessional. I recently joined a list in which the automated message warned new subscribers to wait a bit before posting an introduction, a tactic that will help the group develop more consistent norms.

MUD software offers a unique means for players to control their self-presentations. You can type a description of yourself that other players will read whenever they use the "look" command and add your nickname to it. "Look" is used frequently when a player enters a room, a phenomenon that demonstrates again how eager we are to gather some material to form an impression quickly. On the fantasy role-playing MUDs and other multiuser games, the descriptions embed each character in the MUD's context. On PernMUSH, a MUD styled after Ann McCaffrey's books, all

---

[23] Curtis, P. (1997). Mudding: Social phenomena in text-based virtual realities. In S. Kiesler (Ed), *Culture of the Internet* (pp. 121–142). Mahwah, NJ: Lawrence Erlbaum Associates, Publishers.

players are expected to stay in character unless they enter a special OOC (Out Of Character) room to get help on the software. On social MUDs like LambdaMOO, some descriptions are fantastical ("an impish, mischievous elf carrying the planetary gems"), but Pavel Curtis notes that most players tire of this role-playing effort quickly. They return to a more normal mode of self-presentation, albeit with some degree of wish-fulfillment. He says he can't count the number of "mysterious but unmistakably powerful" figures he has seen wandering around the mansion.

As especially inventive self-presentation by a MUD player comes from SwampFox, who cleverly re-created some stunning nonverbal cues for her first impression. She used motion, sound, touch, dramatic physical appearance, and eye contact, all in a text-only description that appeared whenever anyone typed "look SwampFox" in the same room. She programmed her character to respond automatically to anyone who "looked" at her with the remark, "SwampFox snarls fiercely and swipes her tail at [your nickname] for looking." With nothing but ASCII characters, SwampFox managed her impression like a virtuoso.

THE HOME PAGE ADVANTAGE

Many people are taking advantage of the opportunity to create a home page on the Web, and this provides a richer medium for presenting the persona online. People create home pages for quite a variety of reasons, as I learned when I queried dozens of them. Some said they wanted to share pictures and information with friends and family. One new father was adding weekly updates to his baby photo collection so his relatives around the country could see his infant son's progress. A few said they wanted to provide a community service. One man in the Netherlands, for example, put some information on his home page about how to eliminate a particularly aggressive virus that was penetrating computers, mainly in Europe. Those who had been infected quickly found his site through search engines and encouraged him to keep adding to his store of information about how to get rid of viruses. He did, and is very proud that his site has become a solid and useful addition to the Web. A number of people, particularly those in the high-tech fields, are putting their resumes online, along with samples of some of the software and multimedia applications they have worked on. This gives prospective employers an opportunity to see considerably more than just the hard copy version of the individual's work experiences.

Many people are using their 5 or 10 MB of free disk space to promote a cause or voice a personal protest. Gary North, for example, maintains his own Y2K doomsday site with apocalyptic warnings about what is going to happen when the clocks reach midnight, January 1, 2000. He says, "I don't expect you to believe me … yet. That is why I have created this site."[24]

Other reasons people mentioned for creating a personal Web site: "Everyone else was doing it," "I wanted to let people know about me," and "I had to do something with that free disk space." Unlike the email address, the home page is not primarily aimed at giving our acquaintances an easy way to communicate with us, though most home pages offer the visitor a chance to send the owner an email through a single click. The home page is more like a billboard, or an ad in the yellow pages. It's an inexpensive way to create an impression, polish your online persona, and tell the world something about yourself and your interests. We can create a finely crafted self-presentation for the whole world to see. We can display our ideal selves, complete with retouched photos, creative essays, artwork, poetry, musical creations, and lists of achievements. We can add numerous links to our favorite spots on the Web, showing off our diverse interests and cosmopolitan tastes.

Not everyone uses the free disk space that comes with their Internet account to profile themselves, of course, but the personal home page, the kind that serves as an introduction to who you are, is becoming more common and also much easier to do because of advances in software. With the exception of a few European aristocrats in the first age of self – the Renaissance – people have not had such an opportunity before. Without any of the costs of land, labor, or building materials, we can make our billboards as simple as a brief description with a photo, or as elaborate as a multimedia multipage spread, complete with music, animations, and rich graphics. We can fill them with as much autobiographical detail as we like, either true or reconstructed, and add links to our previously unpublished poetry, novels, and drawings.

The personal home page phenomenon is taking off with incredible momentum, and commercial sites whose revenue comes from advertising rather than end-user fees are offering even more free disk space to patrons. GeoCities, for example, offers free space and many tools for their patrons to engage in *homesteading* – that is, building their home page. They apparently discovered that people are very intrigued with their new billboards and will spend considerable time on them; advertisers will pay for access to these people. This aspect of the personal home page craze bears some resemblance to those *Who's Who* books that profit

[24] North, G. (1998). Gary North's Y2K Links and Forums [Online] Available: http://www.garynorth.com/ [29 October, 1998].

chiefly from copies sold to the people – and their proud parents – whose names and brief bios are listed.

Eleanor Wynn, of the Oregon Graduate Institute of Science and Technology, and James E. Katz of Bellcore, reviewed many such home pages and found that most of the creators were not trying to create an alternate identity that differed dramatically from their own selves: "A key feature is that they move in the opposite direction of what cyberspace postmodernists claim; rather than fragmenting the self, personal home pages are attempts to integrate the individual, make a personal statement of identity, and show in a stable, replicable way what the individual stands for and what is deemed important."[25] The creators often blend aspects of their public and private lives in surprising ways, partly because the audience for their creation is not well understood. While the audience for a professional resume provides a social context that constrains the contents, the audience for the home page is, quite literally, anyone on the planet with Internet access. Friends and family might drop by, but so might coworkers, employers, or strangers from another part of the world. Thus, many people aim for an integrated and holistic self-presentation.

A typical home page, a conglomerate of hundreds I have seen, looks like John Q. Citizen's:

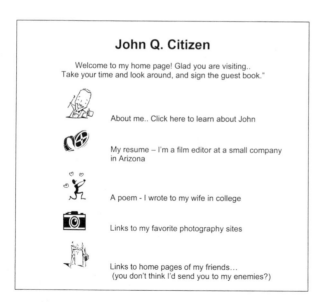

---

[25] Wynn, E., and Katz, J. E. (1997). Hyperbole over cyberspace: Self-presentation & social boundaries in Internet home pages and discourse. *The Information Society* [Online], *13(4)*, 297–328. Available: http://www-slis.lib.indiana.edu/TIS/hyperbole.html [1998, March 24].

This simple and easy-to-create example contains many of the elements that appear on personal Web pages all over the Internet, including links to a brief autobiography, a professional resume, some personal poetry, and links to hobby sites and friends' home pages. With his text, category selections and clip art choices, the creator seems eager to craft an integrated and well-rounded self, and feature his work life along with his humor, warmth, and close relationships.

On the positive side, home pages allow us to experiment with our online self-presentations, share information about our lives with significant others, and get feedback from people who find our Web site. One potentially negative feature of the proliferation of home-grown home pages is that they seem to be contributing quite a lot of chaff to the Internet. The net is, arguably, the world's largest, cheapest vanity press with distribution channels that far exceed anything even the megapublishers can imagine. It also has virtually unlimited shelf space, but the cataloging process is not very well-developed yet. Search engines often bring up dozens of irrelevant personal home pages when you enter keywords that happen to appear on them, creating quite a lot of clutter and distraction when you are searching for information.

FOCUS ON SELF

Tinkering with a personal home page can be very absorbing and time consuming. It can also promote an increased focus on the self and a heightened, and perhaps exaggerated, sense that others are watching us with interest. I am reminded of the work of developmental psychologist David Elkind, who studied the characteristics of egocentrism in adolescence. Young people can be rather absorbed in their self-images and mistakenly assume others join them in that absorption. Elkind found that one feature of this egocentrism is a preoccupation with the *imaginary audience*. During this stage in life, many people seem to overestimate how much others are watching and evaluating, so they feel unduly self-conscious about the impression they are making.[26]

When we create a personal home page, we do not know much about the people who look at it or how much time they spend on it. Software tools can provide tracking information, such as statistics on the number of hits, graphs showing peak usage times, or the Internet addresses of the computers your visitors use. Although Web marketers wisely pour over

[26] Elkind, D. (1967). Egocentrism in adolescence. *Child Development, 38,* 1025–1034.

these reports, not many homesteaders use them. Even when they do include a simple hit counter, the creator may underestimate the number of hits she herself contributed, or forget to subtract them from the total.

Outside of these personal home pages, it is often nearly impossible to decipher how many people attend to anything we post on the net. But the mere fact that millions of people *could* be scrutinizing our creations may inflate our perceptions of the audience's size. The same principle applies to online discussion forums, such as newsgroups and mailing lists. On a mailing list, for example, any post sent to the list name will land in the email inboxes of everyone who subscribed, and you can tell how many people are subscribed by querying the listserver. However, you have no idea how many people on the list are deleting your post as fast as a piece of unsolicited commercial spam. Some may be deleting entire discussion threads, or just using the delete key liberally to remove excess, low priority mail.

Another common destiny for posts sent to mailing lists is the auto-mated filer. Most email software has a means for the recipient to file mail automatically into local folders based on various criteria, such as a string of text contained in the subject line or sender email address. For exam-ple, if I subscribe to a mailing list called GARDEN, I can use the filtering function in my email software to file any mail posted to that mailing list before I even see it. This reduces clutter in the inbox and also saves time, but any message filed this way could easily be treated the same way we treat those flyers and pamphlets we toss into a corner pile. That is where everyone drops incoming mail that seems too important to toss out right away, but not important enough to open immediately. We intend to look at those automatically filed list messages when we get the chance, but often, that chance never comes. Those messages, even the whole folder, could find their way into the recycle bin when the recipi-ent finally decides it's time to free up some disk space, just as we toss those old magazines and pamphlets out when the pile gets too high and we think that corner could use a houseplant instead.

The characteristics of the Internet, then, may be encouraging us to spend unnecessary time polishing our online persona for an imaginary audience, one whose size might be in the millions, or might be close to zero. People who subscribe to a mailing list but never post anything are called *lurkers,* a name that reinforces the illusion that there are hundreds, maybe thousands of people out there sitting in the audience with their eyes glued to the stage, following the action intently. Another name for many of them might simply be *deleters.* When we see our own words and

Web site on the Internet, a medium that reaches every corner of the globe, we may be too hasty to conclude that our audience is large and that they are hanging on our every word.

A difference between the imaginary audience effects we see in adolescents, and the ones that may be flourishing because of the Internet's unlimited shelf space and indeterminate audience size, is that we have far more control over our self-presentation on the Internet compared to what we had in high school. Even with very limited technical ability, we can tinker with digitized photos and completely bypass any concern about facial blemishes. We decide exactly what to say and how to say it, and which personality traits we want to feature.

MAKING THAT KEYBOARD WORK HARDER

The desire to form impressions of other people, and to manage our own impressions in social settings, are fundamental human characteristics that do not disappear just because we now do these things on the Internet. The difference is that we are not expert at using the cues at hand, nor are we sure how to manage our own self-presentations. This keyboard, for example, can be a rascal when it comes to the nuances of human communication. The Caps Lock key is, inexplicably, much too large considering how rarely we use it. If I slip and press it by mistake, my colleagues might think I AM SHOUTING AT THEM. The colon and right parenthesis:) are far harder to locate, but even this blunt socioemotional instrument can add a warmer and friendlier tone to a discussion.

On the Internet, we are struggling with a very odd set of tools and pushing them as hard as we can. Homo sapiens are both set in their ways and amazingly adaptable, and right now, all of us are learning some painful and awkward lessons about impression formation online. I look forward to the time when the kinds of "interaction rituals" that Goffman described will stabilize on the net and the business of forming impressions will be more predictable, reliable, and familiar, and much less prone to those hazardous misperceptions. There is something reassuring about knowing instantly where people stand in a social situation – by their postures, their clothing, their business cards, or even their position in a taxi. But I also enjoy being a part of this highly unstable phase when the ground keeps shifting under our feet and the old rules don't apply.

That online acquaintance I mentioned earlier sent me a few more messages during the next two years, none of which did much to improve the first impression he had made. But my lingering concerns about how inexperienced we all are in the online impression business made me avoid any abrupt, relationship-terminating replies. I did not want to make what social psychologists call the *fundamental attribution error.* We attribute other people's ghastly behavior to their basic natures, to their boorishness. When we, ourselves, do something embarrassing or rude, we blame unfortunate environmental circumstances. If I SHOUT online, it is because that Caps Lock key is so wretchedly misplaced by hardware manufacturers. If a stranger does it, I conclude that the person is unnecessarily brash.

I finally ran into my email acquaintance at a conference and learned how mistaken my initial impressions about him were. His contagious smile instantly belied the cool and arrogant image he had projected at first. Stroking his graying beard, he said, "I don't really know how to do this Internet thing, but I'm learning." We all are.

ONLINE MASKS AND MASQUERADES

"You'll never get him outta there," pronounced the raven-haired woman relaxing on an overstuffed sofa, filing her long, pointy nails. "Of course, we will – those brainless fiends know nothing of the plan – or our abilities." The elegantly dressed gentleman opened a leather-bound notebook, scribbled a few lines, then passed a note to the woman on the sofa. Her eyes widened and she quickly rose, grabbed her cape, and followed the man out the door. "Let's see how they like a little chemical warfare," he smirked, uncorking a small bottle and placing it on the floor.

A hack novelist's contribution to the net's vanity press? Not exactly. This was a scene enacted on one of the Internet's role-playing arenas, in this case, a vampire game. The players were typing their lines and describing their actions in a chat window, improvising the performance around a vague plot as they went along. This particular role play is based on *Vampire: The Masquerade,* a popular storytelling game ordinarily conducted in real life, but that has now migrated onto the net with considerable success.[27] Players spend many months developing their online vampire characters and creatively participating in plots of assassination, clan war, kidnapping, and romance.

Because the never-ending plots unfold 24 hours a day, 365 days a year, the players are not always clear about the difference between IC (in character) and OOC (out of character). The theater's conventions require players to type any OOC remarks inside double parentheses, but several have told me that many participants are often neither OOC nor IC. They are somewhere in between, playing a fictionalized role as

---

[27] The elaborate rules and clans of the real-life game are described in Rein-Hagen, M. (1992). *Vampire the masquerade.* Clarkston, GA: White Wolf Game Studio.

though it were their real selves, taking the vampire wars, murders, and plots of revenge rather seriously. As one vampire player explained, "Lots of people start out playing something totally different from themselves but most of us can't help bringing our own personalities into the character eventually."

"Without lies humanity would perish of despair and boredom," wrote Anatole France in the 1920s. If the converse is also true and lies bring excitement and joy, we have found one reason for the Internet's allure. The characteristics of the online world trigger a wide assortment of role plays, deceptions, half-truths, and exaggerations, partly because anonymity and the absence of visual and auditory cues allow them, and at the same time insulate us from the consequences. Even when we are not exactly anonymous on the net, the physical distance and low social presence make us feel less inhibited, less likely to be detected, and a little less under our superego's thumb.

Psychological research on patterns of lying suggest humanity is in no danger of perishing. In a diary study, college students reported telling an average of two lies a day. People out of college slowed down a bit, but still reported about one lie a day. Some were the little white lies people tell to avoid hurting another; others, however, were the self-serving lies designed to enhance the impression the person was trying to make.[28] Since lying is not exactly a desirable behavior, we can imagine that these people may not have been entirely forthcoming about their lying and may have been underreporting their daily deceptions. They might also have been engaging in a bit of motivated forgetting; it is easier on your self-concept to let memories about misdeeds get a little fuzzy.

Deceptions come in many varieties. A relatively benign form is simple role play, in which you deliberately masquerade as another character and take on a new personality to match. At Mardi Gras, you might sport a Don Juan mask and black cape, and temporarily lose your usual shyness with women. In the online vampire clubs, you may become a debonair and artistic primogen of the Toreador clan, or a feral Nosferatu whose grotesque, animal-like appearance offends even the most tolerant vampires. The key ingredient in this form of lying (assuming you can separate IC from OOC) and the element that makes it fun and relatively harmless compared to other varieties, is that everyone knows it is a mask. The masquerade itself has rigid rules of play, ones we learn very early in life.

---

[28] DePaulo, B. M., Kashy, D. A., Kirdendol, S. E., Wyer, M. M. et al. (1996). Lying in everyday life. *Journal of Personality and Social Psychology, 70(5)*, 979–995.

THE ORIGINS OF ROLE PLAY

Role playing, as a category of play, emerges in toddlers before their second birthday. The preschool years are the golden age for pretense and symbolic play, when children turn sheets into Superman capes, chairs into forts, and closets into secret caves with hidden dangers and treasures. Almost any object is a candidate for a prop in a child's theatrical arsenal, and imaginative children can find exotic uses for the most humble household articles.

When the role play includes other children, a special culture emerges with very strict rules about how to enter the play, maintain the pretense, and make an exit. Holly Giffin studied this kind of make-believe for her doctoral research and observed the existence of an extremely important one called the *illusion conservation rule*.[29] The players are expected to stay inside the play and avoid any references to the fact that the stage is just a stage, or that "it's only pretend." The illusion must be conserved; out-of-character remarks aggravate the other players because they interrupt the fantasy and diminish its power. If they must leave to answer a nature call or go home for lunch, they are expected to adapt their exit to the illusion's script, at least insofar as their imaginations will allow.

On a school playground, one of these sociodramatic plays emerged that showed how these rules control the action. Jackie, an imaginative 5 year-old, began using a stick as a telescope from the top of the Jungle Jim, and his younger playmate Sid shouted, "Ahoy, Captain!" from below. Spontaneously, and with no discussion, the curtain on the pirate play went up and the unspoken, but clearly understood rules for participating were put into effect. Sid clambered up to the top and handed Jackie a piece of paper saying, "Here's the map, Captain." From below, another boy shouted, "Hey, I want to play!" Jackie, however, did not acknowledge the newcomer except to point the telescope toward him and announce [to Sid], "Enemy pirate ship approaching. Man the guns." The intruder needed no other hint that he was violating the illusion conservation rule with his OOC entrance, and deftly switched into character as a marauding pirate foe. Later, when the bell rang to line up and return inside, the players wound down the drama as gracefully as they could by stowing their pirate gear under the seesaw and shouting, "Next

---

[29] Giffin, H. (1984). The coordination of meaning in the creation of a shared make-believe reality. In I. Retherton (Ed.), *Symbolic play*. New York: Academic Press.

time, Bluebeard, you'll walk the plank!" The children dropped out of the pretend mode and into the line.

The clear demarcation children attempt to establish for such games creates a special frame of unreality inside the larger, real-life reality frame. Once they cross the boundary into the role-play frame, they are in a different world where new rules apply. The rules can be just as demanding as those in real-life, sometimes even more so, and they serve to protect the play-frame against leakage from the surrounding real world.

Children begin losing interest in elaborately constructed role plays by age 5 or 6 and turn instead to other forms of play. They become far more interested, for example, in games of skill and chance in which they can compete against one another without leaving their real-life identities behind them. These games have equally stringent rules but the improvised make-believes and role plays so common in young children have virtually disappeared by the time they enter middle school. By the teenage years, adolescents are experimenting with their identities in other ways but they are certainly not doing spontaneous sociodramas of pirate battles between math and chemistry classes.

LEAKAGE ON THE INTERNET

As children, we easily absorbed the illusion conservation rule and all the other strictures that apply to role plays. As adults on the Internet, that concrete wall that separates the reality frame from the role-play frame becomes a flimsy, permeable membrane. Those hard and fast rules that Giffin described, the ones that are consensually adopted by children to define the boundary between real life and pretense in preschool, are only vaguely understood on the Internet. Sometimes they are clear, or at least they seem so. At other times, these boundaries are subject to considerable leakage.

Clear examples occur on the multiuser games in which players are sternly cautioned to stay in character at all times. One player might choose the warrior role and start the adventure with many strength points but few points for wisdom, soul, or cleverness. The game itself directs players toward certain behavior patterns based on their choices, and anyone choosing warrior is not just expected to conform to that role, but is pushed toward it by virtue of the capabilities the character possesses.

In other cases, the membrane is more permeable and Internet participants move fluidly between the real and unreal frames of the environment. A very intricate example of a case in which participants moved this way was described by researchers at the Hebrew University of Jerusalem, who studied synchronous chat sessions.[30] Lucia Ruedenberg-Wright, one of the researchers, used *Lucia* as her nickname on the chat channels and started interacting with *Thunder,* a systems operator. *Thunder* first toys with channel names, inviting Lucia to join him on channels with playful names such as -),/, +bagelnosh, +hsonlegab [bagelnosh spelled backwards], and finally +weed. *Thunder* adds a description for the channel that ultimately becomes the site for the play: ***The topic is:ssssssssssss hmmmm wheres all that smoke from? +weed.

Lucia joins the channel +weed and within moments, more join in. *Kang, Jah, Rikitiki,* and others eventually find the channel called +weed and push their way into it. The role play, suggested by the channel's description, begins.

Thunder passes a joint to *Lucia,* and *Kang* adds the comment, "they might be sushpishus, huh?:-)," deliberately mispelling "suspicious" to stay in character. After several interchanges, *Thunder* starts playing with the keyboard to role-play the marijuana party, given the limitations of ASCII. He first uses ":-Q" to represent a man smoking a joint, and then :| to indicate a man holding his lips together to keep the smoke in his lungs. Finally, he creates a complete scenario, read as smoke joint, inhale twice, let smoke out, then experience pleasure, using the following symbols:

```
\ :-Q :-| :-| :\ :\sssss :-)
```

The rules that governed this IRC performance were conceptually similar to those that control the preschoolers' role-play games, though obviously far more complex. This role play required enormous creativity to maintain the illusion, but the strictures were there. Anyone joining the channel was expected to pretend to be stoned, and use all the creativity they could muster to do it.

The researchers identified not just two frames, the real and the unreal, but five. The first was real life, which is the same as preschoolers identify. The second was "let's play IRC," a frame characterized by reduced accountability and a willingness to talk about almost anything. The

[30] Danet, B., Ruedenberg-Wright, L., and Rosenbaum-Tamari, Y. (1997). Hmmm ... Where's that smoke coming from? Writing, play and performance on Internet relay chat. *Journal of Computer-Mediated Communication* [Online], *2(4)*. Available: http://jcmc.mscc.huji.ac.il/vol2/issue4/danet.html [1998, May 20].

rules that apply to this frame are not well established or consensual, the way they were for the preschoolers involved in the pirate role play, so misperceptions and miscommunications are common. Sometimes the talk can be serious, sometimes playful, sometimes deceitful and treacherous, and it is often difficult to know which is which.

The third frame is "Let's have a party." Now the players begin to flirt and play word games, but the metamessage is that we are here to have fun. Nothing serious. This is when *Thunder* experiments with the channel names and keeps changing them. *Lucia* is not able to type fast enough to actually join him.

"Let's pretend" is the theme for the fourth frame, and it begins to dictate the rules for a virtuoso simulation of smoking marijuana. The players still occasionally slip back to real life, or to "let's have a party," but there is a tentative emergence of certain rules for this chatting session, ones that require the players to join in a role-play game. Finally, the fifth frame of "performance" begins. *Thunder* and *Kang* experiment with keyboard versions of the marijuana smoking exercise, and *Thunder* culminates the performance with the ASCII characters just given. *Lucia* serves as the audience, congratulating the performers for their artistry with limited tools.

On the Internet, we have some enchanting opportunities to engage in such light-hearted role-plays, ones that would not work well in real life. The troubling aspect of this form of play, however, is that the line between real life and role play is sometimes fuzzy and may not always be consensually understood or agreed upon. Unlike the children playing pirates, participants in an Internet role play may not know what the ground rules are, or when people are switching from frame to frame.

Consider, for example, the "Let's play IRC" frame. As I mentioned in a previous chapter, social chatters are constantly subjected to two questions: Are you male or female, and how old are you? Even when a person's nickname suggests one gender or the other, people often inquire anyway. At one point early in this chatting session, *Kang* said to *Lucia,* "lucia=female as i suspect?" Later, *Kang* types a strategic probe to learn Lucia's age, first in lower case, and then, a bit more persistently, in all caps:

```
<Kang> so lucia single long?
<Kang> SO LUCIA SINGLE LONG?
```

Lucia finally replies "SINGLE ALL MY LIFE," coyly deflecting the question. *Kang* comes back more directly, with "how long has your life been so far?" but *Lucia* ignores the query. She could, of course, have been male, and she could have answered anything to the age question. While *Kang* thought they were in the "Let's play IRC" frame, *Lucia* could easily have decided to jump to the "Let's pretend" frame and given any answers she chose.

The fundamental issue here concerns our understanding of the rules of the Internet social environment, and whether we consider it to be subject to the same rules as real life, the rules of childhood role play, something in between, or something entirely different. If everyone is playing a role and everyone knows about it, then there is little problem. But what happens when you jump to a role-play frame in which your online persona is markedly different from your real-life self, and the others do not? This is where role play begins to blend with the less benign forms of deception.

ROLE PLAY DANGER AREAS

Is it acceptable to swap genders and "role play" on the net in the guise of the opposite sex? Are you comfortable with the idea that some people develop intimate online relationships with people whom they deceived in that way? What do you think of a teenage boy who pretends to be in his thirties? Or an octogenarian who plays the role of a 20-year-old to feel young again? Is it permissible to hint you are a drug addict on a support group when, in real life, you are a scientist studying drug addiction? Should you post long confessionals without a word of truth in them, just to enliven the discussion and see the reaction? Clearly, that illusion conservation rule that gave shape, form, and structure to our childhood role plays is very tenuous on the net.

Gender-swapping is an aspect of role play that has caused Internet users to form into opposing camps. For example, Elizabeth Reid discovered some very diverse and passionate viewpoints on such activity among MUD players.[31] Some participants felt it was a clear violation of ethics and considered it to be despicable and perverted. One player said, "I think if you get off on pretending to be a female you should go and dress up and go to some club in San Fran where they like perverts – just don't go around deceiving people on muds." This reaction is

[31] Reid, E. (1995). Virtual worlds: Culture and imagination. In S. Jones (Ed.), *Cybersociety: Computer-mediated communication and community* (pp. 164–183). Thousand Oaks, CA: Sage Publications, Inc.

particularly revealing because the MUD itself promotes considerable role-playing and people create bizarre descriptions of themselves, such as those I mentioned in the last chapter. A player can become an elf, a lizard, a 10-foot-tall Amazon, or a wild swampfox. Despite the acceptability of such fantastical self-presentations, a number of players object strongly if you dare to deceive others about that central trait of gender. For them, the frame for online communication should generously permit all kinds of role-playing, but should draw the line at gender deceit. This particular construction of the frames for real life and online life, and for the membrane between them, is very strict about this issue.

Other players argue that men who pretend to be females are not necessarily perverted, but are "cheating" and violating rules in another way. A MUD administrator for a fantasy role-playing game on a Boston host showed me the system statistics that summarized the gender characteristics of registered players. Only about 25% were female-presenting, and they tended to receive more attention and chivalry in the form of hints and gifts, and occasionally received more harassment. The administrator also knew that a fair number of those female-presenting characters were actually male. From the data people confidentially submit to him when they request a character, he guessed that only about 15% were really female and the rest were gender-swapping so they would get more help on the game and solve the puzzles more quickly.

Some men choose female characters to learn something about what it feels like to be a woman, although they may not realize the consequences the deception may bring. Steve Silberman, a writer for *Wired* magazine, posed as "Rose" in a chat room, though he felt shamefully dishonest about it.[32] His first lesson came as he began receiving one message after another from people who had ignored him in his male persona. Some messages were friendly, some were come-ons, and a few were nasty, brutal, and harassing. Silberman said, "I was shaken by how quickly uninvited male adoration could take on a violent edge." He settled into a conversation with "Adam," an actor who shared the love for poetry that Rose included in her online description and began disclosing more personal information and intimacies. When Adam became amorous and suggested meeting in real life, Silberman confessed his true gender with heartfelt regret about his betrayal and deception.

[32] Silberman, S. (1995). A rose is not always a rose. Available: http://www.packet. com/packet/silberman/nc_today.html [1998, May 20].

In the lighthearted *Rules of the Net: Online Operating Instructions for Human Beings,* authors Thomas Mandel and Gerard Van der Leun offer 250 pages of opinionated and uncompromising rules covering behavior online.[33] Strangely, they have little to say about gender-swapping except for this cryptic remark: "You are allowed to change your sexual orientation or gender. At will or just for fun. But be prepared to suffer the consequences." The omission is especially puzzling because Tom Mandel was one of the targets of an infamous gender-swapper on The WELL, that pioneering online computer forum based in the San Francisco Bay area. Mark Ethan Smith, a middle-aged woman in real life, taunted Mandel as an oppressive sexist until her acerbic, relentless flaming led to suspension of her account.[34]

A widely publicized and notorious story of online gender-swapping involved the Joan/Alex chimera, a.k.a, the "case of the electronic lover."[35] Alex was a New York psychiatrist who used the nickname *Shrink, Inc.* to chat on CompuServe, and began having online conversations with women who assumed he was actually a female psychiatrist. Titillated by the immediacy and intimacy of the conversations in which people thought he was a woman, he began logging on as "Joan" and created an elaborate and detailed persona to go with his new nickname. Joan was handicapped and disfigured, but emerged as a model of the determined female who could overcome all odds to establish relationships and surmount her disabilities. Women flocked to chat with Joan, and some experimented with lesbian netsex, but when the most determined insisted on meeting her in person, Alex had to end the charade. He first hinted at a serious illness and then said she was going to the hospital, where Alex would write her out of existence. Unfortunately, Alex got too caught up and embellished his masquerade with some telling details of time and place. Online friends who wanted to send flowers and show sympathy discovered that Joan had not been admitted to the hospital.

---

[33] Mandel, T., and Van der Leun, G. (1996). *Rules of the Net: On-line operating instructions for human beings.* New York: Hyperion.

[34] Smith did not try to conceal her true gender though she did demand that others refer to her as "he" for political reasons. Hafner, K. (1997). The epic saga of The Well. *Wired,* May.

[35] Van Gelder, L. (1991). The strange case of the electronic lover. Charles Dunlop and Rob Kling (Eds.). *Computerization and controversy: Value conflicts and social choices.* New York: Academic Press. Sherry Turkle, Professor of Sociology and Science at MIT, reported other versions of this legendary "case of the electronic lover" in Turkle, S. (1995). *Life on the screen: Identity in the age of the Internet.* New York: Simon & Schuster.

The fury over Alex's deception was immediate, but the feelings of betrayal were complex and varied. Some were angry at any gender deception, while others, less concerned about online gender-swapping, were outraged by the thought that Alex was using the online "Joan" persona to front for him so he could hear intimate self-disclosures from women and also, experience lesbianism vicariously. Most, but not all, agreed that Alex violated some trust or other. They do not agree, exactly, about what trust that was or why his behavior offended so many people. The play within a play can cause all sorts of problems when others don't know the frame in which you are operating.

Oddly, the online community is far more generous toward women who pretend to be men, and it is rare for Internet users to show outrage at this gender deception. How much women do this is not really known, though MUD administrators report that women gender-swap far less frequently than men. More commonly, women choose gender-neutral names, especially to avoid online harassment.

Gender-swapping, or any deliberate demographic disconnect between your real self and your online persona, could be considered fanciful role-playing, or it could be classified as outright lying. What we reveal to others online is so easily exaggerated or falsified that it makes the environment a very tempting place to conduct a few experiments.

IDENTITY EXPERIMENTS IN THE INTERNET LABORATORY

When we alter characteristics of ourselves on the Internet – even fundamental ones like age, race, or gender – we might not think of ourselves as liars or con artists. Like Silberman, we might feel more like researchers, or experimenters. We are playing with our own identities and trying out different hats to see how they feel and how others will react to them. Though deception is a key ingredient, it may not seem quite the same as lying for personal gain.

Experimenting with identities is an important part of lifespan development, and those identity crises we experience, particularly in our youth, are valuable to personal growth. If we don't try things out, we never know what fits best. That exploration is not confined to adolescence, as many people assume. Especially in fast-paced industrial countries where lifestyle and career options are abundant and change quickly, many of us return again and again to questioning our values and beliefs, and then re-establishing a firm commitment to a set of life goals. This alternating pattern is known as MAMA, an acronym that stands for moratorium/achievement/moratorium/achievement.[36] During the moratorium part of the cycle, we feel that self-doubt and confusion about who we are and what we are doing with our lives. Once we sort things out again, we reach the state of identity achievement with a deeper sense of self.

On the Internet, the opportunities for cycling through MAMA, or for remaining permanently suspended in a moratorium status, are magnified many times. We can re-enter that moratorium status every night, experimenting with identities we never got around to while we were teens, or that were off limits for logistical reasons or the basic laws of physics. We can subscribe to a philosophy mailing list and discuss Descartes, pretending to be a professor or a hermit in a mountain cabin. We can join IRC chats to talk with gay men and women with far more ease than we could enter a gay bar. The newsgroups are awash with brittle political discussions, and we can leap into any acerbic debate, joining either side at whim. We can post fictional confessions about our abused childhood to support groups, or even send fake suicide notes to alt.suicide. The possibilities are endless, and for some, they are extremely enticing. The chance to experience some of those alternative identities, especially ones that would be nearly impossible to experiment with in real life, may be too attractive to ignore.

Besides the pace, a significant difference between the real-life MAMA pattern and MAMA on the Internet involves the consequences. If we experiment with a new identity on the net, we can simply disconnect if things get too hot and the consequences get out of hand. Unlike Silberman, most people who role play as a dramatically different person on the Internet probably do not confess. They simply vanish if they tire of the game or sense suspicion. There are thousands of other groups they can join that know nothing about those previous experiments. We are not able to withdraw from such exercises this easily in real life. If we join a gang or march in protests, we would not be able to disentangle so easily from those identity experiments. We might wind up with a tatoo, a criminal record, or a drug addiction. If a married man is seen at a gay bar, the rumors would be difficult to quell. The consequences limit our experiments in real life, but on the Internet, those consequences are much reduced.

The Internet is an identity laboratory, overflowing with props, audiences, and players for our personal experiments. Though many people

[36] Archer, S. L. (1989). The status of identity: Reflections on the need for intervention. *Journal of Adolescence, 12,* 345–359.

stay close to their home self and just tinker with a few traits they wish they could improve, especially their extroversion, others jump over the line between impression management and deception. We may cling to the belief that our experiments are harmless diversions, but the dupes in our laboratory may not agree.

THE DUPES IN THE EXPERIMENT

Social psychologists know a great deal about deceptive experiments since they sometimes use deception in their research. Strict professional guidelines and review panels control the use of such deception, especially to ensure that the subjects in any experiment suffer no ill effects and are fully debriefed after the event. To learn more about certain kinds of human behavior, researchers have little choice but to contrive cover stories to hide the true purpose of the experiment so the subjects will behave as naturally as possible. Without the deception, many people would try to please the experimenter, or behave in ways that will make them look as good, moral, and socially desirable as possible. Fortunately for researchers, human beings have a strong truth bias. Despite warnings about "believing none of what you read and half of what you see," we tend to take input from our sensory systems at face value. If we did not, the world would be a chaotic place, indeed.

Some experiments involving deception might simply mislead the subjects about the true purpose of the research. Others might lead the subjects to believe something about themselves that isn't true, to learn more about how certain attitudes or beliefs influence their behavior. For example, as subjects, we might solve a few easy puzzles and hear "Congratulations! Only 10% of the subjects were able to solve those," as a means to manipulate our feelings of self-esteem. Or we might be randomly assigned to the "low-self-esteem group" that confronts impossible puzzles and be told that "90% of college students can solve these in five minutes or less. Perhaps you'll do better next time." After the debriefing, subjects usually laugh about the deception and – thanks to the truth bias – only rarely suggest they knew something was up all along.

Psychologists walk a tightrope when they use deception to uncover truth about human behavior, and the issue is a controversial one among researchers. Although the guidelines governing such research are demanding, it is not always easy to guess how different human beings will be affected. On the Internet, by contrast, the amateur deceptive experiments have no such guidelines, and no professional insights to help predict the potential harm they might do. Even well-meaning Internet users who never intended to cause trouble for others might stumble into a situation in which their identity experiments go awry.

Consider Adam, the other player in Silberman's gender-swapping experiment. How did he feel when he learned he'd been courting a man online? His initial reaction was, "I suspected it." Though we can't be sure, of course, this strikes me as unlikely, given the natural bias to believe what others tell you, at least at first. Whether Adam had questions about Silberman's real gender the remark helped avoid the "gullible dupe" stigma, and also helped Adam preserve his self-esteem. Human memory is a shifty thing, and even if Adam had no suspicions at all, it would not be difficult for him to engage in a little revisionism so his memories of the feelings he had matched his hindsight. Perhaps the incident would cause Adam to anxiously reflect on his own sexual orientation. At the least, his truth bias would have suffered a near-mortal wound and he might have a very difficult time establishing a close relationship with anyone online again. The world becomes a deceitful and treacherous place to people who fall victim to scams. Fool me once, shame on you; fool me twice, shame on me.

Adam very graciously let Silberman off the hook by suggesting he suspected the charade, and his courtesy continued. "I'm disappointed, of course. But there's obviously something beautiful about you that I saw, and that someone who will love you one day will see too." This generosity in the midst of a painful deception is remarkable, and its effects on Steve Silberman were not trivial. He deeply regretted betraying this man and said he never went online with a female screen name again.

DETECTING DECEIT, OFFLINE AND ON

With online identity experiments on the rise, people on the Internet are charging their deceit-detector batteries. Psychological research on deception, however, shows that most of us are poor judges of truthfulness, and this applies even to professionals such as police and customs inspectors whose jobs are supposed to include some expertise at lie detection. For example, police officers watched videotaped statements, some truthful and others deceptive, and were told to pay attention to facial expressions, body movements, gestures, and vocal cues such as the pitch and tempo of the voice. Even with training, these officers did little better than chance at guessing the truthfulness of the statements. Ironically, those officers who were most sure of their judgments, most confident they were trapping the liars, were most likely to be wrong.[37]

Despite these unpromising results, there are clearly some people who are rather successful at detecting deceit, though the cues they use to do it are far from clear. Liars do not emit any uniform set of clues to help people detect the lies, but there are a few characteristics that seem to reappear in experimental studies. Some examples are overcontrolled movements, reduced rate of speech, more vocal pauses, and higher voice pitch. It appears we have to concentrate when we lie, and the effort diminishes some of the spontaneity of normal human interaction. Poker players, at least the ones who usually win, learn much about decoding deceit in their playing partners. David Hayano found that the best knew very well that few hard and fast rules apply to the behavior people show when they aren't telling the truth.[38] Instead of relying on deception-detection cookbooks, the poker experts analyzed each of their opponents individually, often keeping lengthy notes about the playing styles and idiosyncrasies of each one. In principle, each player has his or her own set of "tells" that reveal a bluff or a winning hand, perhaps through a cough or an almost imperceptible smile. Of course, poker is an endless cat and mouse game, and players contrive "anti-tells" they hope will mislead their opponents.

Practically all the cues people attempt to use to detect deceit are nonverbal. The pauses, the vocal pitch, the tiny lapse in facial expression, the overcontrolled body movements, are invisible on the Internet, unless you are using interactive video. Even if we were experts at spotting a lie, which we most certainly are not, we would be sorely disadvantaged online. The fact that it is so easy to lie and get away with it – as long as we can live with our own deceptions and the harm they may cause others – is a significant feature of the Internet.

DECEIT AND SUSPICION: DANCE PARTNERS

The dance of deception needs two people, at least; one sends the lie and the other receives it. Although few people can accurately tell a lie from truth when they just watch the performance, we do a little better when we have a chance to interact with – verbally dance with – the deceiver. If

---

[37] Kohnken, G. (1987). Training police officers to detect deceptive eye witness statements: does it work? *Social Behavior, 2*, 1–17.

[38] Hayano, D. (1988). Dealing with chance: Self-deception and fantasy among gamblers. In J. S. Lockard, and D. L. Paulus (Eds.), *Self-deception: An adaptive mechanism?* Englewood Cliffs, NJ: Prentice Hall.

things seem amiss, perhaps because the sender is elaborating too much or avoiding our eye contact, our suspicions are aroused and we send out a few strategic probes. Most of the time, we don't want our dance partner to know we suspect anything – at least not yet – so we must do a bit of clever concealment ourselves.

Judee Burgoon and her research colleagues find this dance incredibly complex, with moves and countermoves, feints and parries, and with no simple patterns.[39] They conducted some experiments in which each member of a conversational pair were given information that led to a bewildering assortment of suspicions about their partner's truthfulness. As expected, the subjects were not very good at detecting actual deceit, but they certainly noticed when their partner became suspicious of them because of some misinformation the experimenter provided. A suspicious person seems to have a difficult time hiding their thoughts as they probe for more evidence of deceit. As they try to conceal their feelings, they smile more, nod, use more eye contact, and try to suppress those little tell-tale signs of nervousness such as finger drumming and hair twirling. Their concealment strategy was not very effective. The attempt to camouflage their suspicions was spoiled by "leakage" of nervousness, especially in their voices. Their speech suffered from pauses and nervous vocalizations, and the interviewee couldn't help but notice. Suspiciousness is, apparently, very hard to conceal.

On the Internet, we do get a chance to dance with our partners, though it is mostly through typed text. The communication channel lacks all those nonverbal cues we try to use, ineptly perhaps, to detect deceit or suspicion, and their absence would seem to make it quite difficult to either detect deceit or notice when someone is becoming suspicious of our words. We can't see overcontrolled hand motions, and we can't hear hesitant pauses or raised pitch.

Without the benefit of visual or auditory cues, is there any way to tell if someone is being truthful? Just from an online interaction? Could Adam have really suspected anything? And if he had, would Silberman have noticed? Burgoon and her colleagues found that the nonverbal cues were the ones people relied on the most, but the content of the messages played a small role. There was a tendency for truthful subjects to use words in a slightly different way compared to nontruthful ones. Their words were

[39] Burgoon, J. K., Buller, D. B., Guerrero, L. K., Wallid, A. A., and Feldman, C. M. (1996). Interpersonal deception: XII. Information management dimensions underlying deceptive and truthful messages. *Communication Monographs, 63,* 50–69.

somewhat more likely to be complete, direct, relevant, clear, and personalized. These are generally the same characteristics we use to judge the credibility of messages that appear in print, and that are intended to persuade us to vote for a candidate, buy a product, or contribute to some cause. It is possible that an Internet user who is deceiving through typed text could arouse suspicions by evasive and indirect answers, so perhaps Adam eventually did begin to suspect something was amiss.

Our own stereotypes about how certain people *should* behave will also trigger suspicions about truthfulness and deception on the Internet. These will be primitive, indeed, but as we discussed in an earlier chapter, we are cognitive misers and use stereotypes and categories routinely to save time. For better or worse, we expect people to act in predictable ways, given their age, sex, occupation, race, or status. We expect teens to use plenty of current slang, and anyone in a teen chat room who does not might be suspected of age-deception. Also, people might wonder whether someone who liberally adds "kewl" to his conversation is really a minor, even though he claimed to be older. We think women are more emotional than men, so a character with a male name who liberally displays emotion might trigger our suspicions. Using stereotypes to trigger suspicion about gender is particularly annoying to some women on the MUDs. Nancy Deuel studied gender relations on a MUD and quoted one participant as saying, "It seems to me that if a female character shows any bit of intelligence and sexual recognition, people will think she's a male IRL (in real life). If she flirts shamelessly and has a 'smutty description,' people will think she's a male IRL."[40]

The stereotypes are flimsy crutches, but the ease with which people can experiment with identities on the net, and the difficulty we have detecting such experiments, makes people feel more vulnerable. We seem to use certain kinds of stereotypes even more heavily online to make judgments like this than we would in real life because we have little else to use. We will explore those online gender stereotypes in more detail in a later chapter.

PROS AND CONS OF THE INTERNET'S IDENTITY LAB

On the Internet, we have a new laboratory for experiments, one that is far more flexible and open-ended than the one we have in real life. The

---

[40] Deuel, N. R. (1996). Our passionate response to virtual reality. In S. C. Herring (Ed.). *Computer-mediated communication: Linguistic, social and cross-cultural perspectives* (pp. 129–146). Amsterdam: John Benjamins Publishing Company.

possibilities for constructing and sculpting new identities, and then trying them on for size, are remarkable. Some of our new "selves" might be vaguely formed, very temporary, and barely more than "pilot" identities. Their owners might discard them quickly. Others may coalesce into richly detailed personas whose life onscreen seems even more real than real life. Many of these new identities may simply add a bit of polish or mystery to the self we already know in real life, and these experimental enhancements may lead to very positive consequences. Playing a person who is a little more outgoing and confident on a MUD, for example, could affect the individual's offline behavior, and there is much anecdotal evidence to support this. If the role player's online extraversion is rewarded by others, if he or she gets more respect and more attention, the player may generalize the behavior to real-life situations and shed some of that painful shyness.

The danger zone for this laboratory emerges when the frames of reality and role play have no clear boundaries – for ourselves, certainly, but also for others we meet online. The masquerade is no longer a consensual Mardi Gras where everyone knows a mask from a real face, and there is no illusion conservation rule in operation. At this point, some auditory alarms should go off. Role play, in that context, is just another word for deceit. The consequences and the societal outrage are evident when it is an obviously clearcut case, such as a child molester who goes into teen chat rooms, pretends to be 13 years old, and tries to collect phone numbers and addresses. Yet the Internet is an enabler for many different kinds of experiments. There is little agreement or understanding about how valuable these are to the role players, or whether they might harm the dupes in the experiment. What we do know, however, is that the lab is open for business, 24 hours a day, and a great many people are conducting experiments.

GROUP DYNAMICS IN CYBERSPACE

I can still remember the adrenaline rush when the "Leaders' Club" president informed me that my application for membership was approved. This was, I believed, the elite in-group in my high school – filled with the smartest and coolest students, the best athletes, and all the most popular people. The club was difficult to get into and current members voted on the worthiness of each applicant. It was demanding about the behavior of its members, and a time sink as extracurricular activities go. Once we emerged from the solemn initiation ceremony, we were allowed to wear green corduroy vests over our white gym suits with our names proudly embroidered on the back. Now, of course, I recognize that the Leaders' Club used a standard psychological recipe for creating a cohesive group with strong feelings of belonging, loyalty, and commitment. Group symbols, initiations, challenging entrance requirements, and heavy time demands were some of the ingredients.

Can you create any of that online?

"GROUPNESS"

Skeptics have always wondered whether cohesive groups could really emerge at all in a computer-mediated environment. Some believed that the lack of the usual social cues and the transitory nature of so many online interactions would make it unlikely that genuine and satisfying groups could develop. Certainly, forums that are intended to support a cohesive group come and go with alarming speed on the net. If you subscribe to a mailing list whose title interests you, for example, you might find that the list is virtually dead and the former participants have long since departed. If you post a message to one of these fossils, you might receive a response from some who say they forgot that they were even subscribed, and they hadn't received any mail from this list in ages. There are thousands of newsgroups out there, for example, that started strong, meeting some need the participants perceived. The focus might have been professional, academic, or recreational. But many are now deserted, virtually boarded up except for an infrequent commercial announcement or cross-post that happens to include them. On the Web, innumerable chat rooms and discussion forums are built by online hosts hoping to attract a crowd of lively and engaging guests. Many never draw more than the occasional curious visitor who looks around, finds nothing going on, and leaves. I am reminded of rows of cafes and clubs whose disappointed owners naively believed would become vibrant watering holes, but whose chairs and tables remain empty.

Despite the ephemeral and fragile nature of so many forums on the Internet, there is evidence that a very strong sense of "groupness" does emerge regularly, though the magic that creates this in one group but not another is not entirely clear. Joan Korenman and Nancy Wyatt attempted to untangle some of these variables by investigating the patterns of participation and the attitudes of the participants on a mailing list called WMST-L.[41] The mailing list is an unmoderated forum for people involved in women's studies from an academic standpoint, and it includes teachers, researchers, librarians, program administrators, and an assortment of others interested in the topic. From the list's inception in 1991, the number of participants and postings grew steadily. In August 1991, for example, 28 people posted 51 messages, but by January 1993, there were 365 messages posted by 193 different people. An important point to note about these statistics is the relatively broad-based participation. On many lists, a few people take center stage and hold the vehement discussions, while others watch (or lurk), making only rare comments.

Korenman and Wyatt sent out surveys to the participants to learn what bonds were holding the group together from their own points of view, and how much "groupness" was really present. In answer to a question about what was satisfying and useful about the group, "information" was most often mentioned, but many also mentioned a "sense of community" and "discussion of personal experience." Based on an

[41] Korenman, J., and Wyatt, N. (1996). In Herring, S. C. (Ed.). *Computer-mediated communication: Linguistic, social and cross-cultural perspectives* (pp. 225–242). Amsterdam: John Benjamins Publishing Company.

analysis of the messages themselves, this mailing list appears relatively free of flames and other kinds of antagonistic posts, although disagreement and discussion about sensitive issues were common. Apparently the group members found this environment to be a worthwhile and welcoming place to discuss personal issues, and this points to that elusive but very real sense of "groupness".

Some people develop extremely deep commitments to their online groupmates and the ties may become far stronger than those that link the individual to real-life groups. Author Tom Mandel, a controversial participant in one of the earliest online community experiments (The WELL), posted his feelings about his virtual group experience just before he died:

> *I could start off by thanking you all, individually and collectively, for a remarkable experience, this past decade here on the WELL. For better or worse – there were a lot of both – it has been the time of my life and especially great comfort during these past six months. I'm sad, terribly sad, I cannot tell you how sad and griefstriken I am that I cannot stay to play and argue with you much longer...[42]*

Yet even as people grow to care for and commit to their groups, they have ambivalent feelings and sometimes step back to probe the strangeness of the experience. Eric A. Hochman, a member of another early online community called ECHO (East Coast Hang Out), offered these comments in a discussion about the nature of the online world:

> *I started thinking about this when, for about the thousandth time since I've been online, someone said to me (in reference to ECHO) "Those people aren't real!" And while I would argue that point, I think ECHO is, in some ways, its own separate little world, one with its own mythology, jargon, and social order; in other words, it has its own culture. An interesting one, because rather than it being an external thing that we adapt to, or have imposed on us, we're collectively creating it, here and now, as we post.[43]*

Defining the term *group* is difficult enough without prefacing it with the even more elusive *virtual* adjective. One succinct definition states that a group is a collection of two or more people who are interacting

---

[42] Mandel's post was reprinted in Hafner, K. (1997). The epic saga of the Well. *Wired*, May.
[43] In Shirky, C. (1995). *Voices from the net*. Emeryville, CA: ZD Press.

with and influencing one another. The definition seems clear and satisfying enough until you begin to think of humans on elevators, or in theaters, or in the same subway car. Though these characteristics are apparent in tightly knit work and social groups, they may be far less obvious in elevator passengers, at least until the car jerks to a stop between floors and passengers' faces turn pale. The amount of interaction among people who are in physical proximity can vary dramatically depending on the circumstances, and one small change in the environment could quickly turn a collection of individuals into something that fits neatly into the traditional definition for the word *group*.

Just as real-life groups vary a great deal, virtual groups can be of many different types. Many consist primarily of people who already know each other and are simply using the net as a way to keep in touch and share ideas between face-to-face meetings. The researchers who were the original net pioneers often approached the medium in this way. Other virtual groups might draw together people with common interests via the net who do not yet know each other in person. Time and circumstances permitting, some of these people might eventually meet in real life at conventions, professional meetings, or social gatherings. From many such personal experiences, I know it can be a strange event to finally shake hands with someone you have been communicating with over the net for a long period of time. Surprises are inevitable as the impressions you received from the individual's online contributions are suddenly enriched by face-to-face contact.

On the far end of the spectrum are the virtual groups whose members have no real expectation of ever meeting in real life, despite their common interests. These are the ones in which any sense of "groupness," if it is to emerge at all, must arise from the dynamics of online communication.

Fuzziness around the definitional edges is not uncommon in social science terminology, but those characteristics – interaction and influence – are the two that will be most useful as we try to understand the nature of online groups, and compare them to their face-to-face counterparts. The interaction and influence factors were very clear to Mandel and Hochman, as you can tell from their remarks. People do indeed interact on the Internet, and they can influence one another – sometimes quite powerfully. Nevertheless, the ways in which these processes unfold are not the same as they are in real life, so it is not surprising that people have ambivalence about what it means to belong to an online "group."

We know from decades of research that the presence of other people affects the way we behave, even when they are strangers and we might never see them again. Let's now see how some of these influences work in real life, and then examine how they unfold online. I'll begin with some classic studies on human conformity, a term that sounds terribly out of place in any discussion of the Internet, but one that, in my view, is a key element in the very existence of online groups, especially those that remain entirely in the ether.

CONFORMITY

That madcap producer Allen Funt once orchestrated a *Candid Camera* segment called "Face the Rear," in which he planted several confederates on an elevator. All of them faced the back of the car rather than the front, and none cracked so much as a smirk. The unsuspecting "star" of the video hopped on the car and looked about with a puzzled expression. Confronted with a unanimous, silent, and serious-looking group that seemed to be following a strict rule about which direction to face, the subject turned and faced the rear as well. On a subtle cue, the confederates turned to the left, and the star did the same. On another cue, the group removed their hats, and again, the subject followed suit. Though the naive *Candid Camera* subject looked anxious and uncomfortable, he readily conformed rather than break rank with the odd group choices.

Solomon Asch, the creative social psychologist you might recall from the experiments on impression formation, wondered how deep the tendency to conform actually goes. Would, for example, people under group pressure disregard or at least question the information they receive through their sensory systems? In a pioneering research program, he brought subject after subject into the laboratory to sit with a group of four other people and make perceptual judgments. The experimenter holds up a card with one vertical line on the left side and three other vertical lines labeled A through C on the right. One by one, each person in the group is asked which of the three lines is closest in length to the line on the left.

The correct answer on each of the cards was obvious to anyone not legally blind, but the four other people in the room were not really subjects at all. They were confederates of the experimenter, instructed to give the same wrong answer on certain turns. Like the *Candid Camera* star, the real subject of the experiment faced a troubling situation. His turn was always last, so one after another, he heard each person insist that an obviously incorrect answer was the correct one. Should he go with his own senses, even though everyone in the room thought differently? To even Asch's surprise, the real subjects went along with the group more than one third of the time.[44]

A remarkable feature of this experiment was that there was no particular punishment or consequence for disagreeing with the rest of the subjects. The only pressure to conform came from within, and it was even more startling than the conformity on the elevator because the subjects had to deny their own sensory experience in order to go along. Some probably began to doubt their own eyes because of this subtle group pressure, while others may have remained privately convinced that their senses were intact but chose to conform to the group rather than risk group censure.

More than 30 years later, a group of researchers tried to replicate Asch's original experiment using an environment that resembled the Internet.[45] Five subjects were formèd into an online group, and each sat in front of a microcomputer. The program began by presenting the instructions. Each subject was told that the microcomputers were all networked to the central computer, so each person could see the judgments the others in the experiment were making.

The network was a ruse and the computers were not actually connected at all. After some more instructions about the length-judging task, each subject was asked to enter a three-digit number that would be used to "randomly assign" the order in which the subjects would choose. This was another ruse; regardless of what number the subjects chose, they all were assigned Station #5. They all thought they would be choosing last.

```
                        Case #3
        1                      ———

        2                   ———

        3                 ———

        4                   ———


        FRED:   Please enter choice for case 3 ->   2   Thank You.
        JOHN:   Please enter choice for case 3 ->   2   Thank You.
        KATHY:  Please enter choice for case 3 ->   2   Thank You.
        JILL:   Please enter choice for case 3 ->   2   Thank You.
        JIM:    Please enter choice for case 3 ->
```

[44] Asch, S. (1955). Opinions and social pressure. *Scientific American,* November, 31–35.
[45] Smilowitz, M., Compton, D. C., and Flint, L. (1988). The effects of computer mediated communication on an individual's judgment: A study based on the methods of Asch's social influence experiment. *Computers in Human Behavior, 4,* 311–321.

Imagine you are Jim, and Case #3 just popped up on the screen. Beneath it you slowly watch the display as the choices appear. First Fred chooses 2 and the program responds with a vacuous "Thank You" with a capitalization error, reminding you that it comes from a mindless computer, perhaps programmed by someone who got As in computer science and Ds in English. You might think, "Huh? Fred must have gone afk" (away from keyboard). Then John's response appears, and you wonder whether John just made a typo. When Kathy and Jill finish entering their preposterous choices, the cursor blinks, waiting for your response. You probably do some blinking yourself, wondering whether your eyesight is failing.

In this setting, the degree of conformity didn't disappear, but it dropped dramatically. Asch, for example, found that the number of subjects who made no errors, that is, the number who refused to conform to the group on any trial, was just 25%. In this study, fully 69% of the subjects made no errors. A tempting conclusion is that there is something about the computer-mediated communication environment that reduces our tendency to conform to a unanimous group position, physical presence being one of them.

Though the word *conformist* is not a particularly pleasing or socially desirable one, especially to people who grow up in individualistic cultures, conformity is to a large extent the glue that keeps a group, or even a whole society, together. A successful group needs a certain amount of predictability, and one way to achieve this is by inculcating this willingness to conform from childhood on up, whether we are aware of it or not. For better or worse, it appears that a computer-mediated environment strips away some of the features that contribute to our tendency to conform in a group setting. Physical presence is absent, and anonymity is quite possible. Status cues that might indicate whether some individuals are experts are often lacking. And symbols that might lead us to believe that the people we are communicating with are similar to ourselves, that they are people we would like very much and would want to like us, may also be invisible.

Yet customs and conventions *have* emerged, and tightly knit and successful groups flourish on the Internet. It seems that new strategies were needed to bring about the compliance and conformity so essential to a viable community. If we can't just glare at you as though you'd just grown two heads when you dare to disagree with a unanimous group position, we must find other ways to exert pressure on you to conform to basic group norms if we want our communities to thrive.

CONFORMING ON THE NET

Internet conformity sounds, on the surface, almost like an oxymoron, yet quite a number of group norms have evolved over time because people are willing and sometimes even eager to conform. Why, for example, do people generally write most of their emails using a certain style? A plausible answer is conformity.

Linguistically, much email falls somewhere between a paper memo and a phone call, even though it could have become something quite different. We might have developed a much more formal style with guidelines for placement of date, ASCII art letterhead, salutations, and closings, just as we did for business letters, and for the most part, adopted for faxes as well. However, the original uses of email by the academic and research community established the medium as far less formal and more spontaneous. The rapid transmission of messages helped push it toward informality, and the informality led to the need for more socioemotional content and lots of shortcuts in the form of abbreviations and simplified spellings. IMHO, BTW, ppl, and thx are all examples of email conventions that are widely used and understood. They are almost nonexistent in paper memos. The signature file with the author's favorite quotation surrounded by asterisks[46] is also an email convention, not present in other forms of text-based communication.

When an email digresses from this informal, quasi-conversational pattern, it stands out. Imagine receiving an email that more closely approximates a business letter than those with which most of us are familiar. It might have well-designed ASCII art as the letterhead, the appropriate indents for date, complimentary closing, signature block, the recipient's full name and physical mailing address, the correct spacing between salutation and body, and conventional symbols such as "enc." to indicate an attachment. I have received very few emails like this, and the first time I did I assumed it must either be a joke or some spam from a marketer who knew little about Internet culture. Even when I receive email messages whose function and format are already very well established in the letter format, such as cover letters from people applying for a job, they still usually follow that informal Internet style. This shows how powerful the email convention actually is, and how just using the Internet to deliver a communication can override other conventions about how it should be formatted and the style that would ordinarily be appropriate.

---

[46] This convention is so widespread that it has become the target of sarcasm; a common phrase inserted between those asterisks might be, simply, "Insert quotation here."

A study of emails exchanged among undergraduates at the State University of New York in Plattsburgh[47] showed that students used the medium for quite a number of different things, but again, their style began conforming to a pattern regardless of the purpose. Even those students who had never used email before learned the norms quickly from one another and turned email into quasi-conversation. You can derive some of the general norms by looking at a few of the samples in the table. Misspellings, punctuation errors and deviations, and ungrammatical sentences are perfectly acceptable, even preferred. Crude jokes, flirtations, puns, and sarcasm were all common. The students insisted that email would be used in certain ways, even though they knew big brother was watching. (They were all warned when they logged in that all their messages were being recorded and would be studied by researchers.) Any student who might choose a more formal style would have appeared quite out of step.

Work comments (26.4%)	`Fortran sucks!`
	`Computers are bogus. My program is wrong. I failed. Get the rope.`
Salutations (6.6%)	`Bye`
	`Helllllllooooooooo [Stuart]. So how the %^&* are you? Me.`
Threats and put-downs (8.8%)	`[Paul] eats worms`
	`Hi there! Your computer is going to blow up in ten seconds! 10 9 8 7 6 5 4 3 2 1. … I guess I was wrong. Bye.`
Crude Flirtation (16.4%)	`Hi! I got your message! I'm looking forward to your slobbering kisses.`
Humor and symbolic (23.2%)	`Um uh um uh um um um um uh um uh`
	`Demon! ! ! ! ! ! ! ! !`
Social plans (23.2%)	`Wednesday at 4:00 - OKAY?????`
News and sharing (24.2%)	`I'll take that 4-6 shift Columbus moday if you want-`
Refined flirtation and relationship establishment (45.3%)	`Hi! You don't know me and I don't know you except by sight. I am just seeing if this really works. It should make your day Mor&`
Work on relationship and love messages (27.2%)	`I can only stand so much rejection!!!!!!`

[47] McCormick, N. B., and McCormick, J. W. (1992). Computer friends and foes: Content of undergraduates' electronic mail. *Computers in Human Behavior, 8,* 379–405.

Email among colleagues and professionals will be less informal, but it still tends to follow that quasi-conversational pattern. In fact, the strong norms surrounding email style led Peter Danielson to lament its tedious homogeneity. He argues that the relentless uniformity makes it far harder to sort the incoming mail and wastes his time. If you look at the pile of postal mail you received this week, you might find newsletters, engraved envelopes, window envelopes with your name and address peering through the transparent covering, flyers, colorful catalogs, seductive inducements from Publisher's Clearinghouse announcing "You have won $10 million" (sent via bulk mail), and an assortment of other packages. The tendency to conform, however, along with the structural limitations of the email medium, have led to an undifferentiated stream of unsortable mail, at least until you read a fair amount of the contents.[48] This is no doubt one reason why Internet users are so outraged by spam, even though they receive mounds of paper junk mail.

Although the tendency to conform shows itself in the emergence of group norms like the ones for email style, the ability of the group to pressure a wayward individual to conform is lessened. The lack of physical presence may make our natural tendency to conform weaker, and the opportunity to hide behind anonymity may weaken it further. To compensate, Internet participants have adopted some stronger methods to encourage conformity, or even demand it, and protect their groups from chaos. One technique is to simply post some rules in an obvious place.

THE SIGN ON THE DOOR

First timers in an elegant three-star French restaurant often peer around the room, watching how others behave, to learn the acceptable patterns of behavior. They observe how experienced patrons handle the forks, speak to the waiter, or hold their wine glasses. Those *Candid Camera* stars could immediately grasp the social convention in the elevator the moment they stepped on the car. Newbies on the net, however, don't have those subtle cues available to them. You can't glance quickly around a strange newsgroup or mailing list, for example, and notice that everyone is wearing a tie or dress suit, or that use of any real names would be unacceptable. When you enter a chat channel with an ambigu-

[48] Danielson, P. (1996). Pseudonyms, mailbots, and virtual letterheads: The evoution of computer-mediated ethics. In C. Hess (Ed.). *Philosophical perspectives on computer-mediated communication* (pp. 67–94). Albany, NY: State University of New York Press.

ous but intriguing name like #Elysium, you may not realize that the group is actually a vampire role play and you will be kicked and banned if you violate the masquerade. To compensate, and to help newcomers avoid embarrassment, many Internet niches post a sign on the door.

Guides that give people advice about *netiquette* are becoming common, and newbies are directed to them regularly. One example is an online book by Virginia Shea, sometimes called the Miss Manners of the online world.[49] These provide general rules about online behavior and many seem strangely, almost trivially, basic. Rule 1, for example, is simply "Remember the human." This rule reminds the net user that humans are on the other side of the screen.

As you enter each niche in which you can interact with others in some way, you will often find (or be directed to find) specialty signs that apply to the virtual habitats of specific groups. Many groups on Usenet have FAQs (frequently asked questions) that explain the purpose of the group and the rules for participating. Some warn newcomers about off-topic posts or provide guidelines about how you should quote remarks from a person to whom you are replying. In some Internet locales, the rules are extremely explicit and violators are subject to instant ban. The owners of many chat channels, for example, warn in their titles that you will be kicked out if you are simultaneously chatting on some channel they find reprehensible, such as #snuffsex or #incest.

Apart from fairly standard and informative warnings such as "No Parking," "No Smoking," or "Shoes and Shirt Required," we rarely see signs that so bluntly state the requirements for appropriate behavior in real-life situations. Imagine how strange it would seem to see a "Grocery Store Etiquette" sign that listed behavioral guidelines analogous to those you see on the net signs:

- No cutting ahead of other patrons in the checkout line.
- Pay in full at the cash register.
- Do not move items to different shelves where they don't belong.
- Do not block aisles with your cart.
- Don't steal food.
- Respect the store manager and clerks.
- Do not eat the vegetables until you pay for them.
- Be courteous to other grocery store patrons.

[49] Shea, V. (1994). *Netiquette*. San Francisco, CA: Albion Books. The online edition is found at http://www.albion.com/netiquette/index.html

When you do see real-life signs that seem to grossly underestimate our human ability to grasp social conventions appropriate to the occasion, they are memorable. A tavern in rural Texas had conspicuous signs posted that reminded patrons about acceptable behavior. Two examples were "No Spitting" and "No Fighting." In the men's room, as I learned from my husband upon his return, there was another sign that suggested the tavern owners had a sense of humor and were aware they might be going a bit far with their written rules. The sign there read: "Men: Do not eat the urinal cakes."

The rules of behavior for face-to-face situations, from the board room to the church, are generally unwritten, but they are very extensive. Our lifetime of experience within our own cultures gives each of us ample time to build up knowledge about all these rules, and the physical presence of others is generally enough to ensure conformity when the rules seem to shift a bit or when we are in a strange situation and unsure of the rules. We willingly watch what others do, note what fork they use to pierce the shrimp, and face the rear of the elevator if we determine that rearward positioning is the social convention. The Internet, though, is a global environment with people from many cultures, and not many ways to convey social rules. Stronger measures are needed to get the job done, and the blunt sign on the door is one example. Another example is the verbal reproach.

THE ARCHED BROW

If a group participant fails to read the sign or ignores the rules, group members will escalate their pressure to ensure conformity by simply raising a virtual eyebrow, reminding the offender gently – or not so gently – that certain behavior is not acceptable. In the vast majority of cases, this typed arched brow is enough to bring the person into line. Margaret L. McLaughlin and her colleagues conducted a study of these conformity-inducing reproaches and the way they unfolded on USENET groups.[50] They saved messages from five very popular newsgroups called comp.sys.ibm.pc.games, rec.sport.hockey, soc.motts (members of the same sex), rec.arts.tv.soaps, and soc.singles, and found almost 300 reproach episodes. An episode could consist of several posts. The first was the offense itself, and the second was the reproach in which the

---

[50] McLaughlin, M. L., Osborne, K. K., and Smith, C. B. (1995). Standards of conduct on Usenet. In S. G. Jones (Ed.), *Cybersociety: Computer-mediated communication and community* (pp. 90–111). Thousand Oaks, CA: Sage Publications.

offender was criticized or corrected in some way by another participant. A third might be a reply from the offender, apologizing, making some excuse, or disputing the charges.

Based on these episodes, the researchers developed a taxonomy of reproachable conduct as follows:

TYPE OF OFFENSE	EXAMPLES
Incorrect/novice use of technology	Message with header but no lines Double signature Confusing the "reply privately" and "reply to group" options Posting multiple copies of the same article to group Attributing quotes incorrectly
Bandwidth waste	Excessively long signatures Multiple email addresses Surface mail address, telephone numbers Selecting default distribution (world) for tests
Violation of networkwide conventions	Changing the subject line without apparent reason Posting commercial announcements Posting sensitive material more suitable for private email
Violation of newsgroup-specific conventions	Failing to use "spoiler" warnings for game solutions, TV/movie plots
Ethical violations	Reposting/forwarding private email without permission "Creative" editing of others' quoted posts Posting personal information about others
Inappropriate language	Flaming Course or vulgar language Personal attacks or insults
Factual errors	Mistakes with respect to names, dates, places Errors in summarizing others' posts

The reproaches range from the mild correction to the truly vicious attack on the offender. Some groups were particularly vocal about any perceived violations, and all in all, reproach episodes made up about 15% of the network traffic during the period. Clearly, there are a lot of mistakes to be made on the Internet, and a lot of people eager to tell you when you make them.

Reproaches from fellow players also occur in the Internet's gaming communities, especially ones in which the participants have, or are eager to develop, a high level of group cohesion. On Legends of Kesmai, the adventure metaworld in which players work together to slay dragons and collect treasure, I watched a very simple but effective reproach episode. Two knights sparring in the gymnasium had dropped their heavy dragon scale armor on the side of the ring. This armor is difficult to acquire on Kesmai, and quite prestigious to own since it shows you are canny enough to waste a powerful dragon and drag its body to the tanner to make scales for you. Another player dressed as a wizard wandered into the gym and stood on the square with the armor, apparently watching the boxing match. He left after a few minutes, and then the boxers jumped out of the ring to retrieve their armor. "Hey! He took it!" The culprit was still lingering near the gym's entrance, and the boxer reproached him with a simple, straightforward remark: "Don't steal other people's things on Kes." The wizard replied, "Sorry, I didn't know – I'm new." He returned the armor, and the knight answered, "np :)" (no problem, smile). There is nothing in the program's software that prevents players from moving up the ranks by acts of thievery or treachery against other players, and certainly some choose that route, but a surprising number of Kesmai inhabitants conform to the emergent norm of cooperation once they grasp it from the other players.

The effectiveness of reproaches is probably quite high. Though some people will continue doing what they were doing or even escalate the behavior that led to the reproach, most seem to respond to the public chastisement by either conforming or leaving the group. For the few who do not, there are other more drastic means to protect the group from destabilization. A moderator can stop posts, for example, and participants can use their email filters to automatically delete any postings from a particular offender. In the chat rooms, an operator can maintain a long list of nicknames and IP addresses who are considered "banned" – if they attempt to enter the chat room they will be immediately kicked out.

The MUDs and other multiplayer games have their own escalation schemes for encouraging, and sometimes demanding, conformity about various rules of conduct. A character can set the command to "gag" another player if that individual is bothersome in some way. The comments from the gagged character still appear to others in the room, but just not to the one who did the gagging. Pavel Curtis notes that this facility is very rarely used on Lambda. In one survey, just 45 players out of 3000 were gagging other players. An obvious reason is that the "gag" command has one big drawback: the gagged player can still be heard by everyone in the room, so the one doing the gagging is at somewhat of a disadvantage, although the screen scroll may be less aggravating and cluttered.

A more potent threat to players who fail to heed reproaches on Lambda is *toading*, a term that evolved from the MUD administrator's power to alter a character's appearance in the direction of a hideous amphibian. The character's own description is temporarily inaccessible, and anyone who looks at the toaded player sees a text description of something quite revolting. On the MUD, however, the term came to mean permanent banishment of a particular character. Now, a system is in place by which players who have a gripe about another character can begin a petition process to toad the offender, and other players can vote on it.

IN SEARCH OF THE LEVIATHAN

Conforming to social conventions and adhering to laws that restrict our freedoms are, from a philosophical perspective, things we do to preserve our existence. We give up certain freedoms to earthly authorities in order to live in a predictable and safe world, interacting peaceably and fairly with our fellow humans. Thomas Hobbes proposed the concept of the Leviathan, defined as "that mortal god, to which we owe under the immortal God; our peace and defence." The Leviathan might simply be a system of government that we empower to resolve disputes, justly we hope. It might also be the head chieftain who has the power of life or death over tribe members. That particular mortal god is elusive on the Internet. One might wonder whether any Leviathan could exist at all in cyberspace, given how sprawling and decentralized it is.

As a doctoral student in government at the University of Texas at Austin, Richard C. MacKinnon insightfully argued that there is indeed a Leviathan on the Internet, one to which most people willingly give up freedoms in order to preserve the value and energy of the medium itself.[51] There is still very little formal Internet regulation in most countries, but MacKinnon believes the Leviathan is there anyway because we want the Internet to flourish, and sense it will not unless we build a framework of trust and establish means to ensure compliance with, at the very least, netiquette. We also have some fear of injury from unlaw-

---

[51] MacKinnon, R. (1995). Searching for the Leviathan in Usenet. In S. G. Jones (Ed.), *Cybersociety: Computer-mediated communication and community* (pp. 112–137). Thousand Oaks, CA: Sage Publications.

ful others, for our personas certainly, but also for our reputations and even physical selves. This, too, motivates us to build a Leviathan-like creature to whom we can relinquish certain freedoms in return for orderliness.

The Leviathan emerges, for example, in our eagerness to establish some groups as "moderated." The anointed moderator, almost always an unpaid volunteer, can choose which messages to censor and which to pass along to all the subscribers, and can edit as he or she sees fit. In many cases, the moderators play a very relaxed role and rarely kill anyone's contribution. Yet the presence of some authority figure can have a calming influence and ensures participants that a means is available to resolve disputes should they arise. Anyone who has watched the membership in one of their favorite discussion forums erode when a small number of participants engage in a public flame war or lengthy off-topic debate may have felt a wistful longing for a firm-handed moderator.

Bill Southerly of Frostburg State University started a mailing list for psychology teachers called TIPS: Teaching in the Psychological Sciences. As the moderator, he wanted to set a collegial tone for the group and ensure that people could express disagreement without flaming one another. In the early days of the list, he had some difficulties because a few participants just couldn't resist adding personal insults to their posts when they disagreed with another member. As the years went by, however, the need for censorship or reproach diminished. The norms of the group evolved and the members were able to convey the list's conventions to one another, with very satisfactory results. Although an occasional flare-up occurs, the willingness of almost everyone on the list to conform to the group's norms has led to a vital community of psychology teachers who have a lively virtual coffee shop to share their professional and personal enthusiasms.

In unmoderated settings, the Leviathan would emerge with more difficulty were it not for human willingness to conform and our eagerness to preserve a productive online group environment. Members of cohesive groups expect new participants to comply with whatever norms and posted signs are in place for the group, and when they don't a reproach may be forthcoming.

More recently, the Leviathan may be getting a boost from the growing realization that our contributions to the net are not as fleeting, nor as difficult to trace, as many had supposed. For example, newsgroup posts are archived and searchable by keyword, so anyone can find your contributions if you used the same email address. Also, Internet Service

Providers are adding their own horsepower to the Leviathan, for better or worse. They have no obligation to continue your account if they receive a complaint, and most have no interest in lengthy investigations to determine if any particular complaint is valid. Bill Machrone, writing for *PC Magazine,* tells of an incident in which an active and sophisticated net user became involved in a flame war, and his opponent finally complained to the ISP. The company simply canceled the writer's account rather than spend time listening to charges and countercharges. Internet service is easy to get in most areas of the country, so ordinarily the writer would not have been too inconvenienced by the cancellation. The writer could simply sign up with another service. In this case, however, the ISP was the local cable company and the *only* provider of high-speed Internet access in the writer's region. The abrupt cancellation based on his opponent's complaint left the writer without high-speed access until some other service is available in the region.[52]

EXPERIMENTING WITH THE LEVIATHAN ON A SOCIAL MUD

The wizards of LambdaMOO experimented with several different methods of establishing the Leviathan in a pendulum-like fashion. It was initially embodied in the system administrators. "Vengeance is ours, sayeth the wizards," was the dire warning prominently displayed in the help files – the sign on the door of the MUD, so to speak. Players with disputes or complaints against others pled their case to these all powerful MUD "gods", and the ultimate punishment – toading – was completely in their hands. But Pavel Curtis, wearied by the psychological and moral weight of playing mediator on his innovative creation, decided at one point to retire from his role as judge, jury, and executioner and institute a far more laissez-faire approach – one that would rely on the judgments of the people at large (whoever they were):

> On December 9, 1992, I posted a pivotal message to LamdaMOO's "Social-Issues mailing list; I titled it "On to the next stage,..." but somehow history has indelibly tagged it "LambdaMOO Takes a New Direction," or "LTAND." In that message, I announced the abdication of the wizards from the "discipline/manners/arbitration business"; we would no longer be making what I glibly termed "social decisions." It was so simple in my mind; there was a clear distinction between politics and engineering. We wizards would just become technicians and leave the moral, political, and social

---

[52] Machrone, B. (1998). Mind your manners. *PC Magazine,* October 20, 1998, p. 85.

rudder to "the people." In the metaphor of that message, I was throwing the baby bird of LambdaMOO society out of the nest of wizards as mothers; in hindsight, I forced a transition in LambdaMOO government, from wizardocracy to anarchy.[53]

Just a few months after the LTAND message, Curtis realized his mistake. He had ripped the wizard Leviathan from LambdaMOO and left nothing in its place. The community began to disintegrate and bitter interplayer disputes escalated, just as Hobbes predicted they might. The turning point came when a brutal cyberape occurred (discussed in another chapter) and one of the wizards took it into his own hands to toad the perpetrator after all – with or without the judgment of the people. To this day, no one may request the character name "Mr.Bungles" on Lambda because that character is permanently toaded. Although most players were outraged at the savage offense, many were even angrier that the wizards had backpedaled on their promise not to interfere by making such moral judgments and executing a player's persona without some kind of due process.

Curtis tried to rebuild some order in the MUD by instituting a formal petition and ballot system, inspired by the voter-sponsored initiative process in California. Any player can start a petition and if it gets enough signatures, it is placed on the ballot for a vote by the players. Rare petitions call for toading of another player, but most are proposals for minor rule changes on the MUD such as the method for determining how much disk space each player is allotted for building rooms and objects. When participants log into Lambda, an automated message reminds them about petitions they still need to vote on, and some are quite complex with considerable debate, pro and con. Though he moved much of the Leviathan closer to an online democracy, Curtis reserved a slice of power for the wizards by insisting that a petition would not become a ballot until they had "vetted" it. To be vetted, the wizards must decide that the proposal is clear, feasible (from a technical standpoint), legal, secure, and *appropriate*. It is the last criterion that gives the wizards a loophole, much like the determination of "offensive" in debates over obscenity.

Did Curtis's rigidly formal Leviathan work? No, not very well, but not because Lambda citizens preferred anarchy. Many were deeply committed to this online community, but the petition system fell prey to yet another potent aspect of group dynamics whether online or off: group

[53] Curtis, P. (1997). Not just a game: How LambdaMOO came to exist and what it did to get back at me, [Online]. Available: ftp://parcftp.xerox.com/pub/MOO/papers/HighWired.txt [27 May, 1997].

polarization, one I will explain in a moment. Curtis notes, "There were long periods, indeed, where many petitions reached ballot stage and none of them passed; it seems to me now that the voting population could never agree on anything of real substance." Also, many LambdaMOO characters carried their usual political apathy into the MUD and didn't really care about the petitions. Many appeared to involve petty little disputes among players anyway, or arcane programming rules, and the residents simply abstained. That outcome of the Lambda experiment should sound vaguely familiar to anyone who goes into a voting booth and is confronted with choices on issues about which they know absolutely nothing.

Finally, the petition system did not work well because it was impossible for the wizards to really abdicate decision-making on social issues. Technology and social policy are tightly interwoven in this virtual community, dependent as it is on a single host and a small group of technically savvy people who maintain and improve it from day to day. In 1996, Curtis posted his third pivotal message to the Social Issues mailing list in which he repudiated his theory of a social/technical dichotomy, and essentially re-embodied the wizards as Leviathan.

LambdaMOO's experiments demonstrate how fragile and elusive an orderly virtual environment can be, and how difficult it is to find workable solutions. This is a social MUD, an Internet niche rarely frequented by the large majority of net users, but the events that transpired as the group tried to get organized as a community are revealing. Internet users are adamantly opposed to any centralized, all-powerful Leviathan for the net at large, and censorship concerns routinely rate high on the list whenever user surveys are conducted. But this means that the earthly authority that most people want and need must come, for the most part, from within – through popular consent and voluntary conformity to whatever rules and conventions emerge within each community. The fact that humans tend to conform to group norms may be one of the key reasons Internet communities continue to thrive and flourish. Through signs on the door, reproaches, and our own willingness to conform, we each become a cell in the body of that mortal god, the Leviathan.

GROUP POLARIZATION

Disagreement often becomes very heated and contentious on the Internet, even when everyone in a group is conforming to the group's written and unwritten behavioral guidelines. The breakdown of the petition system on LambdaMOO, for example, was partly due to the fact that people couldn't seem to come to an agreement about much of anything. Clay Shirky, author of *Voices from the Net*, points out how so many exchanges become polarized on the politically oriented discussions:

> *The greatest loss in public discourse on the net is the loss of moderate voices. In many public political forums, it is almost impossible to develop and refine ideas of real political complexity because there are a spate of constant challenges from the extremes. For instance, people who want to reform welfare have a difficult time talking without being attacked by those wanting to abolish it altogether. With the real hot-button issues, this can become a network of talk radio, where people post, not to elucidate a point or advance a contention, but to hear (read) themselves think.*[54]

Research in social psychology suggests that the phenomenon of group polarization may be partly responsible for the extremism we so often see on the Internet, and the apparent absence of that moderate voice. An individual may hold a relatively moderate view about an issue initially, but after talking with others about it, he may move away from the middle ground toward one of the fringes. And on the Internet, that is what people do: talk, talk, talk. Studies of group polarization in face-to-face settings suggest that the factors that contribute to it are present in abundance on the Internet, so we may not have far to look to understand why that moderate voice is so rare.

Consider the experiments on what psychologists called the *risky shift*. Most people intuitively suppose that groups would be more conservative and cautious in their thinking and decision-making than individuals, and that it makes good sense to appoint a committee (or jury, or board, or task force) when important issues need to be resolved and difficult decisions made. Democratic societies are not all that comfortable with an autocrat, and we routinely put groups in charge to balance and restrain the potential extremism of an individual. But in the early 1960s, a graduate student at MIT was working diligently on his Master's thesis in industrial management and found that surprising things happen when groups are asked to make decisions.

For his thesis, James Stoner created dilemmas in which an imaginary character was faced with a decision and was seeking advice from the subjects in the experiment. Each involved an element of risk, and Stoner wondered whether individuals or groups would choose the more cautious route. One dilemma, for example, involved a fictional writer of genre westerns who yearns for a loftier literary goal:

[54] Shirky, C. (1995). *Voices of the net*. Emeryville, CA: ZD Press.

Helen is a writer who is said to have considerable creative talent but who so far has been earning a comfortable living by writing cheap westerns. Recently, she has come up with an idea for a potentially significant novel. If it could be written and accepted, it might have considerable literary impact and be a big boost to her career. On the other hand, if she cannot work out her idea or if the novel is a flop, she will have expended considerable time and energy without remuneration.[55]

Subjects were invited to choose how much risk Helen should take. They checked a box to indicate they thought she should take the leap if the chances of success for the novel were 1 in 10, 2 in 10, 3 in 10, and so on. After each person in the group indicated his or her choice privately, the group discussed the case and came to a consensus recommendation for Helen. To everyone's surprise, the group decision was actually riskier than the average of the individuals' decisions. After talking it through, the group became less cautious, not more so, and the individuals did as well.

Nothing piques the interest of psychologists more than a counterintuitive finding like this one, and years of research followed. It was important to nail down the underpinnings and complexities of this risky shift – especially because we rely so heavily on groups to make important decisions. We thought that by appointing a group we would be achieving some balance of input and could be assured that good decisions would be forthcoming. It was alarming to find that whatever was going on when people got together to talk led to more extremism, not less.

Though the phenomenon was initially dubbed the "risky shift" because the problems involved some decision about risk taking, later studies demonstrated that group discussion does not necessarily lead to riskier decisions. Instead, talking it over seems to intensify the individual leanings of the group members further toward one of the extremes – pulling them toward one or the other poles. If the individuals are leaning toward caution in some kind of a dilemma, their group decision will be even more cautious. Or if they tend to agree with a particular opinion individually, their group will agree with it even more strongly after they have a chance to discuss it.

Psychologists David Myers and George Bishop showed how this "move toward the fringe" occurs when like-minded people get together

[55] Stoner, J. A. F. (1962). A comparison of individual and group decisions involving risk. Unpublished master's thesis. Massachusetts Institute of Technology, 1961. Cited by D. G. Marquis in Individual responsibility and group decisions involving risk. *Industrial Management Review, 3,* 8–23 (p. 332).

to discuss racial attitudes.[56] They asked high school students to complete surveys about various racial issues, such as how much they favored open housing laws. After scoring the results, they formed groups of like-minded individuals, either prejudiced or unprejudiced. The group polarization effect influenced these people in opposite ways. The groups made up of people who initially leaned toward prejudiced attitudes became more so after group discussion. The groups of relatively unprejudiced students went in the other direction – they became even more unprejudiced after the discussion. In other words, when groups talk things out, they can polarize toward one of the extreme ends.

The question of why people in groups shift toward one or the other end of the attitudinal scale has been a difficult one to answer. Certainly a discussion will allow group members to raise tidbits of information that might not have occurred to each individual separately. Indeed, this is one reason why most people believe a group will make better decisions than an individual. Nevertheless, if the group members lean slightly toward one end to begin with, their tendency to conform could continue to reinforce that same direction in one another as they add their tidbits of information. One might say, "Well, Helen really has little to lose," and another might add, "She isn't proud of herself as a cheap western writer, anyway." Each argument in favor of "going for the gold" would tend to sway the individuals, and thus the group, toward the extreme.

Another element that seems to make group decisions more extreme than their individual counterparts is social comparison. When you don't know what the others think, you can't compare your own opinion to theirs or exhibit your own tendency to conform to the group norm. You might suppose that most people would take a more conservative viewpoint about Helen's dilemma, and that you would be the adventurous risk taker in the group. When you learn that others generally agree with you, you might want to not just conform, but move even further out on the limb to maintain that initial view you had of yourself – of being the adventurous one in the group. As others do the same thing, the group moves perilously close to the ledge.

POLARIZATION ON THE NET

The loss of that moderate voice is partly due to the exaggerated group polarization effects that can occur on the Internet. Consider, for exam-

[56] Myers, D. G. and Bishop, G. D. (1970). Discussion effects on racial attitudes. *Science, 169*, 778–334.

ple, the early studies by Sara Kiesler and her colleagues in which they formed three-person groups who were to work on various problems, either in a face-to-face mode or via computer-conferencing software. The computer-mediated groups took more time to reach consensus, used more uninhibited swearing, name-calling and insults, and made larger decision shifts from their original, averaged, individual positions. In general, they had more trouble coming to agreement than the face-to-face groups and they tended to use more polling and numerical votes.

Russell Spears and his colleagues demonstrated that group polarization can be quite high in Internet-like situations, especially when the people who are working as group members think strongly of themselves in those terms.[57] These researchers sent out questionnaires to their subjects to find out their initial positions on four controversial subjects that had clear "right–left" political overtones. One item, for example, asked the students to state their agreement with the statement, "Nationalized industries should be sold off." They assumed, rightly, that the students would already be leaning toward the left on issues such as this, and the experiment would detect whether their positions became even more radical after various types of group discussion.

Groups of three arrived at the lab, and all were taught the basics of a simple computer-mediated communication system with which they would discuss each of the issues in turn. For half the groups, the subjects sat in the same room during their discussion so they could see one another, even though they communicated by means of the computers. For the other half, though, the subjects never saw one another and stayed in separate offices. This latter condition is closer to the Internet environment where physical distance is great and anonymity high.

To investigate the extent to which each person's feelings of groupness influenced their behavior, the researchers added one additional twist. Half of the groups who would be sitting in the same room, and half of the groups whose members would be lodged in separate offices, were given special instructions that would make them feel closer to their other group members, and make group membership more salient to them. It doesn't take much to get people to identify with a group, as we will see in the next chapter. Sometimes just putting the same color hat on them will work, as long as it is different from the hat color of others in the room. In this case, the researchers encouraged group identity by a

---

[57] Spears, M., Russell, L., and Lee, S. (1990). De-individuation and group polarization in computer-mediated communication. *British Journal of Social Psychology, 29*, 121–134.

carefully worded introduction to the experiment. They were told that their group consisted entirely of first-year psychology students, and they were being tested as members of a group – not as individuals. In contrast, the other groups were encouraged to behave as individuals and group identity was downplayed. They were told that the experiment was designed "to evaluate personal styles in the way individuals communicate, and to investigate person perception." After the computer-mediated discussions, the subjects in all conditions answered the questionnaire again and also guessed what attitudes they thought their fellow group members held about the same issues.

Overall, the groups whose members sat in separate rooms showed about the same amount of polarization as the groups whose members could see one another. Also, those groups who were made to feel more group identity showed about the same amount of polarization as those who were encouraged to be individualistic. The fascinating part of this experiment was in the interaction between those two conditions.

For those whose group membership was emphasized, sitting in separate rooms caused a sharp *increase* in polarization. But for those for whom individuality was emphasized, sitting in separate rooms caused a sharp *decrease* in the polarization phenomenon. In fact, these people actually strayed in the opposite direction when they couldn't see each other, away from the group norm.

You are probably scratching your head by now, wondering what these complicated results might mean for the Internet. Human behavior is notoriously complex in any setting, and these interactions among variables that psychologists are constantly turning up show why we answer so many seemingly straightforward questions with, "Well, that depends."

In this case, a plausible hypothesis is that the Internet-like setting is most likely to create a strong tendency toward group polarization when the members of the group feel some sense of group identity. Group polarization, after all, relies on group influence and the tendency to conform and compare one's own views to those of others around you. But for people who don't feel like they are a part of a cohesive group, the isolation, deindividuation, and physical distance typical of the Internet make them ignore the group's views and go their own way. They do this more easily than people who are in plain sight of their loosely knit group members. They might even show a little psychological reactance in the other direction to demonstrate their own individuality, as they did in this study.

FINDING OTHERS OF LIKE MIND

We may be more susceptible to group polarization online than off because it is so easy to find people who are already leaning the same way we are on just about any issue, regardless of how peculiar. Unlike the people in many of the studies I described in this chapter, we are not randomly assigned to groups and given a particular task to work on. We can proactively choose which groups to join and find like-minded others who are almost certain to reinforce our viewpoints, and move us a bit further out toward an extreme position. In the Myers and Bishop study discussed earlier people who leaned slightly toward prejudiced or non-prejudiced positions were grouped together, and after their discussions, the individuals on each side moved even further away from a moderate position. Those researchers tested the subjects first to decide how to group them. On the Internet, you find your own groups and your choices are almost infinite.

You may know of no other people in your geographical vicinity who happen to believe that a new ice age is imminent, or that Elvis sightings have been documented, proven, and suppressed by government conspiracies. On the Internet, people who share your interest and lean in the same direction as you are just a few keystrokes away, regardless of the issue's obscurity, social desirability, or bizarreness. As people participate in online group discussions with the few others who share their views from around the world, they may well hold biased discussions, experience the influence of group polarization, and move further and further toward extremism. Interacting with a small subset of like-minded others spread around the globe, our framework for social comparison could become rather warped. We could quickly acquire an exaggerated perception of the rightness of our views because we found others who not only agreed with us, but who are even further out on the attitudinal limb. Inch by inch, we would move out on the limb ourselves – toward the polarized extreme – with the support of those like-minded others. Goodbye, moderate voice.

If it weren't for people's natural tendency to conform and for their desire to be a member of cohesive groups, the vibrant virtual communities on the Internet would probably not exist. Yet, the harmony of the groups that emerge on the Internet can be tenuous and fragile because the elements that contribute to harmonious group interaction in real life are weaker, or at least different, on the Internet. We sometimes need virtual sledgehammers to bring about the conformity that is so important to group cohesion, something we rarely require in real-life group settings. Also, the elements that lead to group polarization in real life are present in abundance on the Internet, so we should hardly be surprised when we run into discussion groups whose regular members firmly hold some weird or extreme viewpoints.

Much of what I have been discussing in this chapter thus far involves the "open" Internet, and all the voluntary public forums and communities that attract net users from around the world to engage in group activities. However, companies and organizations are also using the net as well as a variety of computer-mediated software environments to help their employees become more productive. Let's turn now to the virtual workgroup and see how the online environment is influencing their group dynamics.

VIRTUAL WORK GROUPS

Increasingly, organizations are taking advantage of electronic media for group work. The software used to support such group activity includes email, online discussion forums and conferences, and also a variety of software tools that give group members the opportunity to engage in electronic brainstorming, voting, sorting, prioritizing, collaborative document editing, online chatting and interactive video, and collective decision making. The software goes by many different names; examples include group support systems (GSS), groupware, group decision support systems (GDSS), and collaborative technologies. In some cases, the software is designed to be used by people who are sitting at computers in the same room, and the participants shift back and forth from a face-to-face discussion to an electronic activity with a facilitator to guide them. In others, the groupware is available via the net 24 hours a day for asynchronous group work, and participants could be spread across the globe.

Software developers and marketers move much more quickly than social scientists, and the electronic tools are evolving at a breathtaking pace. Managers eager to take advantage of information technology, and put to use the money their companies are spending on it to transform their business and gain competitive advantage, are adopting these tools with enthusiasm. Unfortunately, behavioral research on the effectiveness of virtual work groups and the special dynamics that might arise in the computer-mediated environment is still sparse, and scientists are having a very hard time keeping up because the technology is changing so fast. Yet the effectiveness of virtual workgroups is a significant issue, and we need to better understand how the move from the conference room to the ether affects group dynamics, productivity, and the overall quality of the work they perform. For example, from the discussion of group polarization, we can guess that the moderate voice in a workgroup might be a weak one, weaker than it might have been in a face-to-face setting. Other aspects of workgroup dynamics also appear to unfold differently online, including biased discussions, the influence of minority opinion holders, and brainstorming productivity.

THE BIASED DISCUSSION IN ONLINE WORKGROUPS

In any workgroup discussion, it is unlikely that everyone would start out knowing all the same things – this is, after all, one reason we tend to think groups will make better decisions than individuals. They should, in principle, have the combined information and expertise of all members at their disposal after they talk about it. Each person can share what he or she knows with the others, making the whole at least equal to the sum of the parts. Unfortunately, this is often not what happens, and it is especially not what happens when workgroups get together online to make decisions.

Groups sometimes suffer from polarization because members can be rather selective about what they share with the others. As polarization gets underway, the group members become more reluctant to bring up items of information they have about the subject that might contradict the emerging group consensus. The result is a biased discussion in which the group has no opportunity to consider all the facts, because the members are not bringing them up.

Ross Hightower and Lutfus Sayeed studied this phenomenon in the context of management, wondering how online groups using groupware might collaborate to make personnel decisions.[58] As I mentioned, this kind of software varies considerably, but these researchers took advantage of its synchronous chat and online voting capabilities to support the group's work.

The research involved the review of resumes for three candidates who were applying for a marketing manager position. The investigators rigged the candidates' positive and negative attributes so that one applicant was best suited for the job because he matched the criteria in the

---

[58] Hightower, R., and Sayeed, L. (1995). The impact of computer-mediated communication systems on biased group discussion. *Computers in Human Behavior, 11,* 33–44.

job description most closely. Then they handed out packets of information to their subjects containing a subset of the information from the resumes, so each group member only knew part of the story. Some of the three-person groups assigned to recommend one of the three candidates met face-to-face, while the others discussed the candidates from separate locations using the groupware.

Polarization was common, and you may be dismayed but not surprised to learn that almost none of the groups – face-to-face or computer-mediated – chose the best candidate. They just were not sharing the information in a way that would enable the group to make an objective decision based on the whole picture. The amount of bias in the discussions, though, was particularly skewed when the discussion was held online. The researchers could assess *how* biased the discussions were by examining the actual tidbits the group members chose to share. In a very biased discussion, they would tend to share positive information about the winning candidate and also negative statements about the losing applicants, but they would avoid bringing up negative information about the winner and positive items for the losers. Each item they contributed would thus reinforce the march toward group consensus rather than add complications and fuel debate. This trend was very apparent in the online groups, and more than twice as large compared to the face-to-face groups.

MINORITY OPINIONS IN ONLINE WORKGROUPS

Another group dynamic that appears to unfold slightly differently in online work groups compared to their face-to-face counterparts is the way minority opinions are expressed and received by the group. On the surface, we might suppose that a person who holds a dissenting opinion from the rest of the work group would feel freer to express that opinion in the online setting. The dissenter would not have to endure raised eyebrows or interruptions by members of the majority, or be made to feel uncomfortable about the failure to agree with the others. She could type away at the keyboard, restating her position in a persistent way.

It appears that dissenters do feel more liberated to express their views online than off but, unfortunately, their online remarks have less influence on the rest of the group. Poppy Lauretta McLeod and her colleagues at the University of Iowa explored this aspect of online workgroups using an experimental procedure somewhat similar to the resume reviews.[59] In this case, the group members were all given various bits of information about companies A, B, and C, and their job was to discuss which would make the best investment, either face-to-face or in a synchronous chat. The deck was stacked so that if all information was out on the table, company A was the best choice. However, the most revealing pieces of information were only provided to one individual in the group – ensuring that this person would be a minority opinion holder. These people were especially vocal when their contributions were online and anonymous, but they were also especially ineffective at changing the majority opinion under those same conditions. As a result, the online workgroups wound up making rather poor decisions and bad investments.

One way to interpret these results considers the role of pain–gain. In a face-to-face setting, a minority opinion holder has to stick his neck out and risk censure when he voices his views, and this alone may make the others in the group pay more attention to him. Online, the pain for the dissenter is considerably lower, particularly if the contributions are anonymous, so the gain may be lower, too.

WORKGROUPS AND ELECTRONIC BRAINSTORMING

Group brainstorming emerged on the business scene in the 1950s, after advertising executive Alex Osborn published a how-to book on the technique.[60] Intuitively, it seemed like a wonderful way to stimulate creativity and generate many original ideas very quickly. People were brought together in a room, given a topic, and told to come up with as many wild ideas as they could. Group members were not allowed to criticize one another's contributions, and instead were to improve on, combine, or build on the ideas of others during the brainstorming session. The participants generally loved the technique, and it took hold. Unfortunately, it didn't work. After more than two decades of research on the subject, behavioral scientists came to the conclusion that individual brainstorming was simply more effective. In study after study, groups whose members worked individually developed more ideas, and more original ideas, compared to the same size group working with the group brainstorming technique, primarily because of *production blocking*. In a

[59] McLeod, P. L., Baron, R. S., Marti, M. W., and Yoon, K. (1997). The eyes have it. *Journal of Applied Psychology, 82(5)*, 706–718.
[60] Osborn, A. (1953). *Applied imagination*. New York, NY: Scribner.

group, only one person can talk at a time; if you are listening to the discussion you have less time to come up with original ideas of your own.

Terry Connolly at the University of Arizona points out that software developers rarely read the behavioral science literature and might ignore it if they did read it, so they proceeded with the design of an electronic support tool for group brainstorming – despite the evidence that it didn't work.[61] Participants would sit at their microcomputers and enter their original ideas in one window. After the idea is submitted, it appears in a second window along with the ideas of the other participants. Researchers investigating the effectiveness of this new version of group brainstorming found, to their surprise, that the electronic support made quite a difference in the results. When the group is large, the results from the computer-mediated group brainstorming session were superior.

One reason why electronic group brainstorming works reasonably well when its face-to-face predecessor did not is because the electronic version bypasses the production-blocking problem. With the computer-supported version of group discussion, you can glance at your group members' contribution at any time, but they need not interrupt your train of thought. Also, the computer-mediated environment may trigger disinhibition, so group members may feel freer to express their wildest notions with less concern about negative reaction.

At the moment, much electronic group brainstorming is confined to laboratories in which the participants can see one another and a facilitator guides the activity. However, there is no reason why it can't be used over the Internet, with participants who are continents away from one another. In this case, the early results are promising – a technique that failed in its face-to-face version may work well online because of the features of the medium.

DEVELOPING TRUST IN VIRTUAL TEAMS

For workgroups to succeed, the individuals who participate must develop some trust in one another. In face-to-face situations, this kind of trust evolves as coworkers come to know one another and learn to respect the contributions that each person can make to the team effort. Over time, as they work on task forces, committees, and work teams together, colleagues learn they can rely on one another and trust that

---

[61] Connolly, T. (1997). Electronic brainstorming: Science meets technology in the group meeting room. In S. Kiesler (Ed.), *Culture of the Internet* (pp. 263–276). Lawrence Erlbaum Associates, Publishers.

other team members will perform as expected. This kind of trust has great advantages for a workgroup. Individual members don't have to worry about freeloaders who can't be trusted to do their share or get the work done on time. They can spend less time cajoling and monitoring members' contributions, and more time in productive work.

Corporations are finding many advantages to the kinds of fluid teams the Internet makes possible, with members drawn from subsidiaries around the world and activities conducted in cyberspace. If a team needs a certain combination of skills, the corporation need not be limited by geography when members are chosen. But how do these virtual team members establish a sense of trust so they can work together effectively?

Sirkka Jarvenpaa at the University of Texas at Austin, and her colleagues studied the development of trust in 75 global virtual teams, each of which had 4 to 6 members residing in different countries.[62] The groups worked together for eight weeks on several tasks, including two trust-building exercises and a final project in which the teams proposed a Web site to provide a new service to ISWorld Net, an organization that supports information systems professionals. Predictably, some teams did extremely well while others did very poorly; a key success factor involved the development of trust among the members.

The members of one of the teams that developed a high level of trust exchanged messages frequently, and they all showed optimism, excitement, and a clear orientation toward the task and the project goals. Members shared leadership duties, and they were very proactive – volunteering for specific roles without waiting for assignments. They also recognized that as a virtual team they needed to stay in close contact and meet their commitments, and even during weekend trips the members found ways to communicate. In the early part of the project, some members explained away short absences or failure to meet deadlines because of strikes, sickness, or personal duties, but another quickly pointed out, "Do you know what the devil's grandmother died of? Bad excuses. So therefore, I will stop apologizing – and start working."

By contrast, a team that failed miserably had members who were infrequent and noncommittal communicators. At one point, eight days went by without a single message exchanged. When a member did finally post some ideas for the project, she implored "Can we PLEASE try

---

[62] Jarvenpaa, S., Knoll, K., and Leidner, D. E. (1998, Spring). Is anybody out there? Antecedents of trust in global virtual teams. *Journal of Management Information Systems* [Online], 14 (4), 29ff. Available: EBSCOhost/Academic Search/686763 [1999, February 25].

to respond?", and rarely did any online discussion emerge in which the members reacted to one another's contributions.

Jarvenpaa and her colleagues suggest that the teams who were most successful in the virtual environment were able to capitalize on "swift" trust. They did not have the time or the history of personal interactions to develop trust gradually, the way a long-term face-to-face group might. Instead, the members jumped into the project acting as though trust existed from the start, even though they had no evidence that their groupmates would carry their share of the load. Their initial willingness to show trusting actions led swiftly to actual trust. By interacting frequently, emphasizing the positive tone, volunteering for assignments, and then going that extra mile to meet their commitments, they were able to overcome the obstacles that led to poor performance in many of the other teams.

Given the trends, virtual workgroups should become more common in the coming years, particularly as tools become more sophisticated and people learn how to use them to increase productivity. However, the issue of trust is likely to emerge in many forms because there are still many unknowns surrounding the medium. For example, employees tend to use email and other forms of Internet communications in a relaxed, conversational way, and the use of passwords or encryption software leads people to believe their messages are private. However, "forwarding frenzy" is common in many organizations. Some corporate emails seem to develop a life of their own as the jumbled history of messages, replies, and replies to replies grows longer and longer, and the list of recipients, some of whom may remain concealed behind the blind carbon copy (bcc) line, mutates over time.

From a legal standpoint, the status of corporate electronic communications is still evolving, but courts in the United States are generally holding that it is company property and employers can snoop at will. To further compound the trust problem of virtual workgroups, these communications do not disappear just because the recipient or sender clicks delete. Data centers make backup tapes of the server's disk drives in case of system failures, so messages might be electronically resurrected years later for legal proceedings. For example, prosecutors have used Internal emails from Microsoft in their antitrust case against the corporate giant, to show what the insiders at the company were planning.[63]

---

[63] Associated Press (1998, October 21). Microsoft may have sought control of Sun's Java: Another lawsuit, another allegation. [Online] Available: http://www.msnbc.com/news/207708.asp [1999, March 24].

Much of the research on virtual workgroups involves students working on group projects, so the stakes are lower and the influence of these other trust-related variables may not be so apparent. Clearly, the virtual workgroup offers many important advantages in the business world, but the psychological and cultural dynamics surrounding our use of this technology are changing rapidly. In a world in which a workgroup's "conversations" might eventually come back to haunt the employees or the corporation, the development of trust – swift or otherwise – could be problematic.

5 INTERGROUP CONFLICT AND COOPERATION

I have seen Steiner's cartoon with the caption "On the Internet, they don't know you're a dog" so many times now, reprinted in Internet-related articles and slapped onto overhead projectors at conferences, that I know he must have struck the collective trigeminal nerve. A great hope for the Internet has always been that the virtual world would at least put a dent in discrimination and prejudice. Without cues to detect race, gender, or age we would not be able to indulge in racism, sexism, or ageism. Steiner's cartoon is both meaningful and hilarious because it adds "species-ism" to the list of -isms the Internet can eradicate.

Has the Internet created the environment we dreamed of, one that would be the foundation for a global community where cohesive and satisfying groups would emerge, free of intergroup tension and prejudice? In some ways, yes, but the reality falls far short of what earlier visionaries imagined. We enter the virtual world laden with the psychological baggage of a lifetime and certainly don't abandon our suitcases in the entrance lobby. Our attachment to groups, and the attitudes we tend to hold about our fellow ingroup members, are part of this luggage. So, too, are the prejudices and negative attitudes we often develop toward outgroups – those outsiders who disagree or compete with us, or are just different. We know quite a bit about this thing called the ingroup and why it can have such dramatic effects on our behavior. To explore the dynamics of intergroup tensions and build a launchpad to extrapolate to our behavior on the Internet, I'll go back to one of the most compelling field experiments ever conducted in social psychology. We head now to Robbers Cave, a remote boys' camp in Oklahoma, USA.

THE ROBBERS CAVE EXPERIMENTS

About half a century ago, Muzafer Sherif and his colleagues orchestrated a series of studies on intergroup conflict and cooperation by becoming participant observers in a naturalistic setting – similar to what researchers are doing now on the Internet. However, as camp director and counselors, they could also manipulate the environment and the boys' activities in controlled and systematic ways.[64,65] Stage 1 focused on the emergence of that sense of groupness I described in the last chapter. It began when the boys were randomly assigned to two different groups and separately bused to the campsite. For the first week, they were unaware of the other group's existence. The researchers watched as each one developed norms, hierarchies, and rules. The boys did exactly that, and by the end of the first week, the Rattlers and the Eagles had coalesced into tightly knit groups. A "toughness" norm emerged in the Rattlers, for example, and members conformed by enduring pain and declining rest stops on hiking trips. Sherif repeatedly introduced activities that would encourage cohesiveness and strong group identity, such as a group treasure hunt that demanded full cooperation of all members.

Though subcliques within each group were apparent in the first few days, they disappeared by the end of the week when subtle signs of an outsider presence in the camp began appearing. One evening, the researchers deliberately allowed the Rattlers to wander within earshot of the Eagles as they played on the baseball diamond. The Rattlers wanted to run them off the property, which now became "our" diamond rather than just "the" diamond. The next day, the staff told the Rattlers that another group – the Eagles – was also at camp, and they wanted to challenge them at baseball. The Rattlers responded by saying, "They can't. We'll challenge them first. ... They've got a nerve..." Cohesiveness and group identity shot up dramatically on this news, and "us" and "them" figured prominently in their attitudes and behavior. "They better not be in our swimming hole," muttered one Rattler. Now that controlled con-

---

[64] Sherif, M., Harvey, O. J., White, B. J., Hood, W. R., and Sherif, C. W. (1988). *The Robbers Cave experiment*. Middletown, CN: Wesleyan University Press. This book is a reprint and update, with additional material, of a book first published by the Institute of Group Relations, the University of Oklahoma in 1961. The experiments themselves were conducted from 1949 to 1954.

[65] Sherif, M. (1966). *In common predicament: Social psychology of intergroup conflict and cooperation*. Boston: Houghton Mifflin.

ditions had created two ingroups, each with a threatening outgroup to deal with, Sherif raised the ante and began stage 2.

The events were contrived to generate maximum intergroup friction, especially through intense winner-take-all competitions in a camp "tournament," complete with trophies, prizes, and medals for the winning group in each event. As the rivalry intensified any semblance of good sportsmanship vanished, and the boys burned each others' flags, planned raids on their enemy's cabin, and physically attacked each other. After each tournament contest, the jubilation inside the winning camp was evident while the losing side bitterly argued amongst themselves, blaming everyone and everything for their shameful loss. When the Eagles won the tournament by the narrowest of margins, the tension was at an all-time high and the Rattlers raided their cabin to steal the prizes. It was definitely time to begin stage 3, in which the experimenters arranged contacts between the two groups to try to reduce the intergroup friction.

Just bringing the boys together for a meal or a movie was useless. The Rattlers would enter the building while the Eagles waited, taunting them with, "Ladies first." Catcalls, jeers, and insults were the main styles of intergroup communication, and food fights were common. Sherif predicted these contacts would do little to reduce intergroup friction and as it turned out, they actually increased it because the meetings gave the groups more opportunities to irritate each other. He hypothesized that only one thing would really work: the superordinate goal.

During the last part of stage 3, the researchers contrived some events involving an important goal that all the boys would want to achieve but that neither group could manage on their own. The idea was to create situations in which the individuals in the groups become mutually interdependent. They cleverly "broke" the camp's water supply and the only way to repair it was for the boys to cooperate. On an outing, the camp truck "broke down" and the boys decided – on their own – that all 20 of them working together could win a "tug-o-war" against the truck and pull it uphill. These controlled events worked their magic and slowly the ingroup/outgroup tensions were reduced. No more catcalls, or "Ladies first." Gradually the negative attitudes the Rattlers held about those Eagle stinkers, and that the Eagles held about those Rattler bums, diminished. The members of the outgroup were no longer a homogeneous, stereotyped bunch of losers and intergroup friendships began to emerge.

INTERGROUP RIVALRIES ON THE INTERNET GAMES

On the Internet, intergroup tensions play out in numerous ways, but the elements that create them share characteristics with what happened at the boys' summer camp. When the environment fosters group identity, cohesive groups emerge. When a group feels threatened by outsider intrusion, the members band together more closely, enforce their own rules more stringently, and develop negative stereotypes about members of the outgroup. If winner-take-all competitions are available, intergroup conflict escalates to new highs. If a valued superordinate goal requires cooperation, intergroup tension will decline and those negative stereotypes will dissipate. Some of the multiplayer Internet games, for example, seem almost like recreations of the Robbers Cave experiments.

These gaming environments take many forms, from the synchronous chats to the MUDs and metaworlds, and they have a variety of different themes. For example, some are medieval adventures, while others lean toward science fiction. Contemporary warfare is always popular, along with the more traditional card and board games like bridge or Trivial Pursuit. Regardless of the theme or the sophistication of the graphics, certain properties of the gaming environments affect the way the players act, in much the same way those experimental manipulations influenced the behavior of the Rattlers and the Eagles.

One important element is simply the assignment of players to competitive teams. Aliens Online, for example, creates a highly visual reenactment of the Sigourney Weaver movies in which Marines and Aliens fight head to head. You must join one side or the other when you first create your character and give it a name, so you are immediately dropped into a group environment with built-in intergroup competition. Once in the game, your job is to work with your teammates to destroy the other side. Elaborate missions are organized, leaders emerge, and battles are won or lost. It is not hard to see how the typical patterns of intergroup conflicts would emerge in this environment. People tend to play the same character on the same team whenever they log in, and just like a Rattler or Eagle, they can form strong attachments to members of their ingroup and show contempt for the members of the outgroup. As you might expect, strong leaders emerge on each side to lead the attacks and players are expected to follow the rules in a military-like fashion. The Rattlers and Eagles became more rigidly hierarchical and strict about conforming to norms after the outgroup emerged as well.

In #trivbot, an online version of Trivial Pursuit on IRC's Austnet, intergroup tensions are sometimes exacerbated for the same reasons. The programmed bot greets new players as they enter the room and nags them until they join team 1 or 2. During play, the bot asks questions like, "Who wrote Grapes of Wrath?" or, "Where did Napoleon surrender?" Players quickly type in their response and the bot evaluates them, awarding the point to the team that answers correctly first. The members of each team can name their group – fostering group identity – and players cheer when a member of their own team earns a point. Most of the time the intergroup tensions stay under control, but occasionally little flame wars erupt with name-calling and insults.

If it seems a little strange to you that people would feel some bond with an Internet group just because they arbitrarily joined the Aliens or Trivbot's Team 2, you underestimate how easily we begin to think in terms of ingroups and outgroups. The British social psychologist Henri Tajfel conducted studies in which he assigned people to "groups" based on the most trivial attributes, but found that they developed a feeling of group membership anyway.[66] For example, in one study British teenagers were first asked to evaluate modern painters. Tajfel later let them know that they were assigned to a group that appreciates "Klee" or to a different group that appreciates "Kandinsky," though their actual preferences were totally ignored in the group assignments. The teens within each group never actually met one another, but they formed a bond with their like-minded art lovers, particularly when they had a chance to dispense some rewards. When they were asked to divide money among members of the in and outgroups, they consistently favored members of their own group, by about two to one. Much like the members of the Marines, Aliens, or a Trivbot team, these people never met one another in real life. The label that formed the group in the first place was about as inconsequential as it gets, but they still showed a strong sense of ingroup favoritism. They believed that the members of their ingroup were smarter, better, and more pleasant than the members of the outgroup.

The tendency of people to identify with a group and favor its members, despite the arbitrariness and absurdity of the criteria for group membership, is known as the *minimal group phenomenon*. It hardly seems rational to show such favoritism toward people who become part of your "group" because of a coin toss, a color label (the blue group), or an imaginary pref-

---

[66] Tajfel, H. (1981). *Human groups and social categories: Studies in social psychology*. London: Cambridge University Press. Tajfel, H. (1982). Social psychology of intergroup relations. *Annual Review of Psychology, 33*, 1–39.

erence for a certain type of art, but we do this routinely. Once assigned, we imagine that our fellow group members are more similar to us than they actually are on some far more meaningful dimensions, and that the outgroup is more homogeneous and dissimilar to us than they really are.

While the environment of Aliens Online or #trivbot is a programmed setup for intergroup conflict, many other gaming worlds do not require any automatic group membership. They do not set up a contrived "us against them" environment in which online players join competing teams. However, groups often emerge spontaneously in these worlds anyway, partly because of the human tendency to want to be part of a group we can call the ingroup. In Ultima Online's graphical metaworld called Britannia, numerous player guilds have formed. Although many disappear quickly, a few survive with distinct characteristics and very devoted memberships. The Pluggers, for example, demand a very strict code of honor for anyone who aspires to membership. The following tenets appear on their creative Web site:[67]

```
The Pluggers are a close guild dedicated to adventuring
together. Our mission is to be known for our valor in
combat and honesty in actions. Our tenets are quite simple:

    1. Courage. Courage to stand in the face of diversity.
    2. Integrity. The integrity to be trustworthy and
       dependable at all times.
    3. Honor. Your name is your honor and you must not
       project a negative image of yourself or the guild.
    4. Loyalty. Loyalty to your fellow Pluggers.
    5. Virtue. We are not slayers of the innocent, thieves
       of the unwary, nor scavengers of the misfortunate.
       The Pluggers can be distinguished by our hunter
       green colors and black plate armor. We can be found
       in the areas around Yew if you wish to seek us out.

 - Lord Skyblade
```

The Pluggers certainly know something about the psychological principles underlying group cohesiveness and identity. They have a lengthy initiation for newcomers who seek to join, and they demand that new players develop certain skills such as magic or combat that will be useful to the guild. The hopeful initiate must also pass a formal test: "At the end of your training and initiation, a suitable "test" will be administered

---

[67] The Pluggers' Web Site [Online]. Available: http://www.alliancesports.com/epduvall/guild/guilinfo.htm [1998, February 10].

by our senior members to determine whether or not you are qualified to become a full-fledged member." The more difficult it is to get into any group, the more elite and desirable it becomes. When we work hard to join a group and undergo difficult challenges, our cognitive dissonance kicks in to ensure our attitudes are in synch. The group must really be powerful and worthwhile, we come to believe, if we went through all that to measure up.

The spontaneous alignment of player guilds sets the stage for intergroup conflict even when the game itself didn't require or encourage it. The conflicts can get especially heated when the gaming environment is manipulated in certain ways. When there are scarce resources and winner-take-all competitions, the seeds are sown for intergroup conflict. For example, if two guilds both want to tackle the same dragon adversary and claim the treasure at the same time, their aggression might be redirected toward each other.

Another variable in the environment that heightens intergroup rivalries, one that is especially controversial, is player-killing, or *pking*. One player can attack another and kill that character in order to gain skills and points, steal the character's possessions, or just make trouble. The death is not usually permanent, but the player who was knocked off could lose points and skills, and also suffer the embarrassment of having been taken off guard. When game developers implement this feature, the level of intergroup conflict appears to rise dramatically. The Pluggers, for example, include on their Web site a list of "Most Wanted" and call for their destruction:

```
The following are names of known pkillers, thieves, and
scoundrels on the Atlantic shard. These miscreants will
be attacked on sight outside the protection of city
guards. Due to the fact that we have allied with the
Anti-PK Unification Alliance and have knowledge of many
pkers, we will now list multiple members of the hunted
without descriptions.
```

The management of deviant behavior in online communities – such as the unwanted player-killing that contributes to group tensions in the multiuser Internet games – was the subject of an online panel discussion hosted by moderator Amy Bruckman of the Georgia Institute of Technology.[68] Appropriately, the discussion was held on MediaMOO,

---

[68] Bruckman, A. (1999, January 20). Managing deviant behavior in online communities: An online panel discussion. [Online]. Available: http://www.cc.gatech.edu/fac/Amy.Bruckman/MediaMOO/deviance-symposium-99.html [1999, March 24].

the text-based MUD designed for media researchers. One of the panel members was Raph Koster, a long-time MUD administrator and also a lead designer for the popular Ultima Online commercial game. Speaking as Ptah on the MUD symposium, Koster explains how his company approached the problem in the transcript that follows:

```
Ptah says, "On many gaming muds, you see server code
trying to handle the task of intervening before actual
harm is done, and prevent the antisocial activity from
occurring (eg, the "playerkilling switch")"
Pogo lets Ptah finish
Ptah thanks Pogo—he's almost done, and he knows he is
typically verbose. :)
Ptah says, "What we try to do on UO [Ultima Online] is
give tools to the players to help them identify the
behavior THEY don't like, and then to give them tools to
easily identify and track repeat offenders."
Ptah says, "Then we try to use the code to administer the
punishments—the ultimate goal being reducing the immense
cost of having humans judging, and then acting as
executioner, for a multitude of ambiguous, often
controversial personal disgreements or attacks."
Ptah nods to Pogo.
Pogo says, "thanks"
Amy [to Ptah]: of course scale is a big issue here … how
many users do you have, Ptah?
Pogo says, "Actually, I'll address the first questions
first."
Ptah says, "Right now, UO sees peaks of well over 20,000
users simultaneously every night."
Amy whistles
```

There is still much to learn about how technological solutions can be applied to online environments in ways that will discourage intergroup tension. However, Koster's point about the costs of employing humans to mediate disputes is a good one, and the costs are not just financial. You may recall from the last chapter how Pavel Curtis attempted to diminish the role LambdaMOO administrators played because the wizards were tired of being judge, jury, and executioner. A prominent early member of the Lambda community, yduJ, attended this online symposium and mentioned that "LambdaMOO is still run entirely by volunteers (most of whom are burned out at the moment, so who aren't really paying enough attention.)." The non-technological solution they attempted, which involved ballots and votes by community members, was not effective either:

```
YduJ [to Ptah]: We haven't managed it. We *tried*; we
gave them a mechanism of peer reviewed justice, but the
jerks have completely destroyed that system (voting no on
even the most *obvious* of abuses.)"
```

Kinder and gentler multiuser games on the Internet contain techno-logical features that attempt to discourage intergroup tensions, particularly by putting strict limits on player killing. For example, some games will terminate the player's account if the server records more than two or three incidents over a span of time. Also, many of the games encourage group cooperation by making most of the great quests and challenges all but impossible unless a large group is assembled. The most deadly dragon in the game can become that superordinate goal that draws players together, even when they belong to different guilds or clubs.

PLAYER TYPES AND MOTIVATIONS

Although classic experiments in social psychology can help us better understand the activities in these multiplayer games, we can also gain fascinating insights from the people who actually create and run them. Game developer and MUD administrator Richard Bartle, writing for the *Journal of MUD Research*,[69] offered many of his and his fellow wizards' ideas about the psychological variables that affect the multiplayer environment and how wizards might make programming alterations to tweak the group dynamics – much the way Sherif did at Robbers Cave. Based on their experiences, this group concluded that there were essentially four main motivations for people to play these games, and that most players favored one of the reasons over the others.

Achievers are the first category Bartle identified; this type of player emphasizes game-related goals such as accumulation of treasure or increase in skills. A typical achiever would enter the game intent on

---

[69] Bartle, R. (1996, June). Hearts, clubs, diamonds, spades: Players who suit MUDs. *Journal of MUD Research* [Online], *1*(1), 82KB. Available: http://journal.pennmush.org/~jomr/v1n1/bartle.html [1998, May 20]. Bartle uses suits from playing cards as loose analogies for the different player types. The hearts are, not surprisingly, the social-izers, clubs are the killers (who club people), diamonds are the achievers (who accumulate treasure), and spades are the explorers (who dig deep into the MUD terrain).

mastering some puzzle or the conquest of some particularly difficult monster. The *explorers* are less interested in gaining skill levels or treasure, and seem to enjoy mapping the topology of the game, learning obscure secrets about it, and gathering esoteric knowledge about how the game actually works. The third group is the *socializers,* who join a MUD primarily to interact with others. The focus of their interactions might be the game itself, but it could also include unrelated personal topics as the players come to know each other on a social level. Finally, most MUDs attract a small number of people who get their kicks by harassing others, often using the tools provided by the game to do it. On a game with player-killing enabled, these would be called, simply, *killers.* The Pluggers have a name for them, too: Most Wanted.

To understand the underlying dynamics of the MUD world and the different motivations of the players, Bartle created a two-dimensional graph that plots the four types against two axes: acting versus interacting, and players versus world. The achiever, for example, is most interested in acting upon the MUD world, while the socializer is most interested in interacting with other players. Killers act upon other players, while explorers like to interact with the world as they wander about and collect bits of obscure knowledge.

INTEREST GRAPH

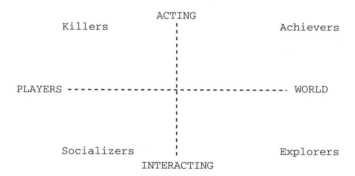

Bartle admits freely he is no psychologist, but his analysis delves insightfully into the motivations and interactions of people he has observed over many years on the MUDs. Intergroup tension, for example, develops routinely among some of the player types because their motives for participating are quite distinct. Socializers and killers, for example, have the most fractious relationship because their motives for participating are, for all practical purposes, mutually exclusive. Remarking on the way killers treat the social types, Bartle points out, "They go out of their way to rid MUDs of namby-pamby socializers who wouldn't know a weapon if one came up and hit them (an activity that killers are only too happy to demonstrate), and they will generally hassle socializers at every opportunity because it's so easy to get them annoyed."

The tension among groups and the population sizes of the different types can quickly change the character of the MUD, or even cause it to die. Just as any habitat can only support a limited number of predators, the MUD world can only support a small number of killers. If they get too numerous, the other player types will leave. A great many socializers will tilt the MUD toward the synchronous chat in term of psychological spaces, and those who participate for the gaming aspects will probably leave. Bartle argues that most MUDs eventually gravitate toward the primarily social, or chat-like environment, or the "hack and slash" arcade gaming environment with considerable player-killing, because it is so difficult to keep the player types in any balance. Few MUDs achieve that balance, but those that do are the most interesting; and may also become the most successful commercially.

Although many aspects of a MUD's survival are out of the control of the administrators, tweaking the programmed environment can have certain effects on the groups, their intergroup conflicts, and their population sizes (as I discussed earlier). Bartle points out that subtle changes in the technology environment can change the balance of player types. For example, adding more innovative communication tools should encourage more socializers. A MUD that allows people to play sound files (e.g., laughter, applause, sighs, snarls) to relate socioemotional content to the others in the room would support a broader range of player communication. If the MUD seems to be drifting too heavily toward socializers and player interactions and the achievers are departing, the administrators could take measures to emphasize the "acting on the world" dimension. They could add a detailed game manual, post maps of the known lands on the Web, raise the rewards for achievement, and develop an extensive level and class system through which the achievers could progress.

The early MUDs were text-based virtual reality environments, created and run by volunteers and offered free to anyone who knew how to log in. People like Richard Bartle learned a great deal about how human beings behaved in these intriguing worlds, essentially microcosms of group conflict and cooperation – much like Robbers Cave. Now, these multiuser games are becoming big business on the Internet, as companies such as Sony, Ultima Online, Fujitsu, and Microsoft enter the fray with highly graphical worlds filled with multimedia elements. Although many people are unaware of how quickly these environments are growing, some analysts predict that the online Internet games will be one of the hottest business of the next decade. And as you will learn in a later chapter, these games can become a serious time sink and can lead to compulsive overuse, sometimes called Internet addiction. The commercial potential is enormous, and the cleverness with which the administrators design the environment so that it achieves the right balance and becomes a place that attracts large numbers of loyal, community-oriented players, will determine which ones succeed and which ones disappear into the ether.

INGROUPS ON THE INTERNET

Intergroup tensions are real enough in the gaming worlds when minimal groups are at work, but what happens when ingroups and outgroups that already have a real life existence move onto the Internet? What becomes of those tensions, and the prejudices and stereotypes that go with them? Does racism, ageism, and other kinds of discrimination against outgroups disappear on the net? Probably not as much as we had hoped, but some of it seems to be diminishing because the cues to outgroup status are not as obvious. The email address might reveal gender and other clues in the address, or the signature file might indicate occupation, nationality, or location, but they would generally not indicate race or age. In social settings, people might inquire about age, but few ask about race in any Internet forum. Contrast this with a real life setting, in which a person's race and age are two characteristics you notice immediately.

Another characteristic that is often used to define boundaries around groups is status, and this, too, appears to be receding into the background on the Internet. There are no first class, business class, and cattle class seats, and there is no Executive Lounge to speak of. This means that in a discussion forum, your words will probably carry more weight than your socioeconomic position or your place on the corporate career ladder.

On the Internet, status is not exactly invisible, but it plays out in unusual ways. Status cues are usually less visible, and groups form without the traditional barriers to participation based on occupation, socioeconomic status, position in the corporate or educational hierarchy, or other factors. In the study Joan Korenman and Nancy Wyatt conducted on the WMST-L mailing list, for example, they found that participants covered quite a broad status spectrum, one that included university faculty, graduate students, librarians, a software designer, a technical editor, a science writer, a research assistant, and a secretary.[70] Even though the list was targeted to academic professionals, a broad range of people participated and the discussion forum supported considerable boundary crossing that might be far less likely in real life. Suppose, for example, an academic researcher started a Thursday afternoon luncheon group to discuss the same topics as the WMST-L list entertains. It would be hard to imagine that this group would attract the diversity of participants, in terms of the usual status cues, that the Internet forum does.

The WMST-L mailing list also shows the "status equalization" phenomenon that has been observed in many studies of computer-mediated communication. Unlike real-life, face-to-face groups, in which status often determines who contributes most and has the most influence in a discussion, the computer-mediated forums tend to allow more participation by lower status members. Sara Kiesler and her colleagues observed this phenomenon in some of the earliest research on computer-mediated group interactions. Three-person groups were asked to reach consensus on several problems, working in a synchronous chat computer-mediated mode, an asynchronous email mode, or a face-to-face setting. They found that in all the groups, one person tended to dominate the discussion, but this was far less pronounced in the computer-mediated groups.[71]

This status equalization phenomenon is particularly intriguing because research has demonstrated that equal status contacts can do a great deal to reduce stereotyping and discrimination of outgroups. Those kinds of contacts didn't work very well for the Rattlers and the Eagles – just watching a movie together was not enough to reduce the intergroup tension. But they have worked rather well in other settings to reduce prejudice. For example, in the wake of the U.S. Supreme Court decision to integrate schools in the 1950s, and civil rights legislation to do the same for housing in the 1960s, researchers found that people tended to drop their discriminatory and prejudicial attitudes more if the contacts were between people of approximately equal socioeconomic status.[72]

[70] Korenman, J., and Wyatt, N. (1996). In S. C. Herring (Ed.), *Computer-mediated communication: Linguistic, social and cross-cultural perspectives* (pp. 225–242). Amsterdam: John Benjamins Publishing Company.

[71] Kiesler, S., Siegel, J., and McGuire, T. W. (1984). Social psychological aspects of computer-mediated communication. *American Psychologist, 39,* 1123–1134.

[72] Hewstone, M. R., and Brown, R. J. (1986). Contact is not enough: An intergroup perspective on the contact hypothesis. In M. R. Hewstone and R. J. Brown (Eds.), Conflict and contact in intergroup encounters; 181–198. Oxford, England: Blackwell.

The status equalization phenomenon, as it unfolds on the Internet, is a bit different from equal status contact, despite the similarity of the terms. To reduce stereotyping and prejudice, it is important to bring together people from the different groups who perceive themselves to be about the same status. On the Internet, status cues are difficult to detect, so there is a tendency for perceptions about status to converge. In other words, since you can't easily tell a person's status on the Internet, you may be more likely to think that person is in your general ballpark with respect to status, particularly if you like that person for other reasons. This could well create an environment in which that all-important ingredient of equal status seems to be present, even when it isn't. This bodes well for the diminution of stereotyping and prejudice, as the research demonstrates. For example, you might be involved in a home improvement discussion group in which the participants discuss remodeling and renovation. If you are a six-figure attorney who dabbles in this as a hobby, you might tacitly assume that the others in the group are not too different from you. Recall that we tend to perceive people who share our interests, whom we like, as more similar to us than they actually are. You might be very surprised to learn that a particularly knowledgeable member of the group is actually an unemployed carpenter's assistant on welfare. If you harbored negative stereotypes of welfare recipients, this news could shake you a bit.

"EXPERT-ISM"

They may not know if you're a dog on the Internet, but they do know whether you are an expert or novice. One characteristic used to define and insulate elitist ingroups on the Internet is expertise, so "expert-ism" is one of those -isms that is probably more prevalent on the Internet than in real life. On some forums, for example, the insider knowledge of the group's history and norms can be the dividing line between the ingroup and the outgroup, with little reference to race, age, gender, or ethnicity. The practice of *trolling* illustrates how the insiders taunt neophytes who try to break into the group, and thereby increase their own cohesiveness and separateness from the annoying intruders. It begins when a veteran group member lays a little bait by posting a forceful but incorrect comment. In a discussion of Star Trek bloopers, for example, the poster would point out that the directors made an egregious lighting error when they showed a shadow on the Enterprise hull from a nearby spaceship. "Light, of course, does not travel in the vacuum of space so the shadow was impossible." This is a troll.

An unsuspecting newbie or two might jump in and politely point out the error, or even ridicule the poster for stupidity. Other veterans would chuckle behind their screens as they watched the newcomers fall into the trap. They would privately congratulate the troller for the success, and perhaps extend the discussion and the complexity of the troll by offering pseudoscientific evidence about light in space. Effective trolling episodes are treasured by the ingroup and the successful troller gains more insider status. The trollee may never learn what happened, or the troller may decide to send a cryptic message containing the acronym YHBT (You have been trolled), which the victim will probably fail to understand anyway. As you can see, in a group like this the observable discussion in the forum is very deceptive. There is an insider subtext underlying it that remains concealed from the newbie outgroup.

An extreme version of an elitest Internet ingroup is the computer underground, the so-called hacker community. The *Jargon Dictionary*, an online and evolving "compendium of hacker slang illuminating many aspects of hackish tradition, folklore, and humor," includes an entry for *hacker ethic* that sums up the norms:

```
hacker ethic /n./ 1. The belief that information-sharing
is a powerful positive good, and that it is an ethical
duty of hackers to share their expertise by writing free
software and facilitating access to information and to
computing resources wherever possible. 2. The belief that
system-cracking for fun and exploration is ethically OK
as long as the cracker commits no theft, vandalism, or
breach of confidentiality.[73]
```

Writing in *2600, the Hacker Quarterly*, an anonymous author says, "To be a hacker, your primary goal must be to learn for the sake of learning.[74] Hackers are actually a fractious lot, but this romantic and exalted vision binds them into a group and separates them from a number of outgroups, including the "lusers"[75] (users who are also losers) and the "wannabees" (those who call themselves hackers but can't hack). The ethic also erects a barrier between themselves and their dreaded cousins –

---

[73] E. Raymond [1996, July 24]. *The Jargon Dictionary. File 4.0.0* [Online]. Available: http://www.netmeg.net/jargon [1998 May 19].

[74] Anonymous (1994). Crime waves. *2600 The Hacker Quarterly, 11(1),* 4–5.

[75] The Jargon Dictionary identifies MIT as the home of this term. While logging in, the terminal screen would indicate the number of users online, but the hacker programmers changed the word *users* to *losers*, and then finally *lusers* as a compromise.

the crackers – who maliciously infiltrate computer systems for their own greed and profit. That same anonymous author wrote, "We hack because we're curious. We spread what we find because segregated knowledge is our common enemy. ... It is our moral obligation to keep our noble, if somewhat naïve, aspirations from becoming subverted by those who truly don't understand."

While newsgroup veterans might use a troll to protect their ingroup, hackers go much further. Journalist Netta Gilboa (nickname: *grayarea*) attempted to enter various hacker gathering spots on Internet Relay Chat and also at live conventions. She reports some very aggressive anti-outsider tactics.[76] They stole her trash looking for numbers and codes, pulled her credit reports, forwarded her phone number and then discon-nected it, and deleted her email before she could read it. Hackers know a great deal about how to manipulate networks, computers, and phone systems, and some of them certainly use that knowledge to harass the outgroups – despite the lofty ethics statement. Gilboa finally achieved some qualified and temporary success in joining the ingroup because a high-status member introduced her.

GLOBAL VILLAGERS: ARE WE A GROUP?

Reading about the digital citizen, the global villager, the net generation, or the superconnected, one can easily get the impression that Internet users themselves form a cohesive ingroup. For example, Jon Katz, writ-ing for *Wired*,[77] summarizes the results of a major survey conducted by Merrill Lynch and the magazine in which the data from the question-naires are broken down according to how well "connected" the respon-dents were. Katz reports, "The survey reveals there is indeed a distinct group of Digital Citizens," and then goes on to generalize about their attitudes, likes, and dislikes. Digital Citizens are "informed, outspoken, participatory, passionate about freedom, proud of their culture, and committed to the free nation in which it has evolved."

I argue against such sweeping generalizations about the Internet "ingroup" in this book because I do not see the data to support it. Just because a somewhat higher percentage of the "connected" support a

---

[76] Gilboa, N. (1996). Elites, lamers, narcs and whores: Exploring the computer underground. In L. Cherny and E. R. Weise (Eds.), *Wired women: Gender and new realities in cyberspace* (pp. 98–113). Seattle, WA: Seal Press.

[77] Katz, J. (1997). The digital citizen. *Wired*, December 68–82, 274–275.

particular cause compared to the mildly connected or unconnected, does not necessarily lead to the conclusion that Internet users are a distinct group, any more than TV watchers, telephone users, or beeper carriers are. The Internet already supports an enormously diverse bunch of people, one that is getting more heterogeneous each day. Like normal human beings in any environment, they are unlikely to unanimously agree on *any* issue. I might also add that surveys such as this compound variables such as simple affluence with connectedness. If a higher percentage of people classified as connected "worship free markets," as they did in this study, one might wonder whether their devotion has more to do with income than digital-ness.

The patterns of electronic communication on the Internet make it even less likely that a consensus will emerge. Bibb Latané and Martin J. Bourgeois demonstrated that the way people communicate on the nets – the extent to which their messages are distributed to others – has considerable impact on the social dynamics of consensus.[78] Some patterns, especially those that are most typical on the net, are very likely to create a majority opinion and also a strong and vocal minority who disagrees.

They created 24-person groups who communicated via email and played the Conformity Game, in which players try to guess what the majority opinion of their group will be. On the first of five rounds, for example, the players were asked whether they thought the majority would be for or against surface mining. Each player came to an individual prediction and then passed it along to a few others in the group. This is how the researchers controlled the patterns of communication.

In some cases, the pattern was like a long and circular street with houses on either side. Each player sent her predictions to her four closest neighbors, but no others. In other cases, the geometry of the social space was more like clumpy families in which the relatives had excellent communication with one another, but few ties to other families. After each round, a player could stick with his original prediction or change it if he thought the information he received from his neighbors warranted a change.

In many repetitions of the game with many different groups of 24, all but a few hold-outs agree with their "neighbors" by the end of the five rounds. People on one end of the row of houses, for example, might all

---

[78] Latané, B., and Bourgeois, M. J. (1996). Experimental evidence for dynamic social impact: The emergence of subcultures in electronic groups. *Journal of Communication, 46(4)*, 35–47.

agree to predict that the majority will be "for" surface mining. But people on the other end of the street went the other way. On most tests, a majority opinion emerged, but so did a strong and stubborn minority opinion, and the players became part of the majority or minority because of their "location" in the contrived social space. This minority opinion was dead wrong, because the goal of the game was to predict what the majority of the players would do. The members of the minority, however, could not really tell they *were* off the mark because of the way the communication paths were arranged. As Pavel Curtis found on LambdaMOO, it's very hard to get any large online group to agree to much of anything. One reason may simply be that the patterns of communication in a large network make that nearly impossible. Even when they *want* to agree – when that is the goal of the game – they don't because the complex communication patterns obscure events distant from your "neighborhood."

INTERNET GROUP POWER

Internet users are not a cohesive ingroup, but once in a while something comes up that raises their hackles and causes them to coalesce in some surprisingly large numbers – especially to fight a threatening outgroup and achieve a superordinate goal that most of them value. Though we might generally stick to our usual communication circles with just a few neighbors most of the time, we might break out and spread the word far wider when the occasion demands it. The Internet supports the wider distribution of protest messages to large numbers of people, and the dissemination alone can facilitate and energize grassroots movements. For example, in the mid-1990s the Internet played an important role in a nationwide campus-based protest against California's antiimmigration measure. The quick spread of information helped students organize protests on 20 campuses and attract more than 2,000 people to a protest march in San Francisco.[79] Usenet groups served a particularly vital role during the Tianamen Square event in 1989. Chinese students in China, the United States, and around the world convened in soc.culture.china to share information, debate appropriate responses, and mobilize their forces.[80]

[79] Eng, L. (1995, January 22). Internet is becoming a very useful tool for campus radicals. *The Journal Star*, p. 8.
[80] Carnevale, P. J., and Probst, T. (1997). Conflict on the Internet. In S. Kiesler (Ed.), *Culture of the Internet* (pp. 233–255. Mahwah, NJ: Lawrence Erlbaum Associates, Publishers.

Some of the events that energize large numbers of Internet users have to do with issues related to the Internet itself, or to problems that the network's existence creates. Free speech is one of those issues, and the Blue Ribbon Campaign for online freedom of expression is one of those that has considerable support among Internet users. The Campaign is jointly sponsored by the American Civil Liberties Union, the Electronic Frontier Foundation, and the Electronic Privacy Information Center, and it distributes information about legislation such as the Communications Decency Act and the Internet Censorship Bill. At one of the Campaign's Web sites at the American Civil Liberties Union, the tools are in place to enable visitors to instantly fax a message to U.S. Attorney General Janet Reno containing a prepared text urging her to refrain from prosecutions under the Child Online Protection Act. You need only enter your name, address and email, and click on send. During the protest over the Communications Decency Act, supportive Internet users were draping their own sites in black to demonstrate their protest. Blue Ribbon Campaign supporters are now encouraged to place a Blue Ribbon symbol on their own Web sites.

An earlier case that mobilized a large number of Internet users involved the protection of privacy in the digital age and a widespread, Internet-based community protest against a product called Lotus Marketplace. In 1990, the Lotus Development Corporation announced they would be releasing a CD-ROM, which its marketers dubbed a "desktop information product." The business version would contain information on more than 7 million American businesses, while the household version would carry easily searchable demographic data and mailing addresses of 120 million Americans from 80 million households. Laura L. Gurak[81] of the University of Minnesota did an analysis of the events that followed, focusing on the role the Internet played as the dramatic community protest got underway.

Soon after an article appeared in the *Wall Street Journal* about the Lotus CD-ROMs, members of a number of discussion forums began posting excerpts of the article and adding comments about the potential threat to privacy. The topic aroused a great deal of passionate interest, as messages were forwarded all over the country to numerous other lists. Gurak quotes a post from a discussion forum called RISKS, one that demonstrates the participant's concern about misuse of so much sensitive information:

[81] Gurak, L. J. (1996). The rhetorical dynamics of a community protest in cyberspace: What happened with Lotus MarketPlace. In S. C. Herring (Ed.), *Computer-mediated communication: Linguistic, social and cross-cultural perspectives* (pp. 265–278). Amsterdam: John Benjamins Publishing Company.

It astonishes me that anyone can imagine they can control how a small piece of plastic, indistinguishable from hundreds of like copies, will be used once it gets out in the world.

Naturally, not all participants in these discussions agreed that the product posed a serious threat to privacy, but the groups themselves began to attract more and more like-minded individuals who were quite eager to do something more effectual than grumbling to one another. Soon the path for more effective protest was opened, as posters spread around Lotus's address, phone number, and the CEO's email address.

Gurak's analysis revealed that the growing and unusual protest lacked any centralized leadership, much like the Internet itself. No one was in charge of the movement, though certain texts and protest "form letters" began to take on a quasi-leadership role simply because they were forwarded so frequently from forum to forum. One example came from Larry Seiler in Boston, who had cut and pasted some text from another email and then forwarded that, along with his own comments, to multiple lists. His note, or modified versions of it, was circulated around the country, weaving its way in and out of multiple lists through those circuitous digital pathways – the same ones that carry Internet humor and hoaxes. Seiler's contribution may have been passed around repeatedly because it struck a resonant chord with the protesters, and succinctly summarized their views:

GREAT! So not only do they have the audacity to print an estimate of your income (which could be quite damaging if they get it wrong, and is an intrusion into your privacy if they get it right), they also have space on the disk for arbitrary comments about you – and they'll be selling this data in volume to mass marketing companies across the country!

Another intriguing feature of this digital community protest was the criterion participants used to judge the credibility of the information sources. Seiler revealed his own credibility yardstick when he said his information came from someone with "an excellent reputation on the internet." This is telling, especially because Seiler's text was one of those that appeared to be circulated most widely in that fractured and leapfrog way. The elusive reputation one earns on the Internet can enhance credibility much like those academic degrees or book awards.

Considerable research in psychology has been devoted to the slippery notion of credibility and its role in persuasion, and two elements stand out: expertise and trustworthiness. In most settings, we are more likely to believe, and be persuaded by, a message communicated by someone who appears to have expert knowledge of the subject, and in whom we think we can place some trust. In one of the earliest studies on this topic conducted back in 1951, before atomic energy was used for much besides bombs, subjects heard a message arguing that building atomic-powered submarines was a feasible thing to attempt. The subjects who thought the message came from the atomic physicist J. Robert Oppenheimer were, not surprisingly, more convinced by the argument than those who thought it was an excerpt from *Pravda*, the Communist Party's newspaper.[82]

In the Lotus Marketplace case, at least some of the evidence people were using to determine the credibility of the information they were receiving was that it emerged from the Internet community itself, those who were involved and vocal in the protest, and not the company or other media. This seemed to be the case even though much information was very difficult to attribute to any particular source, because there was so much cutting and pasting going on as messages were forwarded, appended, edited, and forwarded again. Also, some bits and pieces were factually inaccurate. For example, one widely disseminated and reposted message listed database fields that were supposedly contained in the CD-ROM database about each consumer. On the list were the individual's make of car, stereo, video equipment, and other household appliances, gleaned from warranty registrations. The database did not actually have any fields like this.

Lotus eventually responded to the growing protest by using the Internet to send a formal press release describing the product, but they were not really able to calm the storm because they did not know where all the messages had been distributed. The lack of leadership and any conventional organization in this protest movement, so much like the Internet itself, made any coordinated response very difficult to make. In any case, their response was not well-received in some quarters because the seeds for distrust of the outgroup had already been sown. One poster responded to Lotus's assurances that the data would be protected from illegitimate use with the following sarcasm:

If somebody will send me the $599, I'll be glad to try the experiment of sending in an order in the name of "A. Slimy

---

[82] Hovland, C., and Weiss, W. (1951). The influence of source credibility on communication effectiveness. *Public Opinion Quarterly, 15,* 635–650.

Jerk". Just make your check out to me personally … after all, why shouldn't you trust me as much as you do Lotus.[83]

This case shows how a superordinate goal important to large numbers of Internet users became the lightning rod that drew them together into an effective community protest. Whether the immediate threat to privacy posed by the CD-ROM was real or not, the protest worked and the Internet facilitated it. On January 23, 1991, Lotus announced that it was canceling the product due to "public concerns and misunderstandings of the product, and the substantial, unexpected costs required to fully address consumer privacy issues."

[83] From a posting to comp.society Usenet newsgroup, January 4, 1991, cited by Gurak, L. J. (1996). The rhetorical dynamics of a community protest in cyberspace: What happened with Lotus MarketPlace. In S. C. Herring (Ed.), *Computer-mediated communication: Linguistic, social and cross-cultural perspectives* (pp. 265–278). Amsterdam: John Benjamins Publishing Company.

6 FLAMING AND FIGHTING
THE PSYCHOLOGY OF
AGGRESSION ON THE NET

When John S. required knee surgery, his boss asked if he would stay on top of his job in the finance office via email. John readily agreed, thinking it would make points with the boss and relieve some of the boredom of two weeks in bed. The Information Systems Department loaned him a laptop and showed him how to get his mail using Pine, software he didn't know but that seemed easy enough to learn. All went well the first few days as he routinely opened his electronic inbox and replied to incoming mail. But Pine's opening screen had a second, cryptic option: "News-collection <news>." He moved his cursor and pressed the return key. His laptop monitor filled up with an incomprehensible and seemingly endless list of titles, most with bizarre references to everything from aliens to erotica. Years before the Internet had become a household word, John accidentally stumbled into what some call the Dodge City of the online world: the Usenet newsgroups.

He began exploring and then participating in some of the sports-related discussions and was thrilled the first time someone replied to one of his posts. It wasn't long, however, before another participant, identified as "Tallyho," called him a moron. He had a knee-jerk reaction and spent many hours composing what he thought was a brilliant comeback. Then he logged on several times a day to watch for the reaction. Both John and his invisible nemesis were determined to have the last word, and they exchanged salvos for several weeks. Other participants took sides, tried to defuse the argument, or left the group in disgust. Suddenly, at the peak of the text-based war, John's adversary vanished. Days passed and John's barbs went unanswered. "It was like he just hung up the phone on me. It made me furious, but I guess I won." John never found out what happened to his sparring partner. When I suggested that he (or she) might have been a seventh-grader whose parents decided the Internet was eating up too much homework time, John vigorously denied the possibility. The notion that he just spent weeks consumed by an argument with a contentious kid was unacceptable.

In person, John is not a particularly aggressive man. I've seen him lean on his horn when the car in front is a bit slow to move when the light turns green, and he makes his points forcefully in committee meetings. But it was hard to imagine him involved in a flame war, and the one with Tallyho was not the last.

Many people believe that the Internet is loaded with fighting and flaming, and that aggression in general is higher online than off. Certainly some of the early research on computer-mediated communication uncovered startling levels of name-calling, swearing, and insults – much higher than in face-to-face groups. Aggression is a complex behavior but just as in real life, some aspects of the Internet can cause anyone's blood pressure to soar. To analyze why, let's first examine some possible causes for human aggression.

BORN TO FIGHT?

The sombre fact is that we are the most cruel and most ruthless species that has ever walked the earth; and that although we may recoil in horror when we read in the newspaper or history book of the atrocities committed by man upon man, we know in our hearts that each one of us harbours within himself those same savage impulses which lead to murder, torture, and to war. – Anthony Storr[84]

A very old and probably unanswerable question is whether those savage impulses, as Storr calls them, are inevitable because a tendency to behave aggressively in certain contexts is part of our biological makeup. Thomas Hobbes certainly thought it was, and considered it imperative that societies be constructed in a way that would constrain our aggressive impulses. Psychoanalysts agree, arguing that people carry a death instinct, Thanatos, right along with their instinct toward life, Eros. Aggression emerges when our Thanatos dark side turns outward toward others.

Ethologists such as the late Konrad Lorenz take a somewhat different tack but still arrive at the conclusion that aggressive tendencies have a

---

[84] Storr, A. (1970). *Human aggression*. New York: Bantam.

strongly built-in biological component, and are not completely the result of learning – even in human beings. Lorenz proposed that aggression has considerable survival value for both the individual and the species, when it occurs in certain contexts and with constraints that usually prevent a gruesome fight to the death. Members of the same species fight one another for precious territory and scarce resources, and the winners defend their prizes. In his classic *On Aggression,* Lorenz argues that "aggression, far from being the diabolical, destructive principle that classical psychoanalysis makes it out to be, is really an essential part of the life-preserving organization of instincts."[85] Albeit for different reasons, the ethologists and psychoanalysts think we all have a hostile streak.

Decades of research on the relative contributions of genes and environment to our behavior lead sometimes to deadlock, but more often to the middle ground. Human behavior is influenced by both. Much of what we do, day in and day out, is the combined result of biological and environmental forces. Rather than argue about how much each contributes, most of the contemporary research focuses on how a behavior like aggression is expressed by different people in different settings. Sometimes peaceful people like John sharpen their verbal daggers far more than we might expect, and sometimes a Mike Tyson will enjoy a relaxing and noncompetitive evening with friends. What really matters is that just about everyone's tendency toward aggression varies under different conditions, and sometimes a circumstance that elicits aggression may be only slightly different from one that does not. Even Lorenz agrees with this: "Innate behavior mechanisms can be thrown completely out of balance by small, apparently insignificant changes of environmental conditions."[86]

What circumstances and events cause our blood pressure to rise and Mr. Hyde to emerge? Research on this question has been voluminous, not surprisingly so, given the importance of the topic. It helps us little to argue about the age-old nature/nurture debate as it applies to aggression on the Internet, but it is enormously useful to know how environmental conditions influence our level of aggression. Frustrating circumstances, for example, can easily be the match that lights the stick of dynamite.

FRUSTRATION AND AGGRESSION

Watching John clench his teeth when the car ahead dallies a bit too long, I sense he is very frustrated. The driver ahead is checking his hair

[85] Lorenz, K. (1963). *On aggression.* New York: Harcourt, Brace and World, Inc. (p. 48).
[86] Lorenz, K. (1963). *On aggression.* New York: Harcourt, Brace and World, Inc. (p. 49).

in the rearview mirror and his inattention is thwarting John on the way to a goal. According to frustration-aggression theory, John's frustration can lead to anger, and anger triggers a hostile action – not just a little beep to get that driver's attention, but a loud and prolonged blast.

Back in the 1940s, when rumors of war were spreading and social psychologists were becoming intensely interested in the nature of human aggression, Roger Barker and his colleagues conducted an experiment to see just what happened when you produce frustration in young children.[87] They showed two groups of children a room filled with intriguing toys, but the children couldn't reach the toys to play with them because they were behind a wire screen. For one group, the researchers opened the screen right away and the children rushed in to play. The other kids, though, were told they had to wait. When they finally were allowed into the room many of these frustrated children smashed the toys, broke them, and threw them up against the wall.

Frustration is even more likely to bring out an aggressive response when we are very close to the goal and something, or someone, blocks us from achieving it. Snatching defeat out of the jaws of victory is particularly frustrating in the final seconds of a game, and tensions run very high at sporting events in which this occurs. Researcher Mary Harris demonstrated this phenomenon in lines of people waiting for theater tickets, grocery store checkouts, or other places.[88] Her confederate cut into the line, either in front of the second person in line, or in front of the twelfth person. People who were number two in line were much closer to their goal than those who were number twelve, and it was not surprising that they reacted more aggressively.

THE WORLD WIDE WAIT

Is the Internet environment a frustrating place, one that might make us more likely to show anger when something happens to bother us? Just ask anyone who logs on to the Web using a 28.8 kb/s modem from home during peak usage hours, and you'll hear the same reply. It is too slow, it makes them furious. Computer guru Jim Seymour, writing for *PC Magazine*, grumbles, "Boy, our Web access has gone to hell lately; endless dialing and redialing to get through to perpetually busy lines at ISP; long

---

[87] Barker, R., Dembo, T., and Lewin, K. (1941). Frustration and aggression: An experiment with young children. *University of Iowa Studies in Child Welfare, 18*, 1–314.

[88] Harris, M. (1974). Mediators between frustration and aggression in a field experiment. *Journal of Experimental and Social Psychology, 10*, 561–571.

waits for pages to load; lots of reloading of pages that come in halfway and then die; getting dropped repeatedly.[89]

Web designers eager to please their audiences and attract more traffic by introducing fancy graphics and multimedia elements into their sites are learning the psychological reality of the effects of frustration the hard way. Visitors send them angry letters in the form of "feedback." One of the most widely scorned characteristics of America Online was the company decision to insist that end users download new graphics almost every time they logged in. They promised the time spent downloading would not be charged to the customer's account, but end users reacted with predictable frustration, and anger that the online service would treat the *customer's time* so cavalierly.

For synchronous chatters, lag is a chief cause of frustration. *Lag* is simply the time it takes for your typed message to show up on the screens of the others in the chat room or channel after you press the return key to send it. The word is used as both a noun (The lag is 2 seconds), and a verb (You're lagging!). Chatters can usually find out what the lag is to another person by "pinging" them, and receiving a "pong" in return a few seconds later. Lag times vary dramatically, depending on your own geographic location, the location of your server, the location of the other person's server, the bandwidth and traffic density between them, and ... who knows? Probably the phase of the moon, as well.

When the lag is low, 2 or 3 seconds perhaps, Internet chatters seem reasonably content. When it grows to 8 or 9 seconds, or even longer, the frustration level rises considerably. The server might time out particular end users and disconnect them if their lag grows too long, but in those middle ranges, the chatter experiences a great deal of frustration. The person may not even realize that no one is responding to his remarks because of lag. He may assume that the others in the room are just ignoring him.

As a communication environment, synchronous chat is closest to conversation. How much lag do we usually have in face-to-face conversations? Some work on this subject suggests that the lags range from almost nothing, as in an interruption, to just a few seconds. For example, one study found that the average lag in single-sex conversations was 1.35 seconds, and in mixed-sex conversations, 3.21 seconds.[90] Tolerance

---

[89] Seymour, J. (1997). Web follies: Checking e-mail at 2 A.M. *PC Magazine,* March 25, 1997, 93–94.

[90] Zimmerman, D., and West, C. (1975). Sex roles, interruptions, and silences in conversation. In B. Thorne and N. Henley (Eds.), *Language and sex: Difference and dominance* (pp. 105–129). Rowley, MA: Newbury House.

for and expectations about conversational silences vary with different media, and also, in different cultures. In a face-to-face encounter, that 4-second silence could easily be filled with other nonverbal forms of communication. Cultural differences also exist in tolerance for lag. In Japan, for example, long conversational lags are normal. One Japanese colleague confided to me that an effective negotiating strategy when dealing with American business people was, quite simply, silence. He knew that longer lags are very frustrating and confusing to Americans, a cultural quirk that handed the Japanese negotiator a slight edge.

The lag in synchronous chats, then, is acceptable when it falls at least reasonably close to a typical conversational lag. Christopher Werry of Carnegie Mellon University studied many Internet Relay Chat logs and found that the participants seemed to be constructing their sentences and performing a variety of linguistic gymnastics just to keep that lag within acceptable bounds.[91] For example, he computed the average message to be about six words, even though chatters could have typed much longer messages. The delay in typing, along with the delays in transmission, probably pushes the average message length down in IRC conversations. And as I mentioned in the first chapter, the register for synchronous chat is loaded with abbreviations, and Werry suggests this feature will also help chatters reduce lag. Some examples from his transcripts were "r u" (are you), "c u" (see you) and "t" for (tu es, in French). No doubt chatters also use such abbreviations to save typing effort and time.

"Net splits" are another fact of life on Internet Relay chat, and these occur with regularity. The chatters are connected to various servers around the globe, and the servers themselves sometimes lose connections with one another. You might be logged into Dalnet, for example, connected to your closest server in Texas. Others in the chat room could be logged into Dalnet servers in Australia, Germany, or California. When a split occurs, the messages on your screen make you think you suddenly acquired a disastrous case of virtual body odor. One chatting partner after another departs, leaving you alone in an empty chat room. Angry invectives hurled at the "netgods" are not uncommon when these splits occur.

Delays are not the only source of frustration for Internet users. Recent surveys find that Web surfers report navigation problems as one of their chief concerns, right up there along with censorship and privacy. Finding what you want on the Web can sometimes be quite a struggle,

---

[91] Werry, C. C. (1996). Linguistic and interactional features of Internet Relay Chat. In S. C. Herring (Ed.), *Computer-mediated communication: Linguistic, social and cross-cultural perspectives* (pp. 47–63). Amsterdam: John Benjamins Publishing Company.

particularly if you are not experienced enough to know what is easy to find out there and what is nearly impossible. If you use one of the popular search engines that bring up hundreds of thousands of sites for your keywords, you could easily descend into the cavernous depths of the indexed but unfiltered Web. How will you know if the page marked "No Title" – the one your search engine considered quite relevant based on the algorithm it used – contains anything at all of use? If you are not just browsing or looking for information you already know is out there, the Web can be a very frustrating place.

THE HAIR TRIGGER

You might suppose that reasonable Internet users would recognize that it is the Internet and its erratic worldwide connectivity causing the delays and their resulting frustrations, and they would not vent their anger on their chatting partners, their fellow forum participants, or the dog lying by their computer chairs. However, psychological research suggests that most people are simply not that clear-headed and rational when they become aroused and annoyed. We seem to develop a hair trigger when we feel frustrated and we can easily react aggressively to events that might seem relatively harmless in other circumstances.

Psychologist Leonard Berkowitz argues that almost any kind of unpleasant event can lower our thresholds for an aggressive response. Frustration is one of them, but the key ingredient is that aversive stimulation in general triggers a state of "negative affect." Once in this state, our ability to dispassionately reflect on the events around us declines, and we become more likely to lean toward a negative interpretation of stimuli that under other circumstances we might view as neutral.[92]

If frustrating circumstances lower the threshold for an aggressive response, what is the actual trigger? If we are sufficiently primed, almost anything could set us off because our perceptions are distorted. We might log in to the Internet and find an email from a colleague containing one sentence that reads, "WE NEED YOUR INPUT BY TOMORROW! PLEASE!" In a calmer state of mind, you might laugh and imagine the writer in a begging mode, desperate for your invaluable help on this project. However, if you are in a state of frustration and your perceptions are

---

[92] Berkowitz, L., Cochran, S. T., and Embree, M. (1981). Physical pain and the goal of aversively stimulated aggression. *Journal of Personality and Social Psychology, 40,* 687–700.

being affected by it, you might interpret the email quite differently and feel anger toward this coworker's arrogant and pushy behavior.

At this point, if we respond harshly, we have no trouble believing that we were provoked and the response was totally justified. Someone insulted us and we had to retaliate. Or they needed to be reprimanded. Or we needed to be sure they clearly understood our point of view. We are not likely to attribute our own harsh response to the bad mood we happened to be in at the time.

In one survey, the respondents mentioned that one of the main reasons for their use of verbal aggression was to bolster their arguments, a particularly intriguing response when we think about flame wars on the Internet.[93] They may have been using verbal aggression partly because of that hair trigger resulting from frustration or other kinds of negative affect, but this is certainly not the reason that would come to mind. Recall that theory of cognitive dissonance – we don't like our behavior to be out of synch with our self-concept, and inconsistent behavior and perceptions based on our mood state are not exactly good rationales for verbal aggression. It is easier to maintain a healthy self-concept if we continue to insist that we interpreted the situation fairly and accurately, and that our response was justified.

RETALIATION

How do we determine what constitutes a "justified" response, and what is the appropriate level of retaliation, in our judgment, in any particular situation? According to some surveys, the most provocative kinds of insults are the ones in which someone appears to be attacking our character, competence, or physical appearance.[94] This suggests that certain kinds of events on the Internet are especially likely to trigger retaliation, particularly when the hair trigger is in effect. It isn't surprising, for example, that John flinched when Tallyho called him a "moron," or the recipient of the email responded harshly when he felt his competence was in question.

The very human and ordinary response to a real or imagined insult is to retaliate in kind. The Old Testament's "eye for an eye" is the general

---

[93] Infante, D. A., Myers, S. A., and Buerkel, R. A. (1994). Argument and verbal aggression in constructive and destructive family and organizational disagreements. *Western Journal of Communication, 58,* 73–84.

[94] Martin, M. M., Anderson, C. M., and Horvath, C. L. (1996). Feelings about verbal aggression: Justifications for sending and hurt from receiving verbally aggressive messages. *Communication Research Reports, 13,* 19–26.

rule, rather than the New Testament's "turning the other cheek." In a typical study on retaliation, two subjects may be paired to compete against one another in a reaction time experiment. After each round, the winner chooses the level of shock to give to the loser. The experiment, however, is carefully programmed and there is really only one subject; the other one is a computer program designed to manipulate the wins, losses, and shock levels in predictable ways. As you might expect, the real subjects retaliate in kind. If the computer is programmed as Terminator 2 and delivers large shocks to the subject after every loss, the subject strikes back with at least equal force.[95]

When we decide how to retaliate and how aggressive to be about it, we pick a method and level that, in our minds, matches what the offender did to us, but then ups the ante. In some Internet episodes, it begins to sound like the children's game of raising the stakes: "You're a jerk," "You're a double jerk," "You're a jerk times ten," "You and your whole family are jerks." To the uninvolved, some flame wars sound about this silly.

Others are more serious and loaded with detailed arguments for or against an issue, with the verbal aggression and thinly-veiled character attacks embedded more and more deeply as the controversy escalates. They can go on for many weeks and the combatants may insist that they are not in any flame war; they are just "discussing" a subject and "debating" a point. But people on the sidelines detect the tension and observe language and behavior that might be considered totally unacceptable in real life. Because people experience disinhibition on the Internet and feel relatively free of serious adverse consequences because of physical distance and reduced accountability, they often use tactics that go far beyond what they might use in person. For example, if the discussion between Tallyho and John S. had been held in person, that "moron" remark might have led to a physical confrontation rather than a war of words. It is not hard to imagine a fist fight if this level of verbal aggression had occurred in the stands during a hotly contested sports event.

Flame wars that erupt inside long-standing, normally peaceful groups can be extremely disruptive and discouraging. They can also be very resistant to outsiders who attempt to defuse the discussion. I know a few rare posters who can use extraordinary wit and the skill of a professional

---

[95] Dengerink, H. A. and Myers, J. D. (1977). Three effects of failure and depression on subsequent aggression. *Journal of Personality and Social Psychology, 35,* 88–96. Taylor, S. P., and Pisano, R. (1971). Physical aggression as a function of frustration and physical attack. *Journal of Social Psychology, 84,* 261–267. Ohbuchi, K., and Kambara, T. (1985). Attacker's intent and awareness of outcome, impression management, and retaliation. *Journal of Experimental Social Psychology, 21,* 321–330.

mediator to help the combatants see the lighter side of their behavior, often because they make fun of themselves as they gently chide the participants in the flame war. They avoid the substance of the debate entirely and focus instead on an amusing side issue that could rebuild group cohesiveness. But these people are unusual, and they always run the risk of getting caught up in the war if their own contribution is misperceived. Unless the group has a moderator who can actually stop the posts, the war could actually destroy the group as other members get burned for trying to stop it, and eventually just wander off in disgust.

IN THE EYE OF THE BEHOLDER: WHEN IS A FLAME A FLAME?

Philip A. Thompsen and Davis A. Foulger attempted to nail down what makes a flame a flame, at least in the eyes of group participants who are not directly involved.[96] They concocted a fictional series of posts between Dr. Ski and Snow Pro that became progressively more disagreeable and antagonistic, and asked volunteers from around the world to rate them on a scale from 1 (not flaming) to 7 (flaming). The incident begins when "A Total Novice" asks for some suggestions for a good ski school. In the following samples, all lines beginning with > are quotes from a previous post, following the usual convention in email asynchronous discussion forums.

Message 2, from Snow Pro, in response to a question from A Total Novice:

```
A Total Novice asks:
> Is there a good ski school or learn-to-ski package
> someone could recommend?
Brighton is a good place to learn to ski. That's where I
learned, and I think they offer a special deal for
beginners.

- Snow Pro
```

Message 3, from Dr. Ski, also in response to A Total Novice's question:

```
In response to A Total Novice who wrote . .
> I want to learn how to ski.
Alta is the area I would suggest. Alta has really great
slopes, and a lot of them. I ski there almost every
weekend.

- Dr. Ski
```

[96] Thompsen, P. A., and Foulger, D. A. (1996). Effects of pictographs and quoting on flaming in electronic mail. *Computers in Human Behavior, 12*, 225–243.

The tension between the Snow Pro and Dr. Ski gets a little higher after a few messages in which the two disagree:

Message 6, from Snow Pro, directed to Dr. Ski

```
If Alta has a reputation, it's for crowded slopes. Learning
to ski at Alta is like learning to drive on a freeway! :-)
For those just learning to ski, Brighton offers the best
combination of great snow, comfortable surroundings, and
relaxed pace.
```

– Snow Pro

By Message 9, the character attacks are well underway:

Message 9, from Dr. Ski in reply to a post from Snow Pro

```
Snow Pro made reference to
>the ski snobs like Dr. Ski who go to Alta
Snobs? What a joke! Real skiers like Alta because we take
skiing seriously. Skiing is more than just snow, slopes and
lifts, which is all Brighton offers, and barely that. Only
nerds like Snow Pro would admit to skiing at a pit like
Brighton. :-)
```

– Dr. Ski

Message 10, from Snow Pro in reply to a post from Dr. Ski

```
It's obvious that Dr. Ski doesn't want to carry on a
civil conversation. It's also obvious that Dr. Ski
doesn't know a damn thing about skiing. Let me ask you,
Dr. Ski, is your diploma from a cereal box? :-)
```

– Snow Pro

The ratings showed that people gradually perceive a sequence that begins with a disagreement and gets more heated as a flame war. There is a place where perceptions jump over to the flame side, and this is where the observers detect some tension – as in Message 6. When the character attacks and foul language appear, the perceivers widely agree a flame war is in progress. It is interesting that the little smileys helped to reduce the perception that the messages were flames when they were just disagreements. When the emoticons were added to really nasty messages, however, the smileys just made them look even more sarcastic.

LAB AND FIELD STUDIES OF FLAMING

Some of the earlier research on computer-mediated communication was quite alarming to the researchers. In those laboratory studies by Sara

Kiesler and her colleagues, for example, small groups were trying to reach consensus on several different tasks using face-to-face meetings, asynchronous computer conferences, or online chats. They routinely found a higher frequency of remarks containing swearing, insults, name-calling and hostile comments in those computer users. Compared to the face-to-face groups working on the same tasks, these computer-mediated discussants seemed to express quite a bit of hostility. In one dramatic incident, the level of anger escalated to the point where the researchers had to escort the participants out of the building, individually, so they would not run into each other.[97]

However, as more researchers began studying computer-mediated communication in the laboratory, the patterns became more confusing. They did not generally find those high levels of verbal aggression, though most of them found their volunteer subjects using computers to communicate more task-oriented than their face-to-face counterparts, particularly if they were under time pressure to get the job done. Joseph Walther and his colleagues, for example, examined about a dozen studies in which the researchers were trying to learn something about social and antisocial communication online in controlled conditions.[98] They concluded that friendly, socially oriented messages became more common in a wide variety of online interactions when the subjects weren't pressed for time. Those flaming incidents, however, were really quite rare – even when the clock was ticking.

Internet users were not all that surprised by the earlier results because they had already been seeing some acerbic flame wars break out online in their academic and research-oriented discussion groups. Nevertheless, they also knew that many small groups operated effectively online with few problems. Naturalistic studies of what is actually happening on the Internet show that verbal aggression and flame wars are out there, but they are far more common in some contexts than in others. For example, one survey revealed that flaming was more common in group forums than in private email.[99] Also, some forums establish frequently asked questions (FAQs) that threaten flamers with banishment, while others are

---

[97] Kiesler, S., and Sproull, L. (1992). Group decision making and communication technology. *Organizational Behavior and Human Decision Processes, 52,* 96–123.

[98] Walther, J. B., Anderson, J. F., and Park, D. W. (1994). Interpersonal effects in computer-mediated interaction. A meta-analysis of social and antisocial communication. *Communication Research, 21,* 460–487.

[99] Thompsen, P. A., and Ahn, D. (1992, Summer). To be or not to be: An exploration of E-prime, copula deletion and flaming in electronic mail. *Et Cetera: A Review of General Semantics, 49,* 146–164.

more tolerant of verbal aggression. The unwritten norms that evolve inside each group, and the power of some authority to control aggressive behavior, clearly affect the likelihood of hostile incidents.

REPROACHES

As I discussed in a previous chapter, one way in which people attempt to control flamers and others whose behavior in a discussion group is not in line with the group's norms is to use the reproach. A participant will gently or not so gently remind the posters, either publicly or with a private email, about acceptable group behavior. An example comes from a study on reproach episodes that occurred in several different Usenet newsgroups, including soc.singles. The researchers categorized the posts, first identifying the *offense,* and then the *reproach.* Although the offenders often never reply to a reproach, this one did, and the researchers identified that response as the *accounting.*[100]

The Offense:

Hi, I'm a 23 year old graduate student and would like to communicate with any females on this news net.
- (Posted for a non-net friend) -

The Reproach:

Well, Howdy! Finally a request for a female that doesn't specify species - you wouldn't believe how many people on this net want a woman, which of course means a person. *giggle*

My name is Susa, and I'm a five-year-old Lemur in the Philly Zoo. My measurements are 12-12-12, which is considered quite sexy for a lemur *giggle* we all fail the pencil test *giggle* My hobbies include running around, climbing trees, and picking lice; I hope you have a nice thick head of hair!
I only write to stupid people who post personals on soc.singles; the other ones are too smart for me - we lemurs may be very_cuddly *giggle but we tend to be on the low end of the smarts scale. I know that with that post, you'll be really_dumb for a human, and perfect for me! *giggle*

[100] Smith, C. B., McLaughlin, M. L., and Osborne, K. K. (1997). Conduct control on Usenet. *Journal of Computer-mediated Communication* [Online], *2(4).* Available: http://jcmc.mscc.huji.ac.i/vol2/issue4/smith.html [21 April, 1997].

The Accounting:

```
In reference to my posting a few hours ago . . I have just
discovered that this is the wrong news group! Thanks to
so many people, among others, so if you'll all quit
sending me more messages, I move on.
OK? But those who seem to have nothing better to do feel
free to do whatever you want!
```

Reproachers themselves are often taken to task by participants other than the offender for a variety of reasons. If the offense arose from a lack of knowledge, a sarcastic reproacher might be accused of bullying newcomers. I have seen mailing lists and newsgroups become intensely involved in a reproach episode, with numerous followup postings about the specific offense, the nature of the reproach, and the propriety of the corrective action. The metadiscussion can consume the entire group for quite some time before things simmer down.

OVER-RETALIATION

When you believe that someone did you harm, your most likely response is to retaliate, to strike back, with words or actions. But suppose your retaliation is more than just an "eye for an eye, a tooth for a tooth"? What happens when you thrash someone for merely stepping on your toe? Rationally, you might assume that an apology would be in order, especially if the toe-stepper was not intentionally trying to hurt you. Unfortunately, humans are not always this rational, particularly because most of us have a strong desire to think we are decent and fair human beings. Ironically, our desire to cling to a belief in our own rationality can lead us to some very strange perceptual contortions.

Leon Festinger's widely known theory of cognitive dissonance predicts that we will feel uncomfortable when we do something that does not jibe with our own attitudes, beliefs, or perceptions. This tension motivates us to find some way to bring our actions and thoughts in line again, and while it is not so easy to erase what we did, it is not all that difficult to modify our perceptions. We revise our views of the offender and the offending incident and begin to think of them as worse than they actually were. This mental revisionism can occur whenever we behave aggressively toward someone who didn't really deserve such harsh treatment. Even more alarming is that it also occurs when the person never deserved any retaliation at all.

A study by Keith Davis and Edward Jones[101] is especially revealing because it deals with verbal aggression, something that is so common on the Internet. They invited subjects into the laboratory to watch an interview with someone they thought was another student, but who was really a confederate of the experimenters. The researchers instructed each real subject to provide negative feedback to the interviewee/confederate – to state clearly that the subject thought the interviewee was shallow, untrustworthy, and a generally dull and boring person. Before the subjects made these brutal comments, they generally found their interviewees to be reasonably attractive. But after the interview, the subjects lowered their opinion of the interviewee/confederate and rated that individual as less attractive. Somehow, the subjects had to bring their actions and thoughts into line. Aware that they were verbally cruel to the interviewee they revised their opinion downward so that their actions would not be so far out of line. This change occurred even though the cruelty was not the subjects' own choice. The experimenter had instructed the subject to voice those negative opinions to the interviewee.

Given how eager we are to justify our aggressive acts, and how skimpy the cues are about someone who offends us on the Internet, it isn't difficult to guess that we would paint a very negative picture of the target we just reproached. The post directed to the participant who submitted a brief personal ad struck me as this kind of over-retaliation, filled with other-directed humor, sarcasm, and personal criticism. That reproacher might engage in some dissonance-reducing maneuvers to justify the harsher-than-necessary correction, perhaps coming to believe that the offender was a very unattractive and unsavory character who deserved the rebuke. Admittedly, the participants of soc.singles are probably weary of endless come-ons, but a simple "personal ads are not allowed in this newsgroup" would seem to have been more in line with the severity of the first offense.

ANONYMITY AND PHYSICAL DISTANCE

Anonymity, or the illusion of it, is another potent ingredient in the Internet mixture as it applies to aggression. When people believe their actions cannot be attributed directly to them personally, they tend to

[101] Davis, K., and Jones, E. E. (1960). Changes in interpersonal perception as a means of reducing cognitive dissonance. *Journal of Abnormal and Social Psychology, 61,* 402–410.

become less inhibited by social conventions and restraints. This can be very positive, particularly when people are offered the opportunity to discuss difficult personal issues under conditions in which they feel safer. As we will see in a later chapter, the online support groups are flourishing, partly because many of the participants feel freer to discuss concerns in the relatively anonymous Internet environment than they might in a face-to-face support group within their communities. However, anonymity can also unleash some aggressive behavior under the right circumstances.

Obviously most people on the Internet are not cloaking themselves in anonymity, and they willingly add their names, affiliations, phone numbers, and favorite quotations to their emails and forum contributions. Nevertheless, considerable Internet communication does occur under conditions in which the participants believe, rightly or wrongly, that they cannot be personally identified, and another one of Sara Kiesler's studies demonstrated that this element can make a difference in the way the participants behave. In this variant of their online group decision-making experiments, they compared the interactions of people whose names were attached to their computer-mediated messages to groups in which people were contributing anonymously.[102] The groups working together in the last condition did not know who said what, or the actual names of the others in their group. When they tallied the number of hostile remarks for each group, they found that the anonymous computer-conferencing groups made more than six times as many uninhibited remarks as the non-anonymous groups.

Both of the computer-conferencing groups used a program that simulated today's synchronous chat rooms and the conditions for the anonymous groups simulated these rooms even more closely. Chatters pick nicknames when they log in and can change them at will during or between chatting sessions. This underlies a belief among most chatters that they are anonymous and could not be tracked.

Anonymity on the Internet, however, is a moving target. The tools for identifying Internet users keep improving, as do the techniques available to remain anonymous. The success of any tracking effort rests partly on the determination and skill of the tracker and trackee. However, even though an individual's identity might be traceable, simply the height-

---

[102] Siegel, J., Dubrovsky, V., Kiesler, S., and McGuire, T. (1983). Group processes in computer-mediated communications. Study cited in Kiesler, S., Siegel, J., and McGuire, T. W. (1984). Social psychological aspects of computer-mediated communication. *American Psychologist, 39(10)*, 1123–1134.

ened feeling of anonymity appears to be enough to promote disinhibited behavior.

Services or tactics that enable Internet users to hide their email identities, or at least blur them, pose an intriguing set of problems.[103] Ordinarily, when you send an email to another person your email address is clearly visible in the header, along with the routing information. While your email address may not contain a great deal of information about you, it does contain your username and your Internet Service Provider. Even if the recipient doesn't know your real name, he or she might be able to track you down through legal means, particularly if it involved a harassment issue. However, there are various ways to send email more anonymously, in ways that make it far more difficult for anyone to identify you. For example, anonymous *remailer* services have been available that can disguise the origination of the message, and email headers and addresses can be faked. A degree of anonymity can also be obtained through the use of one of the free email services on the Web, such as Hotmail or Yahoo. Since no credit card information is needed to create an email account on these sites, there is no reliable link between the individual and the email address.

The relative ease with which people can send anonymous or disguised emails is not that different from regular postal mail except that the scale can be far greater. At the moment, sending email is free and very easy to do. You can send as many as you want, to as many people as you want, with no concerns about the postage charges. In other words, one angry person could create considerable havoc with little expense, effort, or consequence.

Another characteristic of the online world that probably makes it easier to let our tempers loose is simply that we are hurling the flames from quite a distance. Internet users span the globe, and any virtual community of people, or conversational partners, could be right next door to one another or half a planet away. They are not in the same room, however, so the physical distance measurement is already several notches larger than it would be in a face-to-face meeting. It is easier to attack someone if they are out of sight and far away. We can't see the injured and pained expression on their faces, and we feel safer and more immune to a counterattack.

[103] Lee, G. B. (1996, June). Addressing anonymous messages in cyberspace. *Journal of Computer-mediated Communication* [Online], *2*(1), 33 KB. Available: http://www.usc.edu/dept/annenberg/vol2/issue1/anon.html [1998, May 20].

THE #$@@!!!& SOFTWARE

Certain features of the software we use may also make it more likely we will express ourselves in angry ways on the net, and that our expressions will sound more provocative. An obvious example is that *send* button. When something or someone irritates us on the Internet, it is quite easy to compose a reply and impulsively fire it off before your blood pressure has a chance to return to normal. Compare this to the same message you would receive in the mail. To answer it, you have to type something up, print it out, address an envelope, find one of those nearly obsolete sticky things called a *stamp,* carry your letter to a mailbox, and drop it in. All of that would take some time, and you might well decide you had overreacted and were about to indulge in a retaliation that outpaced the level of the offense.

Although we use the terms *'say'* and *'said'* to refer to what people do on the Internet, we are not actually hearing their voices. We are reading their words, and as I've discussed before, much socioemotional nuance is missing from typed text. You might not be able to spot the difference between an innocuous or gently teasing remark and a subtly sarcastic or hostile one, and certainly few people are expert at conveying that difference with our Internet communication tools. If your frustration level is high and your hair trigger is ready to go, you might easily make errors in judgment and think messages are provocations when they were never meant that way by the sender.

Another intriguing aspect of the software that might push us a little closer to becoming unwitting flamers is the ability to quote from the sender's remarks – a feature known as *framing.* (You saw some examples in those messages from Dr. Ski and Snow Pro, in which quotations from another began with >.) A widely used tactic in argumentative discourse is to quote your adversary, usually out of context, and then verbally tear the remark to shreds or poke fun at it. Electronic mail software typically offers very easy ways to cut and paste, and automatically include snippets from someone else's message framed with a special character such as the > symbol. This feature is extremely helpful because you can reply to the individual paragraphs inside a message one at a time, and refresh the sender's memory about each issue without actually having to revisit it in your own words. We have no other communication medium that grants this capability; the closest I can think of would involve jotting short, handwritten notes next to the paragraphs on a memo you receive and then returning it to the sender.

In this case, however, you do not have the flexibility to quote out of context as you do on the Internet.

Communications researcher Edward Mabry investigated the possibility that Internet users might be using this framing feature to argue with one another, much as debaters use a strategy known as recounting.[104] A debater will restate and summarize each point of the opponent's position and then refute them, one at a time. This tactic can be very effective because the audience then recalls the opponent's points in the context of the debater's criticisms of them. Mabry examined the data from Project H, that major international collaborative effort involving analysis of about 3,000 posts to newsgroups, bulletin boards, and mailing lists.[105] I mentioned this project in previous chapters; researchers have used the voluminous data from it to test various hypotheses. Mabry's goal was to examine the way the posters framed their messages and the way they used quotations from other posts, and to compare this to the socioemotional tone of the message.

Most of the 3,000 posts fell into a neutral range with respect to socioemotional tone (58.8%), and a large percentage had some friendliness about them (25.6%). About 4.4% contained a message that expressed tension, antagonism, or hostility, and another 11% disagreed or diverged in some way. Framing was used by posters for all kinds of messages, but as posts became increasingly disagreeable and contentious, the senders generally used more framing. The only place this dropped off on one of the measures of framing was in the most extreme messages – the ones with outright hostility. Perhaps if you get that angry you don't pay much attention to the niceties of argumentative discourse. You just scream, "YOU IDIOT!!" and click the send button.

For the lurkers who are not involved, the use of frames also seems to affect whether a particular message will be perceived as a flame. Those people who were watching the tension rise between the imaginary Dr. Ski and Snow Pro rated messages containing the quotes from the other poster as somewhat less flaming when they were just disagreements, but as *more* flaming when the message contained antagonism. Like the sarcastic and phony smiley, a quote from your nemesis's post in a really mean-spirited rejoinder is probably viewed as a patently cynical distortion of your opponent's meaning.

[104] Mabry, E. A. (1997, March). Framing flames: The structure of argumentative messages on the net. *Journal of Computer-Mediated Communication* [Online], *2(4)*, 55 KB. Available: http://jcmc.mscc.huji.ac.il/vol2/issue4/mabry.html [1998, May 20].
[105] Rafaeli, S., Sudweeks, F., Konstan, J., and Mabry, E. A. (1994, January). *Project H Overview: A quantitative study of computer mediated communication* [Online]. Available: http://www.arch.usyd.edu.au/~fay/netplay/techreport.html [1998, May 20].

CATHARSIS: IS LETTING OFF STEAM GOOD FOR YOU?

I think it is fair to say that certain elements of the Internet world may lower our normal constraints about verbal aggression. It is also fair to ask whether this is a good or bad thing. If we have a tendency to react more negatively to minor slights, and vent our anger with language that we would rarely use in any real life setting, are we letting off some steam that might be released somewhere else? Psychoanalysts suggest that we all have aggressive impulses and it does us good to vent them once in a while. If we don't they build up and we may explode against our loved ones, or turn our Thanatos drive inward to self-destruction. Perhaps the Internet gives us a safe playground for catharsis, and when we use it that way we become much happier, kinder, and mentally healthier in real life.

The notion that a cathartic release of aggressive impulses turns down the pressure, lets us "blow off steam," and keeps us from erupting violently sounds attractive and plausible on the surface. Unfortunately, psychological research shows it does not work that way most of the time. Instead, behaving aggressively seems to increase our aggressive tendencies, not reduce them.

One research study that demonstrated this phenomenon involved people who were laid off from a company and were likely to feel some anger about it.[106] When such terminated employees were interviewed just after they received their pink slips, the researcher gave some of them a chance to vent their anger at their employers by asking leading questions. One example was, "What instances can you think of where the company has not been fair to you?" Many of the laid-off workers seized the chance to air their angry feelings. Later, when all of them completed questionnaires that asked about their attitudes toward the company and their supervisors, the ones who had vented their anger showed the *most* hostility. Their catharsis did not release pressure from the steam valve at all. It just intensified their anger.

The widespread belief that catharsis is good for you led to the rapid growth of a Web site called Angry.Org.[107] This site solicited contributions from visitors describing what makes them really mad and posted

---

[106] Ebbesen, E. B., Duncan, B., and Konecni, V. J. (1975). Effects of content of verbal aggression on future verbal aggression: A field experiment. *Journal of Experimental Social Psychology, 11*, 192–204.

[107] Duderstadt, H. (1996). *The world's weirdest web pages and the people who create them.* San Francisco: No Starch Press. The Angry. Org Web site seems to have disappeared but its commitment to catharsis lives on at the time of this writing at http://www.angry.net [1998, May 20].

all the responses. Developer Jonathan Mergy tells why he created this home for catharsis: "I was sitting telling a couple of friends and co-workers about how I'd get angry at people who sent email with dumb questions or comments when I used to run a couple of bulletin board systems in San Francisco. I was also telling them about how I got kicked off a couple of systems for name-calling and ad hominem attacks. We thought it would be cool to have a place that we could just bitch and moan at people." One invective rails at the Post Office:

```
Why do the lazy bastards advertise? They are not in
competition with anybody. If private companies were
allowed to deliver the mail, the Post Office would be out
of business. They don't allow competition! The only thing
postal employees do well is shoot one another.
```

There is no research that I know of that explores whether aggression on the Internet serves any cathartic role, but I think it highly unlikely. For those who get involved in flame wars or other forms of Internet aggression, the research suggests it is more likely to reduce their thresholds for aggression, and perhaps not just against others on the Internet.

AGGRESSION: INTERNET STYLE

In real life, people have an almost limitless array of behaviors they can use to express aggression. They can glare at their victim, or shout verbal insults. They can use physical violence in many forms, from a poke on the arm to a gunshot in the head. Aggression is commonly defined as any form of behavior directed toward the goal of harming or injuring another living being, and it leaves open an enormous expanse of possibilities by which to do it.

On the Internet, this definition serves equally well, though the range of choices is rather different. Verbal aggression in written form, targeted to or about another Internet user, is probably the most widely used form of aggression on the net. The flame wars on Usenet and the personal attacks that occur in some mailing lists are well-known.

Another form of aggression is the hostile Web site that teeters on the edge of libel, but still either falls within the First Amendment or has not yet been hit with a lawsuit. If you get really angry at someone and want to retaliate, you can quite easily take the free disk space that comes with your Internet account and launch a Web site to vilify the offender. A Missouri high school student recently took that opportunity to criticize his teachers and administrators. The school district authorities insisted he take down the page, suspended him, and gave him failing grades for the semester. However, he fought back and a U.S. District Court ruled that the school officials should reinstate him, and make no more attempts to prevent him from publishing his Internet commentaries. According to Judge Rodney Sippel, "Disliking or being upset by the content of a student's speech is not an acceptable justification for limiting student speech."[108]

To air some grievances, people need not necessarily develop their own Web pages. They can take advantage of the sites built as a service to people who want to publicly retaliate. These can quickly grow into a catalog of angry denunciations. *The Dick List*, for example, invites women visitors to express their anger at a man who wronged them by submitting the man's name and a vivid description of his misdeeds. The developer hopes the site will become a kind of consumer's guide to scoundrels, and visitors will be able to search by region as well as by name. Once again, the theme of catharsis underlies the motivation for this venture. In an interview with *Wired* the site owner remarked, "I get a broad range of women, from teenagers to divorced housewives, who are finally getting a grip on their anger."[109]

People can mask or change identities in some Internet locales, so they can also express their aggression by impersonating someone else. On MUDs, for example, players can create "puppets" they control themselves, but whose utterances carry the nickname of another player. Others in the room will see the puppet's actions and words, then misattribute them to the real player. The infamous cyberspace rape case involving Mr. Bungle (discussed in chapter 11) was a heinous example of that kind of aggression through impersonation. In that setting, the victims knew Mr. Bungle was impersonating them with his puppet voodoo dolls, but in others, the victim may not realize it. On IRC, for example, some networks allow you to register your nickname so that others may not use it, but other networks do not. One chatter was very disgruntled by this because he felt his IRC reputation, built over several years in some of the politically oriented chat rooms, might easily be damaged if one of his detractors decided to impersonate him.

The anonymous remailer services offer a unique and innovative way to impersonate others, and they have been used aggressively to damage

---

[108] Student finds speech freedoms on Internet. (1999, March). *Curriculum Review* [Online], 38(7), 5. Available: EBSCOhost/Academic Search/1567787 [1999, March 11].

[109] Lohr, N. (1997). *The Dick List* [Online]. Available: http://www.urbekah.com/housewife/dicks.html [1998, May 20]. Dicks-R-Us. *Wired*, September 1997, page 169.

people's reputations. For example, one individual sent out a racist message to 20,000 recipients across the country under the name of a university professor. As I mentioned earlier, the potential for this kind of aggression far exceeds what an aggressor might have been able to do with just paper and pen, if only because of the scope. Because of the hazard, many government officials will accept email from citizens but only reply via snail mail.

So you can impersonate another individual on the Internet for malicious purposes, and on Usenet you can vent your aggression by canceling messages other people send if you have the right "cancelbot" software. One anonymous vigilante, known only as *Cancelmoose*, finds spam – the unsolicited commercial email advertising – particularly egregious and routinely removes Usenet messages the moose considers to fall into the spamming category. The Church of Scientology used one of those cancelbot programs to delete messages it believed contained copyrighted material, an event that caused quite a stir among Internet users.

Channel wars and takeovers are another, more obscure form of aggression – one that looks a little like Internet gang warfare. If the owners of a chat channel annoy the wrong people – the ones who can read Web sites explaining how to use programs to flood the channel and cause the owners and operators to lose their powers of control – they may find that they have been kicked out and the guerrillas own their channel. A group of self-anointed wizards called IRCarnage publish a braggart's list of channels they have taken over. In the tradition of the old *A-Team* television series, IRCarnage nobly offers to retrieve channels that were taken over by other raiding parties and return them to their rightful owners.

Some might argue that the characteristics of Internet users may predispose this group to behave a little more aggressively than other groups in any setting, whether online or off. The group is still largely male, and men generally behave more aggressively than women do. But regardless of whether Internet users are an especially aggressive subsample of humans, and I don't think they are, it is far more helpful to understand how the environment itself can carry the seeds of trouble. You may think you are a very peaceful sort of person, but the research suggests that the Internet has features that might unleash certain forms of aggressive behavior in just about anyone. If we want to lower the hostile temperature online and stay out of the boxing ring ourselves, it is important to recognize just what those seeds are.

7
LIKING AND LOVING ON THE NET
THE PSYCHOLOGY OF INTERPERSONAL ATTRACTION

Personal Info

Age:35	Smokes:No	Religion:Christian
Marital Status:Separated	Drinks:Yes	Body Type:Average
Race:White	Has Children:Yes	

Description

I'm a 35 y/o separating, straight white male, 5'10", 180 pounds, brown hair, green eyes, and disease free too! I am a Non-Geek-Speaking Network Engineer – It's a job! Write soon! Send Pics!

The search for Mr. or Ms. Right has taken a new twist in the Internet era. Online computer dating services abound, and personal ads posted to Web sites have considerably more reach than their counterparts in local newspapers. The mail-order bride service has resurfaced on the Internet, and potential marriage partners can find and get to know one another over the ether, regardless of their location on the globe. It is probably not a coincidence that the number of visas issued to foreign-born individuals intending to marry a U.S. citizen has risen in recent years. The Internet may serve as the sparring ring for flamers, but it also is a place where strangers can meet, become good friends, and even fall in love.

A question on a humorous "geek test" asks, "Do you have more friends on the Internet than in real life?" However you answer, you should not be surprised to learn that people do form close friendships and romantic attachments online, and some appear to be reasonably durable. Often they begin in one of the Internet's group-oriented environments, such as a MUD, a chat room, or a professional mailing list. Two people discover there is something special between them and start backchanneling – communicating by email. Over time, the relationship might escalate to phone calls, exchanges of information and photographs, and eventually to real-life visits – but then again, it might not. Whatever chemistry exists between the friends or romantic partners may stay just where it is, in the ether.

WHO MAKES FRIENDS ONLINE?

Some people argue that online friendships are little more than casual acquaintances – high-tech pen pals – not real friendships. Without the social presence of face-to-face interaction, they surmise, the relationships simply can't be as meaningful. Geeks may treasure them, but the rest of humanity needs the closeness and immediacy of "being there." The research, however, is beginning to show that online friendships may be both more common, and far deeper than many supposed they could be, at least to the people involved in them.

Malcolm Parks and Kory Floyd at the University of Washington surveyed people who were posting to a sample of newsgroups to learn more about who was making friends in cyberspace, and what they thought about their relationships.[110] The newsgroups spanned the gamut from the computer-oriented *comp* hierarchy to the zany *rec* (recreation) and *alt* (alternative) hierarchies. The goal was to survey a wide range of people, not just the computer gurus, though the sample was limited to people who participated in newsgroups in the first place. This represents a relatively small percentage of Internet users, of course.[111]

Nearly two-thirds of the people who replied to the survey reported that they had formed a personal relationship with someone they met on a newsgroup, and those who said yes were not all huddled in the computer forums. The proportion was about the same for the respondents who hung out in any of the newsgroups. Opposite-sex relationships were somewhat more common than same-sex ones, but only a small percentage (7.9%) were romantic attachments.

The respondents were mostly men (67.7%), a figure that corresponded roughly to the sex ratio online as a whole, at the time. Although women were in the minority, they were more likely than the men to say they had formed an online relationship, a finding that could be explained in multiple ways. Perhaps women make friends online more easily, or they might join the newsgroups with a stronger motiva-

[110] Parks, M. R., and Floyd, K. (1996). Making friends in cyberspace. *Journal of Communication, 46(1)*, 80–97.
[111] A 1997 poll by *Business Week*/Harris found that 20% of the respondents who were online participated in conferences or forums.

tion to affiliate with others compared to men. They could also be making more friends simply because they are in the minority and are approached more often.

The people who were forming personal relationships with their Internet acquaintances were generally the ones who had been participating in the newsgroups for a longer period of time, and were more heavily involved and visible to the newsgroup participants in the sense that they posted more messages. It takes longer to get to know someone you meet online because the cues you are using are limited. Joseph Walther's study of the rhythms of impression formation in computer-mediated discussion groups, discussed in an earlier chapter, demonstrated this phenomenon well.[112] When strangers began working in groups using the computer to communicate, they had rather vague impressions of one another. Over a period of several weeks, they gradually formed much stronger impressions of their group members, either negative or positive. In the newsgroups, this rhythm seems to affect the pattern of friendships, so it is not surprising that the long-time newsgroup participants were more likely to have developed personal relationships.

THE NATURE OF ONLINE RELATIONSHIPS

Despite our earlier misgivings, we now know that interpersonal attraction is alive and well on the net, and friendships and romantic attachments are forming. But what is the nature of these relationships? Are they shallow, erratic and short-lived? Do they truly touch the hearts of those involved? Do they eventually emerge from the ether into other, more traditional forms of contact?

The newsgroup posters who replied to the survey Parks and Floyd sent out told a great deal about the levels of development in their online relationships. Each of them was asked how much they agreed with statements such as, "I usually tell this person exactly how I feel," or "This person and I have a great deal of effect on each other." The researchers chose statements that would delve into several characteristics of a relationship, such as interdependence, breadth, depth, and commitment.

This survey shows that online relationships vary considerably, much like other relationships. Some are extremely intense and lasting; others are weak and short. A series of items, for example, probed the breadth of

---

[112] Walther, J. B. (1993). Impression development in computer-mediated interaction. *Western Journal of Communication, 57,* 381–398.

the online relationship, with statements such as, "Our communication is limited to just a few specific topics," and "Our communication covers issues that go well beyond the topic of any one particular newsgroup." One might suppose that since they met on a newsgroup with a special focus, most of their conversations would revolve around that topic. That wasn't the case. More than half of the respondents said their online relationship covered more territory than just the newsgroup subject.

The responses suggested a moderate level of commitment within the online relationships, but again that varied. Some people enthusiastically agreed with a statement such as, "I am very committed to maintaining this relationship," while others were more lukewarm. Friends depend on one another, and the responses suggested that online friends do that, as well. Most of them heartily agreed with the statement, "We would go out of our way to help each other if it were needed."

People have circles of friends in real life, and within a circle, the person's friends are often friends with one another. They may belong to several such circles that have little or no overlap in membership, making it difficult to throw a party and "invite all their friends." One's friends from work may have few interests in common with the buddies in the sailing club or your friends from church. The respondents suggested that their "net friends" are yet another circle, one that overlaps little with any of the other circles from real life. Though many of them said they had "overlapping social circles on the net" very few had introduced their net friend to any of their real-life friends or relatives. Certainly geography might explain part of this, but since more than a third had met the net friend in person, I wonder whether it is the whole answer. It seems more likely that the net discussion forums offer a setting for its own circles; overlap with other circles may remain low.

When you meet another person on the net, how do you decide that you like that person and would like to become friends? What attracts you to them, and they to you? We know a great deal about how interpersonal attraction unfolds in real life, and we can begin to deduce from this research how the process works online.

THE MAGNET OF PHYSICAL ATTRACTIVENESS

The powerful magnet of interpersonal attraction in real-life settings, dismaying though it may be, is physical attractiveness. Though we profess that "beauty is only skin deep," or that "beauty is as beauty does," the truth is that physical attractiveness is an enormous advantage if you want to be liked. This is particularly true for the opposite sex, but also for members of your own sex. Our stereotypes about good-looking people extend far beyond mere appearance. We judge them as happier, more sociable, warmer, kinder, more likable, more successful, and more intelligent, too.

The physical attractiveness stereotype is so pervasive and potent that it affects our attitudes about others in almost every setting researchers have examined. For example, teachers who are rating the intelligence and potential success of students based on their written descriptions and photographs tend to rate the attractive students more favorably than the unattractive ones.[113] Attractiveness also affects the hiring decisions of personnel officers, the chances of a political candidate, and even the salaries people earn. Should we be surprised that cosmetic surgery is a booming business? One might hypothesize that any surgical intervention that moves you up a notch or two on the attractiveness scale could pay for itself.[114] For romantic relationships, appearance plays an especially critical role. In a classic study at the University of Minnesota, incoming freshmen completed a battery of personality tests and then were randomly matched up for blind dates with one another. After the dates, they were asked how much they liked their partner and whether they wanted to see the person again. It was not their date's intelligence, warmth, humor, or wit that counted. It was looks.[115]

Because we view good-looking people more favorably, we tend to treat them better and pay more attention to them. The positive treatment often tends to bring out their best qualities and make them more confident. An experiment that demonstrated how this spiral of *positive treatment* and *positive response* begins involved men college students who were invited to participate in an experiment on "getting acquainted."[116] The men were paired with women students, but they were to get acquainted over an intercom, not face-to-face. Each man received a portfolio of information about his female partner that included her snap-

[113] Clifford, M. M., and Walster, E. H. (Hatfield) (1973). The effect of physical attractiveness on teacher expectation. *Sociology of Education, 46,* 248–258.

[114] Frieze, I. H., Olson, J. E., and Russell, J. (1991). Attractiveness and income for men and women in management. *Journal of Applied Psychology, 21,* 1039–1057.

[115] Walster, E. (Hatfield), Aronson, V., Abrahams, D., and Rottman, L. (1966). Importance of physical attractiveness in dating behavior. *Journal of Personality and Social Psychology, 4,* 508–516.

[116] Snyder, M., Tanke, E. D., and Berscheid, E. (1977). Social perception and interpersonal behavior: On the self-fulfilling nature of social stereotypes. *Journal of Personality and Social Psychology, 35,* 656–666.

shot, but as you might guess, the researchers rigged this picture. Half the men thought they were talking to a very attractive woman and the other half thought they were talking to someone far less attractive.

To no one's surprise, the men who thought they were talking to a very beautiful woman judged her favorably on many qualities. She was, they surmised, poised, humorous, sociable, and generally quite wonderful. Those who thought they were talking to an unattractive female were far less impressed with her attributes and behavior. The type of photo affected the way the women behaved, as well, although they didn't know which photo their partner was looking at. Independent observers listening to the tape recordings of the woman's part of the conversations afterwards also judged her as more confident and charming when the man believed she was good-looking. The positive treatment by a man who was staring at a beautiful (but imaginary) photograph was enough to bring out the best in the woman on the other end of the intercom, regardless of her actual appearance.

ATTRACTIVENESS IN THE DARK

A student in an online college course remarked to me how he rarely had the confidence to speak out in regular, face-to-face classes. He confided he was not very attractive, and always hesitant to answer questions or engage in discussion. People usually ignored the comments he made in face-to-face classes, so he stopped making them after a while. But online, he found a place where people would not dismiss him because of his looks. The first time he joined in the text-based group discussion, he included some humor along with a thoughtful remark about the topic. Several people responded within a day or two, agreeing with his views and taking his side in the debate. "This never happened to me in the classroom," he said – not wistfully, but with wide-eyed pleasure. Perhaps the Internet's level playing field with respect to physical attributes will bring out his best and give him the confidence to show his qualities – even in real life.

In some interactions, the Internet pulls the rug out from under our tendency to rely on good looks in interpersonal attraction, at least initially. This gives people an opportunity to get to know one another without the weight of all the physical attractiveness stereotypes. If interactive video and voice become more accessible and widely used, the equation will change again. But for the time being, perhaps just for this fleeting moment in history, beauty's power is restrained. Without the physical appearance crutch, how do you decide whether the person on the other side of the screen could be a friend, a romantic partner, or your future spouse? Let's look at some research that explores the *other* reasons people are attracted to one another and see how they might operate on the Internet.

PROXIMITY: WHO'S NEXT DOOR ON THE NET?

Near the top of the list is simple proximity. You become friends with, and you tend to marry, people you see frequently – that girl or boy next door. Often, they work in the same office, live on your block, join the same clubs, or ride the same train every day.

One obvious explanation for the proximity effect is that it provides the opportunity to meet and get to know another person. The other person becomes familiar to you, predictable. The old adage about familiarity breeding contempt is inaccurate. It often does not breed contempt; it breeds liking instead. This phenomenon is so strong it even affects how much we like any kind of novel stimulus, not just people. In a rather odd study, psychologist Robert Zajonc presented many different polygons to subjects for a very brief moment, just 1/1000 of a second.[117] Later, he showed them the same polygons along with many new ones mixed in, and asked them how much they liked each shape, and also whether they remembered seeing it before. The people couldn't do better than guessing on the recall test, but strangely, they "liked" the polygons they'd seen before better than the ones they had not. At some level, and I know this sounds strange, the people had formed a positive emotional attachment to the polygons from mere exposure, even though consciously they were unaware that the shapes were familiar to them.

On the Internet, proximity and the familiarity that goes with it translates into something that might be called *intersection frequency*. This is obviously quite different from the geographical distance that defines proximity in real life. It reflects how often you run into that other person on the net. Your online friendship candidate might be on the other side of the planet, but as long as you intersect frequently by participating in the same newsgroup or mailing list, commenting on the same threads, or playing the same MUD (at the same time), the proximity effect will prob-

---

[117] Zajonc, R. (1980). Feeling and thinking: Preferences need not inferences. *American Psychologist, 35,* 151–175.

ably be there. In fact, it may be even stronger online than off because comings and goings happen so fast in some settings and participation can be quite volatile. Even one exposure to a stranger on the sprawling Internet can trigger the proximity effect the next time you run into that person. Certain software, such as AOL's Instant Messenger or ICQ, helps Internet users get better control over intersection frequencies by letting them know who is online when they are. Once installed, users can enter their "buddy list" and be informed when any of them is online, regardless of which neighborhood they happen to be exploring at the time.

The survey of newsgroup participants highlighted another feature of the proximity effect important for online relationships. People who formed such friendships and those who did not were no different from one another in terms of how much they *read* the postings. They were quite different, however, on their participation rate. The lurkers who posted few messages were less likely to make friends. It appears insufficient to just "be" there. You have to be visible to intersect with others, and on the Internet, that means speaking out. Of course, what you say will affect who, and also whether, people are drawn to you, but this survey demonstrated that Internet wallflowers are less likely to establish personal relationships than those who actively participate.

One reason real-life proximity promotes attraction is that the person's nearness makes you expect – and anticipate – future interaction. If you know you'll see that person again because they live on your block, you are more likely to behave warmly toward them. In a study with a twist ending, Joseph Walther demonstrated that anticipation of future interaction is an important factor in the way people behave toward one another online, as well.[118] The subjects volunteered for an experiment they thought would last many weeks, and when they arrived, Walther assigned them to work in small groups that would communicate via an online chatting system, an asynchronous computer conference, or face-to-face. Some groups were told that they would be working with the same partners for the whole study, while others learned they would be changing partners after each task. Then all of them held their first "meeting" to complete the first task, using whichever medium they'd been assigned to.

When their first "meeting" was over, Walther asked them to fill out some questionnaires to rate their experiences and attitudes toward their

---

[118] Walther, J. B. (1994). Anticipated ongoing interaction versus channel effects on relational communication in computer-mediated interaction. *Human Communication Research, 20(4)*, 473–501.

partners. When they were finished, he surprised them by saying the experiment was over. The results showed that the people who anticipated working with the same partners for a long time communicated in friendlier, more affectionate, and generally warmer ways, compared to people who thought they would work together once and be gone. They also expressed more openness and rapport with one another, regardless of which communication medium they were using.

This simple ingredient could play out in many different ways on the Internet. On a collegial mailing list with a professional focus, for example, you would not perceive the participants as just transient passers-by. Those people are in your profession and presumably have some commitment to it and longevity within it, so the anticipation of extended interaction should be higher than it is in a newsgroup devoted to less work-oriented discussions, such as politics, movies, hobbies, or causes.

BIRDS OF A FEATHER, FLOCKING ON THE INTERNET

Assessing the truth of two mutually exclusive proverbs is a common research agenda in psychology. For example, do "birds of a feather flock together?" Or do "opposites attract?" The answer to this one is in, and it is the feathers that count, not the magnetic forces. In study after study, researchers demonstrated that people tend to like those with similar attitudes and ideas. This finding became known as the *Law of Attraction*. In a typical experiment, subjects check off their opinions about a wide range of topics, such as how much they enjoy classical music or what they think about disciplining children. Then they look at the responses of others and guess whether they would like each one. The findings show a direct linear relationship: the greater the proportion of similar attitudes, the more attracted you are to the person.

The law of attraction predicts liking from the *proportion* of shared attitudes, not the total number, a mathematical quirk that may have relevance to interpersonal attraction on the Internet. For example, you might know about Jane's views on six issues, and know that you agree with her on three of them (50%). Jack has spoken out more; you know his views on ten issues, and you agree with four of them (40%). Even though you agree with Jack on more issues, you will like Jane better because the proportion of similarity is higher. Obviously, we're not doing these precision tallies with our scientific calculators in real life, but the trend is there.

On the Internet, where it is more difficult and time consuming to learn how people think about multiple issues, the law of attraction may cause many "false starts" in friendships. On a mailing list, you might learn from Barbara's posting that she shares your views about welfare reform. Knowing little else about her, your proportion of shared attitudes is now a whopping 100%. If you had met her in real life, you – always the cognitive miser – would have presumed many more of her attitudes from her dress, her age, her appearance, her facial expressions, her speech patterns, and her accent. Your presumptions may have been wrong, but you would have formed an impression anyway – one that included some guesses about Barbara's attitudes on many subjects. If she were wearing motorcycle boots and leather jacket, for example, your stereotype of bikers and their attitudes would leap to mind. The total number of Barbara's attitudes you know about, or think you know about, would be much higher from a face-to-face meeting, so the *proportion* of shared attitudes would probably drop from that 100%.

For his master's thesis at Simon Fraser University, Geoffrey Hultin analyzed messages on a bulletin board system between three people who met online over several months.[119] Rick began the online acquaintance with Janet with the following:

```
Hi there! It's rare to find Chinese people on boards like
these. Tell some stuff about yourself and I'll tell you
some stuff about me and don't worry, I just want to make
friends … nothing to lead to a relationship. Hope to hear
from you soon.
```

His initial attraction to Janet as a friend was based on only two pieces of information: Janet was Chinese (as was Rick) and a participant on the same electronic bulletin board. So far, there was 100% similarity, and Janet responded immediately. Over the months, they exchanged more information, and the proportion of similar characteristics plummeted. Janet reveals she is a bookworm, watches TV, teaches piano, and is a terrible driver. Rick writes he is a car nut, kills his pet fish through neglect, and doesn't like reading. Not surprisingly, their messages got shorter and less frequent, and eventually stopped altogether. The level of interpersonal attraction slipped, right along with the proportion of shared attitudes.

[119] Hultin, G. A. (1993). *Mediating the social face: Self-presentation in computer communication.* Unpublished Master's Thesis, Department of Communication, Simon Fraser University.

COMPLEMENTARY RELATIONSHIPS

Similarity is an exceedingly potent force in interpersonal attraction, but it seems reasonable to suppose there are certain features of other people we would want to be different from ours. Wouldn't a sadist and masochist be happy together? A dominant person and a submissive one? On the Internet, wouldn't someone who likes to answer questions and play the expert be attracted to someone who needs and asks for lots of help? Strangely, most of the research shows that even when a complementary match-up seems like an obvious win–win for two people, we are still more attracted by similarity. This finding seemed so puzzling that psychologists didn't give up on it, and continued to explore situations in which opposites might attract.

One such situation turned up in a study at Stanford University involving women who participated in a very cleverly contrived interaction to see whether dominant people attract submissive people, and vice versa.[120] Before they came to the lab, each woman completed questionnaires designed to measure how dominant or submissive she was in social settings. When they arrived, they learned they would be sharing their views about interpersonal relationships with another woman, and reporting how satisfied they were with the interaction. The interaction was a setup, of course, and the other person was a confederate who just read scripts. All scripts started off the same way, describing a problem with an over-attentive boyfriend, and then the woman who was the real subject expressed her views. The confederate then jumped in with what appeared to be an impromptu comment, but was carefully crafted to show a dominant interpersonal style to half the subjects and a submissive one to the other half. The dominant script read, "Yeah, this is one problem that I'll just have to solve on my own. I guess nobody can solve personal problems for you; you have to figure them out yourself." The submissive script was, "Yeah, what you say makes sense. I don't know why it is, but I feel that I just haven't been able to solve this problem on my own. I guess I really do need help."

Which match-ups would you guess were most satisfying? Did the dominant women feel more satisfied when the confederate displayed a dominant style, similar to their own? Did more submissive women pre-

---

[120] Dryer, D. C., and Horowitz, L. M. (1997). When do opposites attract? Interpersonal complementarity versus similarity. *Journal of Personality and Social Psychology, 72(3),* 592–603.

fer the submissive confederate? Or did complementarity prevail? The results were surprising. The women were most satisfied when the confederate behaved in a complementary way. Yet these same people judged the complementary confederate to be more similar to themselves! It seems we may be happier with complementary friends when it comes to patterns of dominance and submissiveness, though we may not even be aware they are complementing us. On the Internet, the same pattern seems to appear, especially in the technical help arenas. People who like to help others and show off their expertise should like those who ask for and appreciate their help.

THE "YOU LIKE ME, I LIKE YOU, YOU LIKE ME MORE" SPIRAL

When someone likes you, you tend to like that person back. Partly because you are flattered and the other person's attraction to you raises your self-esteem, you have warm, fuzzy, rewarding feelings when you're liked by someone else. Just learning that someone likes you can be quite an ego-booster, and the next time you interact with that person you're apt to act a little differently – a little warmer and friendlier, perhaps. The other person will detect the change and react favorably, liking you more and treating you more kindly. Just as physical attractiveness creates a spiral of positive treatment and positive response, being liked by someone else does, too.

One experiment that demonstrated this reminds me of that "anonymous note" adolescents sometimes use to stir up the social scene. The pranksters send an unsigned note to a classmate targeted to be the butt of the joke, confessing deep admiration and attraction. As the conspirators spread misleading hints about who might have written the note, the target's behavior changes. Believing that someone likes her, she likes the other person more, too, and her behavior changes.

In an actual experiment on this, researchers Rebecca Curtis and Kim Miller conspired to lead their subjects to believe that another subject either liked them or did not like them. When the two met again, the ones who were told their partners liked them behaved in even more likable ways. They disclosed more information about themselves and were friendlier toward their partners compared to the ones who were misled to think their partners disliked them. The partners reacted in their turn by developing a liking for the ones who thought they were liked, and an aversion to the ones who thought they were disliked. The spiral moved rapidly up, toward attraction between the two, or down into the pit of aversion, very quickly. The initial "anonymous note" in this study, the one that misled the subjects into thinking their partner liked or did not like them, was the catalyst that set off the chain reactions. One led to an upward spiral of interpersonal attraction – a mutual admiration society. The other led to repulsion between two people.[121]

In real life, you don't need an anonymous note to detect that someone likes you. They will pay attention to you, smile at you, and praise your many fine attributes. And their attraction to you will usually lead you to like them back, as long as you believe their actions are sincere and not simply a Machiavellian scheme to manipulate you or get something from you.

On the Internet, people are using many of the same clues to learn that someone else likes them, and the results appear to be similar. When another forum participant praises your clever contribution to the discussion, then follows up with an email asking for more information and showing interest, you feel that sense of being valued and liked, much as you would in any other social situation. Even though you haven't seen that person and know little about her, you sense she likes you, and that is powerful news. A big difference on the Internet, though, is that you have fewer methods to show that you like someone else. The most important is probably attention. Responding to a person's message in a group discussion, agreeing with them and supporting them, and referencing them by name, can all be powerful cues and very rewarding to the recipient, especially when some of the other methods we usually use to convey liking are not available. You can't smile, move closer, or nod, but you can say, "As Jack said...," "Melanie had the right idea...," and "I like the way Captain Lopez explained things..."

WHEN THE SPIRAL SPINS DOWN

An intriguing twist in the findings about interpersonal attraction is that sometimes we work harder to gain someone's approval when they are not completely awed by us in the beginning. If we succeed in converting them and they begin to like us later, we tend to like them even more than if they had liked us all along.

---

[121] Curtis, R. C., and Miller, K. (1986). Believing another likes or dislikes you: Behaviors make the belief come true. *Journal of Personality and Social Psychology, 51*, 284–190.

Social psychologists Elliott Aronson and Darwyn Linder dreamed up a creative way to test this phenomenon in the laboratory, one that involved a "plot within a plot within a plot." As each woman subject arrived, she was told the study was about verbal conditioning and that another volunteer would be along soon. (This "other volunteer" was actually a confederate, but the subject did not know that.) The experimenter explained that he needed two people for each set of trials: one would be his "helper", the other would be the subject in the study. He went on to say that since she arrived first, she would be the "helper."

The real subject, who is now playing the role of "helper," was told to listen in on a brief discussion between the experimenter and the other woman and record the number of times the woman used a plural noun. The experimenter said he was going to try to condition her to increase her use of plural nouns with a verbal reward ("mmmmmm") each time she used one. Then the "helper" will take over the conversation, but offer no verbal rewards for plural nouns, and the experimenter would listen in to see if the "subject" continues to use plural nouns more than usual. In other words, will the verbal conditioning carry over to a new conversation with a different person? They would switch back and forth talking to the "subject" until each had seven separate conversations with the "subject."

Aronson and Linder then deviously embedded the final plot within a plot. They told the helper that it was important the subject didn't know the real purpose of the study, so the cover story was that it was about interpersonal attraction! After each conversation between the helper and the subject, the experimenter would be asking the subject her impressions of the helper and an assistant would do the same for the helper. The catch was that the "helper" was listening in to the "subject's" evaluation of herself, painstakingly counting plural nouns. Since the "subject" was really the confederate, the "helper" heard precisely what the experimenter wanted her to hear – a sequence of scripts designed to make the subjects think they were very much liked all along, disliked all along, or that the "subject's evaluation of them changed over time. Some subjects experienced a "gain" – that is, they started out overhearing negative evaluations, but these became more positive with each of the seven interviews. Others experienced a "loss" – the "subject's" evaluation of them got worse and worse.

This experiment should win the purloined letter award in the annals of psychological research. Telling the real subjects that interpersonal attraction was just a cover story needed to deceive, when that was exactly the subject of the study, was very crafty. The ploy worked, and the subjects never suspected that those evaluations they were monitoring were staged.

How did the women react to these overheard evaluations? The ones who experienced a psychological gain liked their partners the best, followed by those who heard positive evaluations of themselves all along. The women who suffered a loss, as their partners started evaluating them negatively halfway through, *disliked* their partners the most. One reason for our greater liking for someone who changes their mind in our favor is that we believe we won them over. We guess their initial negative view was mistaken, and that as they grew to know us better they learned the truth about how terrific we really are. This is a great boost for our self-esteem, even greater than what we feel when someone likes us all along. After all, the latter may be a sycophant, or may just have reacted to some superficial quality (like our good looks).

The dislike we feel toward someone whose evaluation of us drops is also more extreme. We might dismiss the one who evaluated us negatively from the beginning as someone who never got to know us anyway. Yet, what a blow to the ego it is to learn that someone started out liking us, but as they got to know us better, changed their minds.

On the Internet, the effects of these gains and losses on interpersonal attraction are probably similar except for one thing. It is so easy to drop out of an interaction and enter another that people may be less likely to give themselves a chance to experience that gain. If someone shows dislike for you at the outset, you might feel little motivation to try a bit harder to win that person's respect, since you could just start over somewhere else. The number of people "out there" with whom we can interact is so enormous that a single communication expressing dislike may be the abrupt end of the game. In real life, many of the new people you meet are not so easily dismissed. You may intersect with them because they live on your block or work in the next office, and you can't just click your mouse to avoid them. The power of the "gain" may have little chance to affect interpersonal attraction because you never get past that initial contact.

HUMOR

The net is loaded with humor, but are funny people more attractive? When someone makes us laugh, do we like them more? That depends. In a study of social attractiveness, Melissa Bekelja Wanzer and her colleagues asked their subjects to complete some questionnaires about their sense of humor and their social lives. They were also asked to give a slightly different version of the questionnaires to two of their acquaintances, one that assessed what they thought of the subject's humor and attractiveness.[122]

The subjects were generally on target about their own sense of humor, as their acquaintances confirmed. However, their ratings of social attractiveness depended on the *kind* of humor they usually expressed. If other people were usually the butt of their jokes, their social attractiveness was not very high, but if they often targeted themselves, it was. The funniest people in the group also expressed less loneliness, another indication that people liked them and sought them out.

On the Internet, humor can be a powerful force in interpersonal attraction, particularly because it isn't overshadowed by the physical appearance factor. Humor can be expressed very easily on the net in just typed text, and those who excel at it are probably earning extra points on the interpersonal attraction scale. One incident on a MUD showed clearly how people reacted differently to other-directed and self-directed humor. Players can program their entrance messages so that when they join a room all the others there see the customized sentence or two. Cowboy's entrance was, "Cowboy gallops masterfully into the room on his stallion, and as the horse rears to a stop, Cowboy leaps off with aplomb ... catching his foot in the stirrup and landing on the ground with a crash." Several people laughed, but Toby remarked that "Cowboy should get rid of that filthy nag ... we all need extra glue." People helped Cowboy up, brushed him off, and he became the center of attention in the group.

In real life, Toby's comment might have been softened with a wink or grin, but on the Internet, it sounded more hostile and cold-blooded than it probably was. Other-directed humor may not reduce your social attractiveness a great deal in real life because people can see many more of your qualities. But as we have seen over and over, the limited cues available on the Internet tend to magnify certain features of your communication behavior, and other-directed humor is one of them.

Some net communities are awash with humor, and their members find innovative and creative ways to make each other laugh. Nancy Baym at Wayne State University studied the performance of humor in

[122] Wanzer, M. B., Booth-Butterfield, M., and Booth-Butterfield, S. (1996). Are funny people popular? An examination of humor orientation, loneliness, and social attraction. *Communication Quarterly, 44,* 42–52.

rec.arts.tv.soaps or r.a.t.s., a Usenet newsgroup in which participants update one another on soap storylines and evaluate the characters and plots.[123] She analyzed the postings that dealt with a particular plot on *All My Children* over several months, and also surveyed the participants to learn their attitudes about the use of humor. Overwhelmingly, the respondents thought the humorous posts were the best, and for many participants, the light-heartedness was what drew them to return again and again to the newsgroup. One survey respondent remarked, "What makes a r.a.t.s. poster successful is a sense of humor, which many of the AMC posters have, especially Lyle and Granma, who are my two favorite people to read. They also have terrific imaginations." Clearly, whatever the funny posters were doing was adding a point or two to their net-based social attractiveness.

Humorous stories and jokes have appeared in text form for centuries, but the performance of humor on the net often develops its own set of norms. Humor emerged on r.a.t.s., for example, in specialized kinds of wordplays, bracketed remarks or asides, and mocking comments about the inept writers. One poster Baym quotes used frequent bracketed comments as she updated the others on a particular episode:

```
The three of them go to the concert together (Excuse me,
but what happened to Trevor's LIFE?) and stand around
worrying about Carter showing up. Galen is the most calm
of all of them! Steven excuses himself to go beg Brooke
(see One Big Happy Family) to fire Carter. He informs her
that she has a "whacko" working for her. She nicely but
firmly tells Steven she can't help him out. He thanks her
for her "overwhelming" sympathy. (For real! Has she
forgotten Gil, the rapist, and how she felt when no one
would believe her! And when her own husband wouldn't get
him out of their house!)
```

Another way the participants expressed humor in the textual messages was word play and clever phrasings. One poster used long, hyphenated adjectives to describe the emotional states of the characters, such as "rapidly-unhinged-just-got-fired-from-Tempo Carter." This particular poster was regarded by most to be one of the funniest in the group, but he was also controversial because he occasionally used other-

---

[123] Baym, N. K. (1995). The performance of humor in computer-mediated communication. *Journal of Computer-Mediated Communication* [Online], *1*(2). Available: http://jcmc.mscc.huji.ac.il/vol1/issue2/baym.htm1 [1998, May 20].

directed humor. Although the writers and actors were considered fair game for jibes, some survey respondents viewed his occasional taunts of other group members negatively.

SELF-DISCLOSURE

Developing a close relationship with another person requires a certain level of intimacy, of self-disclosure. Gradually, you begin to feel comfortable enough with the other person to trust him or her with your feelings, your dreams, and your self-doubts, and be confident that the other will not reject or blame you. Normally, to achieve this kind of intimacy, we rely on reciprocity. If you tell me something about yourself, I'll tell you something about me. Over time, the exchange deepens and the two people disclose more and more information to one another. The dance of self-disclosure is a delicate one, however, and fraught with potential problems. For example, if you pour out your deepest feelings to someone else too early, or in some setting that seems inappropriate, the other person may think you're unstable.

The newsgroup participants who responded to the survey that Malcolm Parks and Kory Floyd distributed indicated that self-disclosure was an important part of the online friendships. They generally agreed with statements such as, "I feel I could confide in this person about almost anything," or, "I usually tell this person exactly how I feel." Of all the questions on this survey, the one that evoked the most extreme response from the participants was, "I would never tell this person anything intimate or personal about myself." Participants strongly disagreed.

When clinical psychologists first began using computers in their offices, one of the applications, besides patient records and billing, was the computerized interview. Clients would sit at a terminal and answer questions about themselves, their problems, and their beliefs about their own behavior, and the computer would dutifully record the responses. The computerized interview was controversial at first, though it was certainly a time saver. Many practitioners thought the client should be talking to a human being and developing a rapport, so even now, not many use it. However, a strange thing started happening. Clients seemed to be more forthcoming when they were interviewed by a computer compared to when they were talking to a person who was jotting notes. As we will see in a later chapter, these findings led to some intriguing developments in computer-based and online therapy.

The tendency for people to disclose more to a computer – even when they know a person will be reading what they say – is an important ingredient in what seems to be happening on the Internet. Yes, it can be an impersonal, cold-blooded medium at times. Yet it can also be what Joseph Walther describes as *hyperpersonal*.[124] You sit at a computer screen feeling relatively anonymous, distant, and physically safe, and you sometimes feel closer to the people on the other side of your screen whom you have never seen than to the people in the next room. You may reveal more about yourself to them, feel more attraction to them, and express more emotions – even when all you have is an ASCII keyboard. At the keyboard you can concentrate only on yourself, your words, and the feelings you want to convey. You don't have to worry about how you look, what you're wearing, or those extra pounds you meant to shed. "The waist is a terrible thing to mind," as Walther suggests, and online you can reallocate your energies to the message. You can also endlessly idealize those personas with whom you are interacting. Someone you know only as "Moonbeam" who has told you many intimate details of her life – but not her name, address, or phone number – is like a canvas with just a few iridescent brush strokes. You can fill in the rest of that minimalist art work with your imagination.

ENHANCING REAL LIFE ROMANCE ON THE INTERNET

Although most of the research on Internet romance focuses on couples who meet online, the net is also playing an important role in real-life love affairs. People who are romantically involved can use the net to exchange email, chat online, play games together, or build shared Web sites. Especially when they are physically separated temporarily, the net can offer a means to avoid all those expensive long-distance phone calls.

There is reason to think that the text-based communication used in most corners of the Internet may provide a unique way to enrich an ongoing romantic relationship. For example, in a study of the communication patterns of engaged couples, the ones who wrote each other many letters because they were geographically separate were some of the happiest of the group.[125] These couples showed better adjustment and

---

[124] Walther, J. B. (1996). Computer-mediated communication: Impersonal, interpersonal, and hyperpersonal interaction. *Communication Research, 23(1)*, 3–43.

[125] Stafford, L., and Reske, J. R. (1990). Idealization and communication in long-distance premarital relationships. *Family Relations, 39*, 274–279.

also more love for one another, compared to the ones who did most of their communicating in the face-to-face mode or by telephone. Perhaps the increased tendency to self-disclose when you are sitting at a computer screen encourages more openness and intimacy between real-life couples. Though they may start out using the Internet as a convenience, the environment may actually contribute something quite positive to their relationship. The ease with which you can send an email or an electronic "greeting card" over the Web, for example, may also promote more frequent communication between couples.

Jerry and Tamara L. like to log into the Internet games as a way to have fun together when Jerry is on a business trip to a distant city. Carrying his laptop, Jerry can link to the Internet from his hotel room and join Tamara, who logs in from their home computer, for an evening of adventure as they converse with one another, chat with other in-game friends, and explore the virtual world dressed in their avatars' costumes. Another favorite past-time for this couple is the online bridge game. They never have any trouble finding another couple to join them for an evening of cards, and they have made a number of new online friends at the virtual card tables. Tamara explained how she and Jerry could gossip and share secrets when their bridge partners were boring. They both open a separate chat window and type private remarks there, invisible to the other players.

Before they started to spend time together in this way their communication during Jerry's trips was limited to a few phone calls and they both spent the lonely evenings watching television. Now, they are very happy with the new arrangement and even look forward to their virtual evenings together.

VIRTUAL PASSION

Perhaps the least understood component of interpersonal relationships on the Internet is the explicit sexual encounters that occur on MUDs, in chat rooms, and within some of the private rooms of the graphical meta-worlds. The practice of sex in cyberspace goes by many names with slightly different connotations. Examples include netsex, virtual sex (V-Sex), compusex, cybersex, cybering, MOOsex, and tinysex. All indications are that varieties of virtual passion are becoming quite popular, partly because the medium supports and encourages hyperpersonal communication quite well, as we discussed.

The chat rooms of America Online and IRC are especially noted for the abundance of sexually explicit encounters and conversation. For example, a listing of chat channels on IRC's Dalnet returns names such as #AdultBeachHouse, #sexy_n_nude_celebrities, and of course, simply #sex and #cybersex. One called #30–40+flirting explains its purpose in the title *Fantasy*Lust*Innuendo*Subtle*Seduction*We have it all*. At any time of day or night, thousands of people are logged into these channels bearing nicknames such as the ones below who, at 2 PM EST on a Thursday afternoon, were all in #sex:

```
sex Eduardo - fuyoyu Graphix Jetman monir _Paolo pjs13
Kyle_-____ lisabi Maria_21 badgerboy Supremo Dr_Girth
tuzluk smart21 petergirl johnybigodes abangmanja johhnn
^BigD RADEK_18 Raptorhigh i4got97 Barbie_20 AMatuer
Lawyer49m CrazyM pOoh I_AM_A_RADIO wld69 DaRkiCE Keizha
sij lesb^^ mikex Temp` ^Melissa tommygun chelsea21
Jaymeee houseboyslut SexNYCNow joek mememe SEX-BOY-20
JimmyKK rawther @Abusive TTBBQ
```

You can see from this list that people try to convey hints about their age, occupation, intention, or sexual orientation through their nicknames to narrow down the search for a partner and manage their impressions. Lawyer49m, for example, says quite a lot about himself through his nick, and managed to relay his occupation, age, and gender very quickly. Whether any of the information is actually true is open to question, of course. Although it is very difficult to estimate the gender ratios in these rooms, they seem to be predominantly male, perhaps overwhelmingly so. If you join the channel with a female or gender-ambiguous nickname, you will instantly receive several requests for a private chat. Except in the gay channels, a male nickname may be ignored.

Nancy Deuel's exploratory study of people who have participated in such encounters on MUDs led her to the conclusion that the virtual reality aspect of cyberspace provides an innovative and unique world in which people can, with relative safety, explore sexuality and personal expression.[126] The programming environment on a MUD allows participants to be especially creative and to mix fantasy with reality. They can build their own rooms and populate them with bottles of wine, candles, and soft music. One player's room is "gently lit by candlelight which flickers and you feel very relaxed, leaving all your troubles and worries

---

[126] Deuel, N. R. (1996). Our passionate response to virtual reality. In S. C. Herring (Ed.), *Computer-mediated communication: Linguistic, social and cross-cultural perspectives* (pp. 129–146). Amsterdam: John Benjamins Publishing Company.

behind you." Another, more explicit, couple built a Nudist Trailer and placed a sign on the entrance: "If you have clothes please leave them by the door!"

Psychologists Michael Adamse and Sheree Motta collected numerous stories of cyberaffairs, romances, and online sexual encounters through their Web site and found an enormous variety.[127] Some people reported an accidental online meeting in a discussion forum that led to email and photo exchanges, phone calls, and eventually visits. Unfortunately, the unbridled tendency to idealize the person when the usual face-to-face cues are not available led to many unrealistically high expectations and false hopes, and the actual meeting often killed the relationship. Sometimes, however, the chemistry survives the difficult transition from cyberspace to the real world, as it did for Britt, one of the people who told her story to Adamse and Motta. She met Eric, who lived in Germany, on one of the German language channels. After several years and thousands of hours logged into IRC, they met and married. Marriages made in cyberspace were once headline news, but not anymore.

Many of the interviewees never have any intention of meeting their online partner and instead are using the Internet as a safe place to indulge in one-night cyberstands and to explore fantasies and fetishes. The networks carry channels bearing titles that convey both the usual singles-bar atmosphere (hottub, cybercheers), and also almost any conceivable sexual variation, such as Truth_or_Dare_Sex Fun, gayteen, 3waysex, hornywifehomealone, and BDSM. The characteristics of the Internet make it attractive as a place to fantasize about sexual adventures and even act them out at the keyboard from a safe distance. Hyperpersonal communication among consenting adults enters a new and controversial level in this context. Whether this is good or bad news is debatable, and research on the issue will be very difficult to do. Deuel argues that Vsex should be considered a phenomenon of social interaction that many of her interviewees appear to value highly as a form of individualized learning, development, and exploration. Yet stories of spouses who feel betrayed when they learn of their partner's online romances are not uncommon.

The exploration component of sexuality on the Internet can get very far out, and a number of odd corners appear to involve practices that

---

[127] Adamse, M., and Motta, S. (1996). *Online friendship, chat-room romance, and cybersex*. Deerfield Beach, FL: Health Communications, Inc.

could be quite difficult or impossible in real life because of morality, social censure, physical risk, and legal consequences. Channels bearing names like incest, rapesex, toiletsex, extreme_female_torture, snuffsex, kiddiesex, and bifem_dogsex are all out on the Internet, though they are a miniscule proportion of the total. These tiny corners can be the target of sensationalized press, and one might wonder how many of the visitors are mostly gawking to see what is going on, or journalists interested in a story. Nevertheless, there has been very little solid research to determine who actually participates, what their motives are, and how the availability of these anonymous and interactive outlets for consensual sexual deviance affects them.

ROSES ON THE NET

Human beings have been using the written word for thousands of years to express affection and love for each other. In poems, letters, scribbled notes, and even classified newspaper ads of the "desperately seeking Susan" variety, we find ways to say in writing what we are not able to say in person. In retrospect, we probably should have guessed from the beginning that the Internet would flourish as a medium of interpersonal attraction, and that people would find it a wonderful way to get to know each other and even fall in love. We were caught off guard by the early results, as researchers watched groups in laboratories get down to business on the tasks they were assigned, focusing on the immediate problem. Struggling with annoying and frustrating computer interfaces, some of them certainly started hurling insults and foul language at each other. With such meager tools for socioemotional expressiveness, it just didn't seem like a very welcoming place to support intimacy. To be sure, it has many characteristics that can trigger verbal aggression. But now we see that it also has the ingredients to foster very strong and affectionate relationships. Most of them do not unfold in the public Internet spaces, however, so perhaps it is not surprising that researchers were a little slow in catching on.

The relationships that form are vulnerable because of the way humans are, and the way the Internet is. People may disclose too much, too soon, and they may idealize and fantasize in unrealistic ways. The role-playing, deceptions and gender-swapping make the Internet a bit hazardous for developing relationships, and it is not at all uncommon for a person you are growing to like on the net – as a friend or romantic partner – to just vanish into thin air. Yet despite the down sides, I think the Internet's ability to support and nurture relationships between two people is one of its most valuable characteristics. Although some brawling may go on in the public forums, behind the scenes people are sharing stories, listening to each other, feeling closer, and sending ASCII roses.[128]

[128] ASCII Art 3 (1998). Advanced ASCII Art [Online]. Available: http://www.marmsweb.com/ezine/dts4.html [1998, May 30].

PSYCHOLOGICAL ASPECTS OF INTERNET PORNOGRAPHY

Sexually explicit materials are available on convenience store magazine racks, in video rental shops, through 900 phone lines, from adult bulletin boards, and ... on the Internet. Their availability online, particularly to minors with computers and modems, has been one of the most controversial features of the Internet and has also been the principal motivation underlying attempts to regulate and restrict content. In the United States, for example, Senator James Exon of Nebraska brought his "blue book" containing images downloaded from some Usenet newsgroups into the Senate and invited his colleagues to stop to look at them, just when the Senate was about to discuss the Communications Decency Act. The outcome of the debate over the bill was sealed. In 1995, The Senate passed the bill 84–16 to outlaw obscene material online, and imposed fines and prison sentences to anyone who knowingly made indecent material available to children under age 18.

The implications for the Internet and Internet Service Providers were quite far-reaching, but the Senators were in no mood to back down, especially in front of the C-Span cameras. After many changes and compromises, the act was eventually passed by Congress and signed into law, but struck down by the Supreme Court in 1997 as unconstitutional because of its implications for free speech. Yet, its momentum as it traversed the legislative and legal landscapes, and also the worldwide Internet forums, demonstrates how volatile the whole issue of online pornography and sexuality really is.

SENSATIONALIZING CYBERPORN

Most people, especially those who are not on the Internet at all or who use it rarely, get their information from sensationalized news stories of dramatic incidents that occur on the net. Psychologists have found that vivid anecdotes like these can be very influential in shaping our attitudes toward the bigger picture. The principle underlying this is called the *availability heuristic* – we tend to use what readily comes to mind as a rule of thumb, or *heuristic,* to judge broader issues and form our attitudes. When something is easily available in memory because the news features it in sensational ways, we tend to think it is far more prevalent than it really is. For example, most of us grossly overestimate the probability that we will be in a plane crash, and the insurance companies who install quickie life insurance vending machines at the airports take full advantage of our error. We are, of course, far more likely to die in a car accident than a plane crash, but the news makes a much bigger deal out of airplane disasters. For the net, it means that a few sensationalized and widely disseminated stories can bias people's attitudes toward it, and lead them to believe that certain events are more common than they really are.

One such story came from *Time* magazine, whose cover on July 1, 1995, proclaimed "CYBERPORN!"[129] Inside was a detailed expose about the pornography that was being transmitted over the ether. The story triggered the availability heuristic, especially for the U.S. legislators who were, at the time, pondering the wording for the Communications Decency Act, and also for many people who were not very familiar with Internet activities.

The *Time* story featured a summary of a study by Carnegie Mellon researchers[130] that examined the kind and amount of sexually explicit images available for downloading from two major sources: the Internet and subscription-based adult bulletin-board services. The wording of the story, however, often missed that critical distinction, and the Internet began to sound like a den of smut. The first two conclusions read:

> **There's an awful lot of porn online.** *In an 18-month study, the team surveyed 917,410 sexually explicit pictures, descriptions, short stories and film clips. On those Usenet newsgroups where digitized images are stored, 83.5% of the pictures were pornographic.*

---

[129] Elmer-Dewitt, P. (1995). On a screen near you: Cyberporn. *Time* [Online], *146*. *Available:* http://www.pathfinder.com/time/magazine/domestic/1995/950703/950703.cover.html [1998, March 10].

[130] Rimm, M. (1995). Marketing Pornography on the Information Superhighway: A Survey of 917,410 Images, Description, Short Stories and Animations Downloaded 8.5 Million Times by Consumers in Over 2000 Cities in Forty Countries, Provinces and Territories [Online]. Available: http://trfn.pgh.pa.us/guest/mrstudy.html [1998, Mar 15]. The article originally appeared in the Georgetown Law Journal, 83(5).

It is immensely popular. Trading in sexually explicit imagery, according to the report, is now "one of the largest (if not the largest) recreational applications of users of computer networks." At one U.S. university, 13 of the 40 most frequently visited newsgroups had names like alt.sex.stories, rec.arts.erotica and alt.sex.bondage.

In fact, considerably less than 1% of those 917,410 images were found on the Internet newsgroups at all. They were located on the adult bulletin-board sites to which members pay a monthly subscription fee to download images of their choice. Usenet can be an untamed environment, as we have seen, but its newsgroups generate a relatively small proportion of Internet traffic. Generalizing from what happens in a few newsgroups to the whole Internet was not responsible reporting.

The *Time* story prompted an enormous outcry from Internet users, and the magazine soon printed a quasi-retraction, acknowledging that there may have been flaws in the study's methodology and problems in the reporting of it. *Time* editors conceded that the story may be "contributing to a mood of popular hysteria, sparked by the Christian coalition and other radical-right groups, that might lead to a crackdown." In response to the outcries and point-by-point criticisms that were appearing on the Internet, Carnegie Mellon and Georgetown University (whose Law Journal published the research) both began investigations. A *New York Times* article commented on the Internet outcry: "Hell hath no fury like an Internet scorned."

BUT WHAT IS REALLY OUT THERE?

Sensational reporting and hyperbole aside, there *is* sexually explicit material on the Internet. You can accidently run across it. Invitations to visit erotic Internet locales can land uninvited in your email inbox through the efforts of aggressive spammers, who flood the net with blanket messages to any list of email addresses they can target. Furthermore, the nature of the virtual world surely broadens access to a wide range of erotica. The anonymity, physical distance, and perceived lack of accountability in cyberspace may all contribute to some differences in the nature of pornography, its use, and its effects on behavior. From a psychological perspective, pornography may be one of the "killer apps" that has been propelling this technology into so many homes around the world, just as the home-viewing of pornographic movies made the VCR so appealing. When adult videos hit the rental market, the sales of VCRs rose dramatically.

So what is out there? On the commercial side, pornography vendors who avoided the Internet before and stuck with the adult electronic bulletin board market figured out that their materials could be peddled on the Web for a profit. Now that patrons can use credit cards to pay through secure Web servers, the possibilities are endless. Vendors offer a few free samplers, many of which they distribute through those Usenet newsgroups, but then ask interested patrons to enter their credit card number at their Web sites. Before they begin searching the image databases by keywords, looking for whatever material interests them, they must pay up. The interactive Internet world offers many other erotic experiences, new to the pornography industry. "Hot chat" is an example, offered to paid subscribers who can communicate with a sensual employee using typed text. A new twist at some sites is a live video of performers, with whom the patrons can communicate via a chat window and offer suggestions for innovative play.

Another kind of sexually explicit material on the net, however, is not commercial at all, and no profit motive is involved. This aspect of sexuality involves men and women who are not paid to perform, but who are engaging in a wide variety of sexual activities online. I discussed netsex in a previous chapter, and this is one example. Amateurs are also creating Web sites with pornographic pictures of their adventures, or contributing their own works of fiction to a newsgroup like alt.sex.stories. Discussion forums abound, and IRC has plenty of chat channels with sexually explicit titles. Interactive two-way video is also entering the scene through technologies such as CUSeeMe. With this software and a cheap videocamera connected to your computer, you can transmit very grainy and jittery moving images to your Internet friends, and watch theirs in return. Human beings have not had these avenues of sexual exploration and expression open to them in the past, and the Internet offers them. The anonymity and physical distance that affect so many aspects of human behavior online also affect sexual activities.

A study of 150 sexually explicit images downloaded from Usenet newsgroups suggests that there may be real differences between the commercial and noncommercial materials. Michael D. Mehta of Queens University and his colleague Dwaine E. Plaza of York University, first determined whether the materials had been posted by amateurs, or by profit-oriented commercial services as an easy way to advertise their services.[131] Sixty-five

---

[131] Mehta, M. D., and Plaza, D. E. (1997). Pornography in cyberspace: An exploration of what's in Usenet. In S. Kiesler (Ed.), *Culture of the Internet* (pp. 53–67) Mahwah, NJ: Lawrence Erlbaum Associates, Publishers.

percent were from noncommercial sources, and these were less sexually explicit compared to the ones from commercial posters. They were also less risky from a legal standpoint. For example, 25% of the commercial photos included children or adolescents, but only 9% of the noncommercial images hinted at child pornography. Even if the actual models are not under age, this illusion makes the material illegal in some countries.

Precision has never been a prominent feature of the definitions of words like *obscene* or *pornographic,* particularly in a legal context. Our reliance on community standards to decide what is erotic and what is pornographic becomes especially problematic in the age of the Internet, and what is "obscene" in Scandinavia is quite different from what might be thought "obscene" in the United States. Governments attempting to regulate content start stepping on each others' toes. For example, in 1995 federal officials in Germany informed CompuServe that more than 200 of the Internet newsgroups violated German law. Rather than risk prosecution, the company closed off access to the offending discussion forums, but they were unable to do this just for people who were logging on within German borders. All of CompuServe's subscribers in more than 100 countries were locked out, and the uproar was heard around the world. Despite the outcries, Felix Somm, the ex-manager of CompuServe's German operation, was eventually convicted in a Bavarian court in 1998 and given a 2-year suspended sentence for allowing traffic in pornographic materials. He is appealing and may win because of changes in German law. Internet Service Providers now bear limited responsibility for foreign material to which they merely provide access.

For our purposes, however, the legal definitions of pornography or obscenity in different countries are not as important as the psychological impact of the range of sexually explicit material and activity that are available on the net. Is it good? Bad? Indifferent? All of the above? Let's begin by looking at the research on the psychological effects of such materials in general, regardless of where you get them.

PSYCHOLOGICAL ASPECTS OF PORNOGRAPHY

Some social scientists maintain that the use of sexually explicit materials is harmless, and that it can also be functional, healthy, and liberating in some contexts because it provides education, erotic enhancement, an outlet for exploration, and entertainment. It can also be useful in some therapeutic treatment programs for sexual dysfunctions. Others, however, point to the ethical and moral issues involved – particularly the exploitation and objectification of women. Males are far and away the principal users of pornography, and a major concern is that so much of the material depicts women in dehumanizing ways. The fact that most countries restrict the use of pornography in one way or another indicates that many people around the globe believe pornography has some harmful effects, whether the research shows this or not. Behavioral research on its psychological effects was just about nonexistent until the 1970s, and even now the results are not all that clear.

One consistent and not too surprising finding is that erotica is often sexually arousing to both men and women. When people view explicit photos, read stories, watch films, or listen to audiotapes, many report feeling aroused, and physiological measurements confirm this. The critical issue, however, is whether exposure to pornography causes any negative changes in attitudes or behavior, and this is where the evidence becomes more difficult to interpret.

For example, the laws in Denmark were changed in the 1960s so that all restrictions on the production and distribution of pornography were removed. Contrary to what many expected, the incidence of sex crimes such as exhibitionism, Peeping Tomism, and child molestation decreased almost immediately, supporting the hypothesis that pornography is harmless or even beneficial. Perhaps the easy availability of erotic material for people with those inclinations made it less likely they would act them out in real life. However, a study in the United States found that the sales volume of magazines like *Hustler* or *Playboy* in each of the 50 states was related to the incidence of rape.[132] Alaska and Nevada ranked first and second in sales, and these states also had the highest rates for rape crimes. Interpreting these conflicting results is difficult, especially since there are so many variables that affect crime statistics. A significant one for sex crimes especially is the likelihood that people will report them to the police.

Some laboratory-based experimental studies have been conducted, and generally the results have not been very dramatic. Some changes do occur, however. For example, men who viewed extremely attractive centerfolds and watched passionate, consensual sex in videos become somewhat less enthusiastic about the attractiveness of their own real-life partners.[133] Probably, a contrast effect is occurring, such that viewing

[132] Baron, L., and Straus, M. A. (1984). Sexual stratification, pornography, and rape in the United States. In N. M. Malamuth and E. Donnerstein (Eds.), *Pornography and sexual aggression* (pp. 186–210). New York: Academic Press.

[133] Kenrick, D. T., Gutierres, S. E., and Goldberg, L. L. (1989). Influence of popular erotica on judgments of strangers and mates. *Journal of Experimental Social Psychology, 25,* 159–167. Zillman, D. (1989). Effects of prolonged consumption of pornography. In D. Zillman and J. Bryant (Eds.), *Pornography: Research advances and policy considerations.* Hillsdale, NJ: Erlbaum. (p. 458).

beautiful models in sexually explicit settings makes people less satisfied with their lot in life and their own real-life partners. Although the pictures or the movie may have been temporarily stimulating, the longer-term effects on the man's personal relationships may not be promising. After all, he is not likely to meet up with the star of the porn movie.

The lab studies are not easy to do, and researchers are troubled by the many ethical issues involved. It is a very important issue, but *do no harm* is a cardinal rule in behavioral research, just as it is in medicine. One research team pointed out that scientists involved in these studies were "quite relieved to find that erotic presentations in the laboratory did not send sex-crazed subjects dashing into the streets to commit unspeakable sexual acts with passing strangers."[134] However, lab studies have their own set of problems – particularly when the subject under the microscope is such an intimate one, and any behavioral changes would not be likely to show up immediately. Lingering doubts remained about whether pornography might be producing longer-term effects, especially when the material depicts violence.

AGGRESSIVE AND VIOLENT PORNOGRAPHY

When Denmark changed its laws in the 1960s, and when the U.S. Commission on Obscenity and Pornography determined in 1970 that scientific evidence did not support the view that pornography was harmful, most of the erotica on the market was of the nonviolent, consensual variety. But images and stories depicting aggression toward women and sexual violence became more frequent and widely available during the 1970s, probably because the general attitude toward all kinds of pornography relaxed. One study found that the number of rape depictions in hard-core paperbacks doubled between 1968 and 1974.[135] Another noted a five-fold increase in the number of pictures containing sexual violence in *Playboy* and *Penthouse*, between 1973 and 1977.[136]

Psychologically, this aggressive pornography appears to be far less benign than other types, particularly because it may trigger negative atti-

---

[134] Byrne, D., and Kelley, K. (1984). Introduction: Pornography and sex research. In N. M. Malamuth and Donnerstein, E. (Eds.), *Pornography and sexual aggression* (pp. 1–15). New York: Academic Press.

[135] Smith, D. G. (1976). The social content of pornography. *Journal of Communication, 26,* 16–33.

[136] Malamuth, N. M., and Spinner, B. (1980). A longitudinal content analysis of sexual violence in the best-selling erotic magazines. *The Journal of Sex Research, 16(3),* 226–237.

tudes and aggressive behavior toward women in real life. Edward Donnerstein at the University of Wisconsin conducted a series of experimental investigations into the phenomenon and found that the kind of movies men watched affected how much aggression they showed toward women.[137] In one study, he showed men different films, some neutral, some erotic but not violent, and some involving a rape. Later, the men participated in what they thought was a totally separate experiment in which they played the role of "teacher," and were supposed to administer shocks, at levels they themselves could choose, to another subject when he or she failed to learn nonsense syllables. The other "subject" was actually a confederate of the experimenter, and the real point of the study was to find out whether exposure to those films influenced the men's behavior toward women. It did.

The men who watched the neutral film were the least punitive, and chose rather low level shocks for both the men and women "subjects." Watching an erotic but nonviolent video caused the men to show a little more aggression toward the male "pupils," but not the women. The violent rape scene, however, was a different matter. Men who watched that tape increased the shock levels, but only for their female victims – not for the men. Recall that all men were randomly assigned to these conditions. The experiment provided some evidence that exposure to sexually explicit and violent material influenced these men in a way that made them more aggressive toward women.

Much of the aggressive pornography out there perpetuates the rape myth – the view that women say *no* but don't mean it, and that they enjoy sexual coercion. Donnerstein looked more closely at whether men behaved differently toward those women "pupils" depending on the kind of aggressive pornography they watched. He created a film that showed a young woman sitting down to study with two men who have been drinking; she is eventually tied up, stripped, slapped around, and raped. For one version of the film, the last 30 seconds showed the woman smiling, presumably a willing participant. For the other, the narrative explains she finds the experience humiliating and disgusting. Men who watched either version delivered higher levels of shock than men who watched neutral or nonaggressive pornography,

[137] Donnerstein, E. (1980). Aggressive erotica and violence against women. *Journal of Personality and Social Psychology, 39,* 269–277. Donnerstein, E. (1984). Pornography: Its effects on violence against women. In N. M. Malamuth and E. Donnerstein (Eds.), *Pornography and sexual aggression* (pp. 53–81). New York: Academic Press.

and again, only to the women confederates – not the men. But the subjects exposed to the rape myth version of the story administered the highest levels.

In a few of these studies, Donnerstein's confederates sometimes provoked the men by insulting them before the experiment began to learn more about how anger might influence the results. In that last study, for example, all the men were angered before they watched the movies. However, he found that it doesn't make any difference whether men are angry or not if they watch the aggressive pornography that ends with the woman as a willing participant. The outcome is different if they watch the version in which the woman clearly is not enjoying the event. In that case, only the men who were angered showed high levels of aggression toward the women confederates. The calm men showed very little.

The implication is that aggressive pornography, particularly the kind that ends in a positive outcome, is not harmless at all. Anger can trigger aggression in many settings, as we discussed in a previous chapter, but it has special effects when it is combined with depictions of sexual violence. From the research, we can't really be certain whether nonviolent pornography has any negative long-term effects, and it probably depends on who is using it and why. People choose to use sexually explicit materials for a number of reasons – erotic enhancement, entertainment, education, maybe just boredom. But evidence about harmful effects from the violent pornography is more compelling.

VIEWS FROM THE INTERNET

Debates about the effects of pornography are quite common on the Internet itself, especially in the niches in which sexually explicit material is created by amateurs with no commercial interests. A discussion thread in alt.sex.stories.d, for example, began when someone objected to the stories being posted about rape:

```
I only want the stories on line to be with concenting
[sic] adults. Let's not force ourselves upon anybody for
the generous task of showing them the joy of sex. It's
still rape, even if you wind up thinking that the victim
enjoyed it. I'm really sick of these stories that say No
means No until she starts enjoying it.
```

In a response, another poster offered a defense of such material with this argument:

People write about rape fantasies because they understand the difference between fantasy and reality…

So let us question some of the conventional wisdom regarding sexual attitudes and sexual behavior. One popular idea has it that "those who fantasize are those who do." Ergo, the only people who write about their fantasies of raping are those who would actually commit the act of rape.

There's a significant reason why that very idea is DANGEROUS. According to that logic, the several million women who have fantasies about *being* raped are therefore consenting to THAT act. I *do* not believe that a woman who derives erotic pleasure from the *fantasy* of being taken against her will has any desire to experience the *reality* of being raped. Do you?

A significant difference between what is on the Internet and what happens in the commercial world of pornography is the involvement of people who aren't paid, and whose motives for engaging in sexually explicit activities are personal rather than professional. We know nothing about how this knowledge might affect the people involved. For example, when men read an aggressive and violent fantasy story whose author, judging by the nickname, appears to be a female, is the rape myth perpetuated even more than it would be from material obviously created to make money?

A new twist that the Internet adds to the violent pornography scene is consensual interactivity, and psychologists haven't even begun to learn how this could affect the people who participate. One example is Gor, an offbeat subculture based on a series of mostly out-of-print science fiction novels by John Norman. The books depict a violent and primitive world on the opposite side of our sun in which men with honor and courage rule and women are mainly slaves, used sexually and punished mercilessly. Goreans have launched dozens of Web sites, and post an online "newspaper" called the *Gorean Daily Times*. They also have built virtual taverns and bath houses in the form of IRC channels where they log in and live out the Gorean lifestyle as best they can, given the limitations of the medium. The sexual violence and grisly warring got them banned from some networks, but they remain active and defensive about their ways. One Web site describes a Gorean IRC channel as a place "Where men are what they are, and women are as they should be. Thanks to Danath and Strummer it is a place where real life and IRC can come together. Please leave your games at the door."[138]

On IRC, all activity is necessarily consensual because anyone can click off a modem – slaves are not kidnapped against their will. Yet, given the research, one can only wonder how those who visit Internet neighborhoods in which sexually violent scenes are acted out by nonprofessionals will be affected when they leave IRC.

CHECKING IDS

Concerns about the contribution Internet pornography makes to a hostile environment for women are overshadowed by worries about minors. A major concern for any society is protection of its children from harm, and this has prompted endless debate over the Internet. Its accessibility and educational value are key reasons to install Internet connections in schools, and governments around the world are funding such projects. Yet the public remains justifiably concerned that minors will have very easy access to pornography. In the United States, this concern was voiced as a key element of the Communications Decency Act (CDA) of 1996. For example, the "indecent transmission" feature of the act made it a crime to knowingly transmit to anyone under 18 years of age "any comment, request, suggestion, proposal, image, or other communication which is obscene or indecent."

Although the Communications Decency Act was struck down by U.S. courts, legislative attempts to restrict Internet content to protect minors continue. The Child Online Protection Act, signed by President Clinton in the fall of 1998, makes it a federal crime to knowingly communicate material considered harmful to minors for commercial purposes. Penalties range from hefty fines and civil suits to prison sentences. Civil liberties groups are dismayed and are, once again, organizing protests against what has come to be known as the CDA II. A district court judge recently issued a preliminary injunction that protects Internet user from prosecution and fines.[139] Barry Steinhardt, president of the Electronic Frontier Foundation, denounced the most recent attempt at censorship:

---

[138] David DiNardo aka Tarl_Cabot (1998). *Tarnsman of Gor* [Online]. Available: http://www.geocities.com/Area51/Rampart/8770/ [1998, May 30].

[139] Electronic Frontier Foundation [1999, February 1]. Netizens Safe from Prosecution Under Net Censorship Law: Philadelphia Judge Bars Enforcement of Child Online Protection Act. [Online]. Available: http://www.eff.com/pub/Legal/Cases/ACLU_v_Reno_II/HTML/19990201_eff_pressrel.html [1999, March 13].

"It is the height of irony that the same Congress that plastered the salacious Starr Report all over the Internet now passes a plainly unconstitutional law to suppress a vaguely defined category of 'harmful' material. You would think Congress would have learned that 'harmfulness' is in the eye of the beholder."[140]

Nevertheless, even determined legislative efforts are not likely to succeed entirely, so the responsibility for protecting minors is now mainly in the hands of parents, teachers, and librarians who can choose to install various kinds of software to filter objectionable materials, restrict access to particular sites, and even stop a child from transmitting certain kinds of information, such as a home telephone number. An advantage to the filtering software is that parents can choose how much to restrict content based on the child's age and maturity. Rating schemes for adult-oriented material on the Web are emerging, and certain kinds of search services allow users to choose whether they want to include the adult sites in their search or leave them out. For example, on Dejanews (www.dejanews.com) you can search the Usenet newsgroups by keywords to find postings of interest, regardless of the newsgroup in which they appeared. You can choose whether you want to search the "adult" or "standard" database, however.

Children also are learning quickly to protect themselves. In *Growing Up Digital*, Don Tapscott describes the results from online research projects that involved many discussions with children and teens who are using the net.[141] These young N-Geners, as he calls them, were surprisingly relaxed about the presence of pornography on the Internet, and many of them believe people are overreacting. Fifteen-year old Austin Locke, for example, said:

```
Many parents have turned away from the Internet because
of the bad press it was given at the start of its
commercial use in 1995/96 regarding some of the
objectionable sites. What a lot of people don't realize
is that all that bad stuff is outweighed a thousand times
over by the good stuff.
```

[140] *ACLU v. Reno*, Round 2: Broad Coalition Files Challenge to New Federal Net Censorship Law (October 22, 1998) [Online], Available: http://www.eff.org/pub/Legal/Cases/ACLU_v_Reno II/HTML/19981022_plaintiffs_pressrel.html [1998, October 27].

[141] Tapscott, D. (1998). *Growing up digital: The rise of the net generation*. New York: McGraw-Hill.

Many of these young people also thought that adults were overestimating the amount of objectionable material, particularly compared to what they see on the tube. Another 15-year-old, Reanna Alder, pointed out:

```
I have never stumbled into a site I didn't want to see.
Not like on TV where I have occasionally flicked the
channel only to "stumble" into some gruesome murder
scene.
```

HOW MUCH SHOULD WE WORRY?

We know too little about pornography on the Internet – who uses it and how it affects them – to draw many firm conclusions yet. Nevertheless, we do know more about the psychological aspects of pornography in general and we can make speculations, given the nature of the Internet. First, people will probably use pornography on the Internet much as they have used sexually explicit materials they have obtained through other sources in the past, for diversion and sexual enhancement, for example. Second, compared to pornography distributed through more conventional means, Internet pornography will have wider distribution and will be accessible to far more people. This is what the Internet is all about, after all.

Third, the nature of the Internet is likely to trigger that disinhibition we see so often in other aspects of online behavior. People may feel freer to read erotic stories and view explicit images online when they might never have entered an adult movie theater or visited a live sex show. They may also feel freer to explore the fetishes, alternative subcultures, and the deviant in ways that have not really been feasible in the past. This may shift the content of Internet pornography away from the mainstream and toward the more exotic. Although the effects of nonviolent consensual material may not be dramatic, there is good reason to speculate that increases in the availability of and exposure to aggressive pornography can be harmful and may promote aggression toward women.

Finally, one might speculate that widespread and inexpensive access to such an enormous range of sexually explicit materials might eventually diminish people's interest in it – a kind of "ho hum" effect. Preliminary results from the HomeNet study, in which the actual Internet activities of 50 families in the Pittsburgh, Pennsylvania, area are being monitored, suggest that most people are not all that interested in the erotica they can find on the net.[142] Those who do take a peek seem to find their curiosity a transient phenomenon. During the first year of the study, almost half the people who stopped in to look did so only once or twice. It is typically the forbidden that is most desirable. The allure that pornography has for some people may just vanish, or turn into boredom, with familiarity.

[142] Manning, J., Scherlis, W., Kiesler, S., Kraut, R. and Mukhopadhyay, T. (1997). Erotica on the Internet: From the HomeNet trial. In S. Kiesler (Ed.), *Culture of the Internet* (pp. 68–69). Mahwah, NJ: Lawrence Erlbaum Associates, Publishers.

THE INTERNET AS A TIME SINK

When SABRE[143], the airline flight lookup and reservation service, first became available through the Web, I remember thinking what an enormous time saver this was going to be. We could now enter our destinations and retrieve dozens of options, complete with fare codes, rules, prices, stopovers, and type of plane. Enchanted by the convenience and control, I spent many hours looking up alternate flights to remote cities around the globe, weighing all the possibilities and costs for a summer vacation. After 2 hours of frustration with my 33.6 kb/s modem, I learned my lesson. Just clicking on the fare code rules for an attractively priced flight can eat many minutes. The airlines have become quite inventive in their pricing strategies, and their rule book resembles an IRS manual. Putting these online for consumers was a great idea, but in my case I would have been better off time- and frustration-wise if I had just picked up the phone and called an experienced travel agent.

As we push Internet access into every home, school, and business on the planet, extolling its many virtues, we are often ignoring this particular aspect of the online world. It can be a *time sink,* and our own behavior and inclinations help to make it that way. I had a phone right on my desk, for example, and my travel agent's number was right there in my electronic rolodex. Yet like many others, I persisted – for psychological reasons we will explore in this chapter.

The time sink aspect of the Internet has received more attention recently because some of the results from the HomeNet trial, in which online activity in a sample of households in the Pittsburgh area was

---

[143] One such service is Travelocity. After you register and obtain a userid and password, you can also make reservations through the online service. Available: http://www.travelocity.com [1998, May 30].

tracked for a period of two years, suggest that increased Internet use is not necessarily beneficial to one's well-being or social involvement.[144] Robert Kraut and his colleagues at Carnegie Mellon University administered a number of personality assessments to the participants in this study, before they began to use the Internet and then again one or two years later. Special software tracked how much each person was logged into the Internet, and also what kinds of applications they were using. They found that as people increased the time they spent online, they experienced decreases in family communication and also the size of their real-life social circles. Increased Internet use was also associated with greater feelings of loneliness and depression over time. The paradox here is that the Internet is essentially a social technology, one that is supposed to improve and enrich communication and help people feel more socially involved. But these preliminary results suggest something else may be happening, at least for some. Kraut and his colleagues hypothesize that people whose Internet use is higher may be substituting poorer quality social relationships for the stronger ones they had in real life. The result may be growing feelings of loneliness and depression.

On the far end of the spectrum, the time sink can become a giant cavern. Some people appear to be entering into patterns of Internet use that resemble a pathological behavioral disorder, in some ways similar to other forms of compulsive behavior. They spend hour after hour, day after day, online – unable to log off, unwilling to leave their computers – while their former real-life activities and social relationships deteriorate. The labels researchers have used to describe this are controversial. Internet addiction disorder, or IAD, was initially proposed by psychiatrist Ivan Goldberg as a joke, but as more and more evidence of the patterns of excessive use began to emerge, people began to wonder. Is there really a new disorder here that should be added to the psychiatric textbooks? Can people become addicted to the Internet? Whatever we call the phenomenon, it is clear that some people are having a difficult time getting their lives in order because of the amount of time they spend online.

People who enjoy and seek out that sense of control over their environment may be singularly vulnerable to the Internet's time sink. This, as we will see, is one of those psychological aspects of cyberspace that lures us.

---

[144] Kraut, R., Patterson, M., Lundmark, V., Kiesler, S., Mukopadhyay, T., and Scherlis, W. (1998). Internet paradox: A social technology that reduces social involvement and psychological well-being? *American Psychologist, 53(9),* 1017–1031.

LOCUS OF CONTROL

In his clinical practice, Julian Rotter found that people differ in their views about how much external forces control and influence the events in their lives. Some people believe they are at the mercy of circumstances and that if something good happens, they must have been lucky. Others believe they are masters of their own fates and if something good happens, it is because they worked hard and earned it. Rotter began to think of these differing viewpoints in terms of *locus of control*. People who felt their own actions were effectual and had a great deal to do with how events came out possessed an internal locus of control, while those whose beliefs emphasized the role of external forces demonstrated an external locus of control.[145]

Social scientists like to quantify elusive concepts such as locus of control, and Rotter developed a test with a series of paired statements. Test takers were asked to choose between two statements, such as the following sets, and indicate which one they believed more strongly:

In the long run people get the respect they deserve in this world.
or
Unfortunately, people's worth often passes unrecognized no matter how hard they try.
Sometimes I feel that I don't have enough control over the direction my life is taking.
or
What happens to me is my own doing.

The notion intrigued the social science research community, and other studies were conducted to learn how these different personal views related to other patterns of behavior. As it turned out, they had quite a lot to do with many aspects of a person's life. People with a strong internal locus of control are more likely to excel in school, succeed in business, make money, wear seat belts, and practice birth control. People who *think* they can control things behave as though they can; they have an optimistic and positive view about their ability to master the environment. I suggest that they are also more likely to be enamored by the Internet because it gives us so much freedom *to* control.

---

[145] Rotter, J. (1973). Internal-external locus of control scale. In J. P. Robinson and R. P. Shaver (Eds.), *Measures of social psychological attitudes*. Ann Arbor: Institute for Social Research (p. 47).

If you have an internal locus of control, you are especially pleased by technological innovations that let you exercise it. Recall, for example, when the TV remote control first appeared in the market. Now here is a device that empowers us to mute those noisy commercials and jump from one channel to the next at lightning speed. Almost overnight, we changed from a passive couch potato at the broadcasting networks' mercy into a master of our viewing destiny. (We were always empowered that way, of course, but exercising it would have involved *physical* exercise. I did not say people with a strong internal locus of control were any less lazy.) When the VCR came out, we were offered another wondrous opportunity to wrest control of the set away from those external media forces. Assuming we learned how to program the recording timer and make it stop blinking 12:00, we could now record any program we found intriguing and watch it later, fast forwarding over the commercials and pausing at any time for breaks. Even people who could not quite get to the "programmed record" level of expertise could certainly just slap a blank tape in the deck, press the REC button, and then sit down to a family dinner.

In contrast, the phone has always struck me as a prime example of a technology designed to promote an external locus of control. It rings without warning, and you have no control over when the ringing starts or how long it goes on. You have no idea who is calling, and if you *do* answer it, you become enmeshed in the cultural conventions embedded in telephone etiquette. You can't just hang up, for example, and if you apologize and say you can't talk now, you also feel obliged to say, "I'll call you back later." The phone's intrusive nature and its tendency to cause people to lose control over their own time were the main reasons people who first installed telephones in the United Kingdom put them in the servants' quarters. At the time, it was considered grossly impolite to call on another household without advance notice, and the social convention was applied to telephone calls as well.

Enter the answering machine, voice mail, and caller ID. All of these empower us to take more precise control over our telephone answering habits, and like the VCR, these technologies are likely to appeal strongly to people who have an internal locus of control. You can even turn the ringer off completely and just check your phone messages periodically.

As a technology of empowerment, the Internet is phenomenal, or at least it appears so. When you get online, you have complete control over where you go, what you say, what sites you visit, what you read, and what you download. If a Web site's images or animations are too annoying and time consuming to download, you can click STOP and go somewhere else, a pattern of behavior that should not be lost on Web developers who think everyone loves elaborate graphics and animations. This empowerment, though, is to some degree an illusion. Combined with that strong internal locus of control, it can be one reason people slip into the Internet's time sink.

My experience with the online flight lookup service illustrates how that can happen. When I was entering destinations and choosing flight plans, I was in control, finding my own information about things I could never have learned by myself before. Not being dependent on a travel agent who may or may not exert the effort to look up all the possibilities, or who may be getting higher commissions for certain airlines or kinds of travel deals, was a potent draw – especially for someone with an internal locus of control.

Getting on the Internet is not all that simple, and I would speculate that Internet users as a group would score somewhat higher than nonusers on internal locus of control. The mere fact that they take the time to obtain net access would also support that supposition. That they are concerned about the Internet as time sink is apparent from some of the surveys. For example, in one of Georgia Tech's annual World Wide Web surveys, the amount of time it takes to download and view Web pages was the Internet problem the respondents mentioned most frequently. Also, they voiced loud complaints about navigation – not being able to find things they know must be out there. In the most recent survey, this issue came right after censorship and privacy as the most important issues facing the Internet, and for the European respondents, it ranked even higher than privacy.[146] The kinds of people who are drawn to the Internet's style of empowerment may be just the same ones who will be most vulnerable to its potential as a time sink.

SECTION 2

Those enticing feelings of control and empowerment emerge in many ways on the net, and another example involves the Internet user's heightened sense of influence over the distant worlds of politics, commerce, and entertainment. I've mentioned several cases in which

[146] GVU's WWW Survey Team, Graphics, Visualization, and Usability Center, Georgia Institute of Technology (1997). *GVU's WWW User Surveys* [Online]. Available: http://www.gvu.gatech.edu/user_surveys/ [1998, May 30].

Internet users joined forces to effect change, and the world of television is also beginning to take special note of Internet users' views. In a mailing list for fans of an off-beat cable television program called *La Femme Nikita,* the participants have just this kind of influence. The television program, about an elite antiterrorist operation known as Section 1 whose "ends are just but whose means are ruthless," has a kind of cult following, mainly female. The mailing list, known as Section 2, is enormously active as the participants analyze motivations of the characters, share synopses, and trade tapes. Canadian viewers get to see the episodes earlier than others, and they always include an Internet convention known as SPACE FOR SPOILERS at the top of their plot summaries. This is a long series of carriage returns so that readers have to scroll down to see the summary, and won't accidentally read the post if they want to be surprised. The group is articulate and vocal about the show, and not shy about saying what they would like to see happen.

Unlike many television producers, the people responsible for creating *La Femme Nikita* follow the Internet activity very intently, and even participate in it. One email message from Michael Loceff, the chief story editor, sent to one of the leaders of Section 2, showed how seriously the show's creative talent were taking the input they received from their Internet fans. Notice the casual, conversational tone and the use of first names. Joel is Joel Surnow, executive producer, and Chris is Chris Carter, the quintessentially postmodern producer of both *La Femme Nikita* and the immensely popular *X-Files.*[147]

```
Joel is now more concerned with the Internet feedback
than any single aspect of the fan response. Chris
compiles a package of 20-30 emails and letters to the
site once or twice a week and Joel not only reads them,
but comes into my office and reads them to ME. (I usually
have read them by that time). And he's not laughing at
the letters either - if he does laugh it is because
someone is poking fun at the show and he agrees totally.
In story meetings now EVERY session involves some concern
about the Internet population - "they don't want her to
appear too whiny", "this ep won't be great for a first-
time viewer, but we have to service the loyal Internet
population", etc. I understand he even read the various
Internet theories regarding the "mystery" on the air. I
```

---

[147] "This in from Michael Loceff," Electronic posting to lfnspycentral@mailinglist.net from Covert Operations Command Center <warywmn@cris.com>, April 6, 1998.

haven't seen an executive producer as tuned in to the
Internet voice since Larry Herzog in "Nowhere Man."
...
Michael

This is very heady stuff for people who, in the past, might have written an occasional fan letter and received nothing more than a canned response and glossy photo. Actually, this mailing list group probably wouldn't have even bothered with anything so ineffectual as a snail mail fan letter. These TV moguls are at home in this world, right along with their net-savvy fans, and that status equalization phenomenon shows through clearly. When people who have an internal locus of control are able to exercise it in domains such as this, ones that were formerly far beyond their power reach, the lure is extraordinary. However, exercising this kind of power means that you spend more and more time online, and potentially less with your friends and family.

THE ONLINE AUCTION

The Internet opens up vast opportunities for entrepreneurs who can now reach a global market from a mountain cabin in Canada. This technology is certainly driving major transformations in the competitive business landscape, but it is also attracting people with that strong internal locus of control who want to cut out the middleman altogether and negotiate their own deals. If you are looking for that special gift for your significant other or for yourself, you can go directly to what may be the largest flea market in the history of the planet: the online auction.

One example is eBay, which at last count had almost 2 million items for sale. If you have something you want to sell, you can register at the site for free, send in a description and a picture if you have one, and decide on the auction details, such as the exact time you want the auction to close and the lowest price you will accept. Your item will be listed and potential buyers learn what you're offering by rummaging through the virtual auction shelves using categories or key words. The lists of items for sale include current highest bid and number of bidders, and they are sorted by auction closing date and time. Those that are very close to completion are right at the top, highlighted in red, presumably to attract attention and build suspense in the final moments. In addition to the individual buyers and sellers who participate, eBay's online community includes a number of small business owners who offer the same products they have for sale in their local retail shop. In fact, this new age global distribution channel has saved some struggling entrepreneurs from bankruptcy.

Novelist William Gibson, who is credited with inventing the term *cyberspace,* avoided the net for many years and didn't even have an email address. But he was finally bitten by the eBay bug until it turned into an obsession. Gibson collects antique timepieces, and he found the online auction an exhilarating way to hunt for treasures. Describing his excitement, he writes:

> *What if someone else got this watch, this watch I'd never seen but which I now, somehow, was emotionally invested in winning? I began to have some sense of the power of the psychology of auctions, something I hadn't really experienced before.*[148]

The power he describes is amplified considerably because the auction is on the Internet, open 24 hours a day, to anyone with a computer, modem, and Web access. Gibson realized his involvement with eBay was getting out of control and decided to kick his habit with a "binge cure" to get it out of his system. He immersed himself in hunts for serious collectors' items for several months, and eventually became far more selective about his use of the online service.

THE INTERNET'S ADDICTIVE PROPERTIES

Some psychological spaces of the Internet may be so attractive, so absorbing, that they may lead people into very heavy use, even compulsive overuse. In the mid-1990s, the notion that people could become "addicted" to the Internet was often greeted with howling laughter, but as more and more cases came to light through anecdotes and surveys, and people began seeking out professional help, many started to wonder. Amidst the rush to connect homes, schools, libraries, and businesses, some fainter voices were describing behavioral problems that were emerging behind the scenes. As usual, anything that has to do with the Internet and our relationship to it can get blown way out of proportion, and the business of Internet "addiction" has been the subject of some intense debates and hyperbole.

Nevertheless, underlying the sensationalized accounts are people who are having trouble because they spend far too much time online and

---

[148] Gibson, W. (1999). My obsession. *Wired.* January, 104ff.

can't seem to log off. As we will see, certain features of some Internet locales can cause that behavioral pattern to flourish. Kimberly Young of the University of Pittsburgh at Bradford conducted an early study on the phenomenon, approaching it as though it shared characteristics with pathological gambling.[149] She modified a questionnaire often used to assess a person's level of compulsive gambling in an effort to separate people who could be considered dependent on the Internet from those who were not dependent. The screening instrument included these questions; anyone who answered yes to five or more was categorized as "dependent."

- *Do you feel preoccupied with the Internet (think about previous online activity or anticipate next online session)?*
- *Do you feel the need to use the Internet with increasing amounts of time in order to achieve satisfaction?*
- *Have you repeatedly made unsuccessful efforts to control, cut back, or stop Internet use?*
- *Do you feel restless, moody, depressed, or irritable when attempting to cut down or stop Internet use?*
- *Do you stay online longer than originally intended?*
- *Have you jeopardized or risked the loss of a significant relationship, job, educational or career opportunity because of the Internet?*
- *Have you lied to family members, therapists, or others to conceal the extent of involvement with the Internet?*
- *Do you use the Internet as a way of escaping from problems or relieving a dysphoric mood (e.g., feelings of helplessness, guilt, anxiety, depression)?*

Young solicited respondents through newspaper advertisements, flyers on college campuses, postings on electronic support groups dedicated to Internet addiction, and other means, and conducted the survey either by telephone or via the Web. Out of about 600 responses, almost two thirds met the criterion for "dependent." On the surface, this sounds staggeringly high, but if you consider the sample, it is not so surprising. The way she advertised the survey targeted people who were concerned about the subject for one reason or another, probably because they or someone close to them was experiencing the problem.

---

[149] Young, K. S. (1996). *Internet addiction: The emergence of a new clinical disorder.* Paper presented at the 104th annual meeting of the American Psychological Association, Toronto, Canada, August 15, 1996.

Demographically, the dependent group who chose to respond to her survey was not exactly what you would expect if your stereotype of the heavy Internet user is the disheveled male student in his late teens or early twenties. More than 60% of them were women whose average age was in the 40s. Breaking it down differently, 42% fell into the "no employment" category, indicating homemaker, disabled, retired, or student as their vocation. Another 39% were in white collar, nontechnical jobs, while only 8% said they were working in high-tech positions. The nondependents, however, were mainly male, and the average age of this group was mid- to late twenties. As usual, any survey like this has problems, and they aren't all in sampling. For example, the fact that so many women were classified as dependents could be because women, in general, are more willing to seek assistance for various kinds of psychological problems and they also self-disclose more readily. The finding that they made up such a large percentage of this dependent sample may reflect their greater willingness to respond to it in the first place, admit they have a problem, and seek help.

The dependent group said they spent, on average, 38.5 hours per week on the Internet engaged in activities that were not academic or employment-related. This is nearly eight times the average of 4.9 hours per week that the nondependents reported, and it constitutes quite a large slice of time for those people – almost equivalent to a full-time job. In the HomeNet study, participants spent an average of 2.43 hours per week online, which is somewhat less than the so-called nondependents.

Other surveys have delved into Internet overuse, with conflicting results about its prevalence. Victor Brenner of Marquette University, for example, put a survey online that asked many questions about Internet usage habits.[150] Of the 185 responses, 30% reported that they were unable to cut back on their Internet use time. More than half said that others in their life told them they were spending too much time online. These figures are lower than Young's whopping two-thirds majority, but sampling problems plagued this survey, as well. Brenner mentions that a number of curious reporters and researchers stopped in to take his survey, and their responses may have contaminated his results.

---

[150] Brenner, V. (1996). An initial report on the online assessment of Internet addiction: The first 30 days of the Internet usage. Marquette University Counseling Center and SUNY-Buffalo. Available: http://www.ccsnet.com/prep/pap/pap8b/638b012p.txt [1997, December 10]. V. Brenner (1997). *The results of an on-line survey for the first thirty days.* Paper presented at the 105th annual meeting of the American Psychological Association, August 18, 1997.

An online survey answered mostly by Europeans, especially people from Switzerland, found the respondents reported a much lower incidence of Internet overuse. Only about 10% indicated that they considered themselves "addicted to or dependent" on the Internet. This group of 450 respondents had demographics that, compared to Young's sample, were closer to the usual demographic profile one finds in many broad-based Internet surveys, at least at the time of the survey. Over half had completed college degrees, 84% were male, and the average age was 30.

Since all these studies involved volunteers who were, presumably, intrigued by the topic and chose to spend the time (!) filling out the Internet survey or talking to interviewers by phone, any conclusions about the extent of the overuse problem in the Internet user population are tentative at best. You can see why surveys, and the percentages computed from them, can be so frustrating to analyze and interpret and so misleading at times. You can get markedly different results depending on the kinds of questions you ask, how you ask them, who answers them, and how honestly your respondents report their attitudes and behavior. You also should know that definitions of terms like "dependent" or "excessive use" are very slippery in a new and unexplored area like this. It is not surprising that the surveys were coming up with some mixed results, and no one knows exactly what the surveys are measuring.

WHAT IS SO COMPELLING ABOUT THE INTERNET?

Are certain aspects of the Internet as compelling as Black Jack is to a gambler, a sale at Bloomingdale's is to a compulsive shopper, or cocaine is to a coke-head? Here we begin to wander into some unchartered research territory, but Young's study, and many of the anecdotes and case histories that reached her as a result of its publicity, suggest there are indeed some very compelling psychological spaces on the Internet. These are not the usual email exchanges that occupy much online time, nor are they time-consuming searches for information on the Web. Those are the two most common activities people pursue on the Internet, but they are not generally the ones that grab people the way slot machines mesmerize the gambler.

Young's dependent and nondependent respondents showed a startling contrast, not just in the number of hours they were online every week, but in the *way* they were using their online time. The nondependents spent 55% of their time on their email and the Web, a figure that compares reasonably well to other surveys of how people in general are spending time online. Another 24% of their time is spent on other kinds of information gathering, such as library searches or software downloads. The dependents, on the other hand, were spending most of their time in the synchronous communication environments on the Internet, especially the chat rooms (35%) and the MUDs (28%).

Poignant stories from some chat room and MUD users illustrate how alluring these corners can be. Young describes the case of Steve, for example, a friendless, shy, and insecure college student whose life is suddenly transformed when he enters LambdaMOO and becomes the highly respected and charming player, Chameleon: "MUDs are like a religion to me, and I am a god there. I am respected by all the other MUDders. I know that I am playing against other highly intelligent people, and developing the winning strategies and getting stronger at the game gives me a great high."[151] This kind of world is hard for any humdrum reality to compete with, especially for people whose real lives are troubled by low self-esteem, boredom, lack of social support, or unsatisfactory personal relationships.

THE PSYCHOLOGY OF ADDICTION IN SYNCHRONOUS PSYCHOLOGICAL SPACES

Synchronous spaces are not the only compelling Internet environments, but they do seem to be chief culprits in excessive Internet use. What is it about them that draws out behavior that in extreme cases looks like an addiction? To get at the roots, we can look at certain processes that underlie other kinds of addictive behavior, such as compulsive gambling. A particularly relevant one in the context of the synchronous Internet environments is operant conditioning, the focus of much of B. F. Skinner's work.

The Skinner box, a familiar sight in psychology labs, came fully equipped with lever, lights, shock grids, and reward tray and has been used extensively to explore the complexities of operant conditioning. The main principle is really quite simple: we tend to repeat behavior that is rewarded. As we learn to associate responses we are making in the environment to the consequences of those responses, we will make more of those that were followed by something pleasing, and fewer of those that were not. But the details of the process suggest why those synchro-

---

[151] Young, K. S. (1998). *Caught in the net: How to recognize the signs of Internet addiction and a winning strategy for recovery* (p. 69.) New York: John Wiley.

nous Internet niches could be so alluring. For example, timing is critically important to the effectiveness of any reward. If it is delayed too long, the reward will lose much of its power and we are less likely to associate it with the response we made.

The likelihood that we will receive a reward if we repeat a particular behavior is another critical ingredient. There are several different kinds of schedules of reinforcement, as psychologists call them, and some are far more likely to maintain a high level of responding than others. An especially powerful reinforcement schedule is part of what ensures that people will continue to pull that slot machine lever, over and over. This is the variable ratio schedule in which the machine is programmed to deliver a reward after a variable number of pulls. Gamblers know those coins will eventually tumble into the tray, but they don't know how many times they must pull the lever before it happens. They are hoping it will be fewer rather than later, and it is this "not knowing" that makes people return again and again to the one-armed bandit.

A behavior we acquire through operant conditioning can also be extinguished if we don't receive rewards for doing it anymore, but sometimes the behavior can be incredibly persistent even if rewards don't appear for a very long time. With that variable ratio schedule, for example, the behavior can continue for quite some time because the individual is already accustomed to many trials without a reward.

Operant conditioning is a fundamental psychological process that influences all our behavior, not just addictive behavior, but these features of it may help explain why the synchronous Internet environments can be so seductive, much like that slot machine. The reward, however, is not the sound of clattering coins. In the social environments that attract so many people, it is more likely to be recognition and attention from unknown and potentially idealized others, all in the context of faceless and anonymous interaction in which your own persona is under your control.

When you contribute a line of text to a synchronous Internet environment, you may receive a reply within a few seconds, or you may not. The short time delay seems to combine with that variable ratio schedule to create a behavior that is very difficult to extinguish, much like "lever pressing" on a slot machine. The fact that you can make endless changes to your persona's personality, searching for ways to improve that ratio of reinforcement, may make the synchronous Internet environments even more compelling. Although some slot players become superstitious about the style they use to pull the lever because a certain type of "pull" resulted in a reward two or three times in a row, you have far more flexibility in a synchronous chat.

Similar operant conditioning processes seem to drag people into the time sink in the more game-oriented MUDs and chat rooms. Though the rewards are a bit different, the timing is the same and the variable ratio schedule is present. One example is the Trivbot chat room on IRC, where players join one of two teams and answer "trivial pursuit" type questions. The bot congratulates the player who is first to type in the correct answer, the player's team gets another point, and the player enjoys the reward of success.

On the adventure MUDs, the immediate rewards might be the adrenaline rush players feel when they knock off a formidable dragon after a variable and unpredictable number of blows. Unlike the single-user computer and video games, social interaction with other players is widely used in these environments, so social rewards also play a major role. For example, on Trivbot the teammates of a player called Skylark will cheer loudly when she gets a point: they might say "WTG, Skyyyyy!" (way to go), or they might send her a string of colorful ASCII balloons with her name emblazoned on them. A high-level wizard on an adventure MUD will be rewarded with respect, admiration, and even awe from lower-level players who are still solving the puzzles and earning skill points. The individual might rarely receive this kind of social reward in real life, but here, in the MUD, the player can be a king if he spends enough game time developing the character. The canny game developers heighten the effect by contriving the reinforcement schedules very thoughtfully, obviously aware of the psychological principles that keep people glued to their games. For example, gaining a new level is usually quite easy for new players, but it gets more and more challenging as players advance. Thus, the rewards for the new player whose behavior has not yet been strongly conditioned come more quickly. The companies also encourage players to spend a great deal of time in the game by recognizing the top scorers and featuring them in special articles. Becoming a top scorer in most of these games has less to do with skill and more to do with how much time you invest. Yet, other players often treat the top scorers with great respect and deference.

Young's survey respondents that were classified as dependent cited the online chat rooms and MUDs as their chief time sinks, but these are not the only spaces on the net in which the timing and nature of the rewards could lead to overuse. For example, the online auction is not a chat room or a MUD, but the tension that builds during the final minutes, the fast-paced bidding, and the rewards associated with winning may make it more similar to the synchronous spaces. It is not difficult to understand why it became a time sink Gibson described as an obsession, and why he felt he had to "kick the habit."

Another environment that shares many if the same features is the graphical metaworld. The number of people inhabiting these spaces is still low because they require superior computer power and usually cost extra money, but there is good reason to believe they will be right up there with chat rooms and MUDs as more people learn of them and have the resources to join. Let's look more closely at one of the most popular socially oriented metaworlds, The Palace.

LIFE AT THE PALACE

John Suler, a psychologist at Rider University, has been observing life at the Palace and has documented a growing trend toward compulsive overuse.[152] Users pay a fee to join, download the software, and then log into one of the Palace servers, each of which has slightly different themes. They don avatars of their choice, add a few props such as cigars or top hats, and then move around vividly decorated rooms to explore and chat. Overuse is widely recognized, even by the programmers who write the software and gently remind Palace denizens by rubbing it in. When a resident mentions the word *Palace* in a chat session, such as in "Where can I get the latest version of the Palace software?" the program makes an amusing substitution. Instead of displaying what the player actually typed, the output reads, "Where can I get the latest version of *this thing that is eating my life?*" Suler points out, "When the user finally figures out that the Palace program itself is making this silly little substitution of words, his confusion may turn to delight, and then, perhaps, to a self-conscious, even worrisome realization."

In these richly graphical virtual communities, part of the attraction is that – like the patrons of Cheers – everybody knows your persona and you will be greeted warmly. If you are pleased with the way you have managed your self-presentation as you gained a reputation in one of the worlds, the way Steve was happy with his Chameleon character, for example, you will be eager to maintain it. Building an online persona

---

[152] Suler, J. (1996). *Why is this thing eating my life? Computer and cyberspace addiction at the "Palace."* [Online]. Available: http://wwwl.rider.edu/~suler/psycyber/eatlife. html [1998, May 30]. Suler, J. (1996). *Computer and cyberspace addiction* [Online]. Available: http://wwwl.rider.edu/~suler/psycyber/cybaddict.html [1998, May 30].

takes time, imagination, and creativity. As I discussed in chapter 2 on the psychology of impression formation, you have some unique tools to accomplish this absorbing task on the Internet, and some people do a very good job. You're unencumbered by your physical appearance or other aspects of your real life, and you can change or modify your persona's appearance or personality at will. If you type fast, think quickly, and have a sense of humor that survives the transition to a chat window, you will be noticed and liked. On the Palace you can also use avatars, and of course you can choose whatever you like. An extraordinary number of people at the Palace are, like the citizens of Lake Woebegone, above average – at least in looks.

Suler insightfully points out that this often frustrating business of maintaining your virtual reputation and managing your online self-presentation can be another key ingredient in compulsive overuse:

> One of these frustrations can, paradoxically, foster addiction in some people. Because Palace feels like a new, pioneering territory with lots of potential rewards, a land rush has set in. Lots of new users are showing up. Among the increasing flood of people, if you want to develop and maintain friends ... if you want people to know your name ... you HAVE to keep coming back. The more time you spend there, the more people get to know you, the more you are considered a member who is "one of us." If you haven't signed on for a few days or longer, you may feel like you are losing ground, that you will be forgotten. You don't want those relationships you developed to fade out. So you feel compelled to go back and reestablish those ties. For many people, it is precisely those social ties that keep you coming back. Without them, the Palace would be just another video game addiction that would quickly wear off.

NEWBIE DISEASE?

Young found that dependents and nondependents in her study were quite different in terms of the length of time they had been on the net. Those categorized as dependents were mostly newbies – about 83% had been online for a year or less. The nondependents, however, were mostly veterans – only 29% had less than a year of Internet experience. The figures might suggest that people who are going to get hooked, get hooked quickly, within the first few months of their online adventures. Another interpretation, however, is that being "hooked" is a temporary phenomenon for some people, a disease from which newbies can recover. After the rush and excitement of these virtual worlds wear off a bit, and Internet users recognize that they may be spending too much time with nonproductive activities, many may just grow out of it and drop their faceless personas.

In *The Psychology of Addiction,* Mary McMurran points out that addictive behavior is not necessarily progressive and that fluctuations and movements in and out occur routinely.

There is a continuum of levels of involvement depending on the current situation and his or her skills for coping with that situation. For example, many people will drift in and out of problematic substance use consequent upon finding or losing jobs, being in a stable relationship or breaking up from their partner, and having good living accommodation, or finding themselves without a home.[153]

The same is probably true of excessive Internet use. People who find themselves "caught in the net" can shake loose, especially if they recognize the problem and take steps to address it.

An ex-Palace "addict" wrote to John Suler to explain how – and why – he quit the habit. He was affected by Suler's Web site about Palacoholics, and began to wonder if he could ever achieve self-actualization, in the sense that Maslow described it, by sitting on his rear interfacing with avatars:

I thought I'd drop you a note saying "Thank you." I've been on the Palace ever since I entered college back in September, and I found that it was slowly but surely sucking away my time and social life (small as it was). ... I had become addicted, and I had even tried to stop once or twice, but got back on after a few hours of my supposed permanent exit. ... In any case, around 2:00 AM, I transferred my registration code to a deserving guest, and asked the wiz to banish me. I made a nice little dramatic exit, and wiped that sucker clean off my hard drive. (Interestingly enough, I found that rollerblading is an adequate alternative for Palace, so whenever I get the urge to Palace, I just hit the streets instead.)

Certainly, some people who are prone to excess in other contexts and for different reasons may have great difficulty controlling overuse of the Internet, especially if they become enmeshed in the interactive chats, MUDs, and metaworlds. Ivan Goldberg, who started the mailing list called Internet Addiction Disorder, emphasizes how important it is to look at the person behind the compulsive behavior, at their reasons for

---

[153] McMurran, M. (1994). *The psychology of addiction.* London: Taylor & Francis, Ltd.

doing *anything* to such excess. He has certainly heard from a wide range of people who have joined that list and shared their experiences with one another. Clearly, the compelling corners of the Internet may not be the only place that a person can lose control of his or her life.

NAMING THE AFFLICTION: ADDICTION? OVERUSE? SELF-INDULGENCE?

In addition to the controversy about the extent of Internet overuse, a heated debate is swirling around the issue of what we should call it. Though some are using the term *Internet addiction disorder,* many scientists are alarmed by this loose use of the terms *addiction* and *disorder.* No such disorder is listed in the *Diagnostic and Statistical Manual of Mental Disorders IV* (DSM), the master document published by the American Psychiatric Association that classifies mental disturbances. Before that would happen, considerably more research would be necessary to validate its prevalence, symptoms, prognosis, and treatment. We have very little to go on now, other than anecdotes, a few surveys, and our societal concern over the impact excessive Internet use is having in some people's lives. The Internet is such a rapidly moving target that this kind of research will be difficult, to say the least.

Based on the case histories that have surfaced, no one denies that excessive involvement with certain psychological spaces on the net can have serious effects on a person's life. For example, students who begin spending extended hours in chat rooms, MUDs, and graphical meta-worlds, have little time for studying, socializing, and even sleeping. They may skip classes, pull all-nighters, and watch their grades plummet. The Internet never sleeps, of course, and there are always more dragons to fight and chat rooms to visit at three or four in the morning. At a large university in New York, the dropout rate among freshmen newcomers rose dramatically as their investment in computers and Internet access increased, and the administrators learned that 43% of the dropouts were staying up all night on the Internet. Anecdotes from people whose spouses have become hooked on the net also abound, and they are especially poignant when they involve a cyber love affair. What does someone do when they see a spouse spending hour after hour online, insisting on privacy, and becoming irritated when questioned about such activities?

Despite the alarm, many researchers find the disease label of *Internet addiction disorder* to be premature or wrong-headed. Also, concern about the way so much of what we do is pathologized by mental health professionals is very real. Perhaps in many cases it is more a matter of self-indulgence and lack of self-control, more like spending too much time gabbing at the water cooler. The loose application of the "A" or the "D" word in conjunction with the Internet may just add to the growing list of pathologies and that could have more negative than positive consequences. There are psychologically compelling areas of the Internet that can devour far too much time if we let them, and we are beginning to understand why. We now have enough anecdotes, case histories, and preliminary surveys to identify the characteristics of these psychological spaces, and also to recognize that some people may be particularly susceptible to their attraction. However, the Internet is not cocaine, alcohol, or nicotine. And people who understand why the Internet can be such a time sink may be able to get the problem under control and get back to more productive activities.

10

ALTRUISM ON THE NET

THE PSYCHOLOGY OF HELPING

Just as in real life, the news rarely carries stories of how humans behave kindly, even nobly toward one another on the Internet. While stalking, cybercrime, mass protests, or pornography rings grab the attention of journalists, the less-sensational human interest stories might be treated more as filler for the back of the magazines. Yet behind the scenes, random acts of kindness occur regularly, and people might be surprised to learn how altruistic net users can be.

RANDOM ACTS OF KINDNESS: INTERNET STYLE

Paradoxically, the net's psychological spaces seem to support and encourage high levels of altruism, when at the same time they can release higher levels of aggression. For example, the net has a long history of volunteerism, and thousands of people give their free time to staff help desks, maintain servers, offer assistance to newbies, and moderate discussion forums. Those telecommunications lines are carrying speedy replies to calls for help – right along side the seedier and meaner bit streams.

People on the net are willing to help one another in small and sometimes very large ways. Helpful replies to requests for information are extremely common, and the willingness of so many to provide assistance is one of the main reasons people participate in discussion forums. Someone sends a short message to a mailing list about boating: "Does anyone know where to get information about good sailing schools?" The replies may flood the participants' mailboxes for a week or more. There is nothing like a good question to bring out helpfulness on the Internet. If you want to break into a discussion group on which you've been lurking for a while, but have been reluctant to post anything, try asking a question. You will probably experience the exhilarating reward of a prompt and helpful reply from a total stranger.

In the Internet games, helping is also quite common. If you run out of virtual money in a blackjack game, your neighbor at the table might offer to spot you some cash through the chat window. Of course, it is much easier to loan play money than real money to a stranger, but the kindness is still appreciated and the helpful mood is infectious. On a hack and slash adventure MUD a new player might receive valuable weapons and armor from some of the veterans, and also tips about how to move up through the ranks. As I mentioned in an earlier chapter, the game's features can have a dramatic influence on how much aggressive behavior you see; they also have an influence on how much altruism the players show toward each other. If the goal of the game is to beat the other players – as it is in the Internet version of Monopoly, for example – you are not likely to see much interplayer helping. If the players are working together to defeat a common enemy, the picture changes. That superordinate goal that requires teamwork brings out more altruism.

Some of the most dramatic and meaningful examples of altruism on the Internet occur in the emotional support forums. Psychologist John Grohol wandered into the newsgroup alt.support.depression when he became seriously depressed after learning that his childhood best friend had committed suicide. The newsgroup is filled with people who are willing to listen and support one another during long bouts with depression, and their doors are open 24 hours a day, 7 days a week, 52 weeks a year. Grohol was a graduate student in psychology at the time, and the experience with his online helpers drew him deeper into the Internet support arena, a vast network of small groups whose devoted members laugh and cry together, boost each others' spirits, and share each others' ups and downs. The groups exist on the Web, in newsgroups, mailing lists, and chat rooms, and Grohol eventually became a prominent member in several of the groups that focus on psychological problems. Now he also helps people start new groups in the alt.support hierarchy when none of the existing groups quite fit.

Research on the psychology of helping – or prosocial behavior – took off in the 1960s because of the shocking case of Kitty Genovese that captured the news for many months in 1964. She was returning to her New York apartment building when an assailant attacked her with a knife. As she screamed for help, dozens of people heard her and came to their apartment windows to watch, but none assisted her. No one even called the police for over half an hour as she pleaded for help, slowly bleeding to death from stab wounds. The entire country was haunted by this tragic event and many blamed the callousness of New Yorkers. At the time, it was far easier to believe that normal people, like you and me, would have rushed to her aid and that there must have been some dreadful character flaw in all those heartless people who just watched from their windows. As the research progressed, however, it became clear that most people would probably have done exactly the same thing under the same circumstances. The environment and the situation at that apartment building contained many of the elements that reduce our willingness to offer help. It is true that some people are more altruistic than others in almost any situation, but all of us are affected by the characteristics of the situation. Under some circumstances, we will be the Good Samaritan and in others, we are less likely to assist.

On the Internet, situations that involve altruism are almost never this dramatic, of course, but the decades of research on the psychology of helping turned up some interesting features that may help us understand why people often behave kindly toward strangers on the net, perhaps more so than they would in similar real-life situations.

BY THE NUMBERS

An element of the situation that influences whether we will offer assistance to a stranger is simply the number of people around. When many people are present, the chances that any one of them will help drops dramatically. Bibb Latané and James Dabbs demonstrated this by taking hundreds of trips in an elevator. When the researcher dropped a pencil or coin, the odds that someone would retrieve it for them were much higher when there was only one or two other people compared to when the elevator was packed.[154] In other words, you are more likely to receive assistance when there are fewer people present, not more. There may be safety in numbers, but not if you need help.

One reason for this numbers effect is that in a real-life situation, many of the bystanders in a large group may not even notice that someone needs help if they don't speak up or attract attention. On that elevator, you might be standing on the other side and not see that the person dropped a pencil. On a crowded urban street, a pedestrian falling into a

---

[154] Latané, B., and Dabbs, J. M. Jr. (1975). Sex, group size and helping in three cities. *Sociometry, 38,* 180–194.

faint might be overlooked by most of the bystanders hurrying by. In fact, some research suggests that helping may be less likely to occur in cities compared to less densely populated areas simply because of this "noticing" factor. Just the noise and commotion in crowded areas may make it more difficult for anyone in distress to attract attention. One study, for example, showed how the noise from a power lawnmower could decrease the tendency to help a person with a broken arm who drops a book. The book dropper was a confederate of the researchers who on some trials was wearing a cast, and on others was not. When the noise level was low, the bystanders helped the person with the cast 80% of the time, but when the power mower was roaring, they only helped 15% of the time. This was the same rate of helping that bystanders showed when the person had no cast on.[155] Apparently, the bystanders didn't even notice the cast when their senses were bombarded by the lawn mower clamor.

Assuming a bystander does notice an event, the next step is to interpret it. You might see a person stumble and fall on a sidewalk, but your interpretation of that sight will very much affect whether you provide any assistance. If you see a whiskey bottle in the person's hand, you would interpret it one way. If you see a white cane you would draw quite a different conclusion.

Humans are highly social creatures, and another reason you have a smaller chance of receiving assistance when large numbers of bystanders are present is that people tend to rely on one another to interpret events around them. We take our cues about the relative seriousness of any situation from the others around us. In another experiment, Bibb Latané and Judith Rodin staged an accident involving a female researcher at Columbia University to find out whether the male subjects in the next room, who were filling out questionnaires, would rush to help. The woman handed the men some forms to fill out and then departed to her office next door. After a few minutes, she pressed the play button on a tape recorder with the volume control high enough so that anyone next door would be sure to hear it. The sounds clearly signaled an emergency, just as though she had been standing on a chair to reach a high shelf and fell off, injuring her ankle. She screamed, then moaned, "Oh, my God, my foot ... I ... I ... can't move it."[156]

---

[155] Mathews, K. E., and Canon, L. K. (1975). Environmental noise level as a determinant of helping behavior. *Journal of Personality and Social Psychology, 32,* 571–577.

[156] Latané, B., and Rodin, J. (1969). A lady in distress: Inhibiting effects of friends and strangers on bystander intervention. *Journal of Experimental Social Psychology, 5,* 189–202.

When there was only one man in the next room confronted with this simulated emergency, the chances that he would rush to help were very high. Seventy percent of these men left their seats and raced to assist. But when there were two men in the next room who were strangers to one another, the chances that either of them helped her dropped dramatically – to only 40%. The men were looking to one another to interpret the seriousness of the situation and, seeing few signs of alarm in the other, decided it was not very serious.

The same kind of thing happened in another experiment in which the researchers rigged a room vent so it would start pouring out smoke on demand. When a man sitting in the room filling out questionnaires saw the smoke, the chances that he would stop what he was doing, investigate it, sniff it a bit, and then report it were about 75%. Put a couple of other men in the room with him, though, and the numbers effect pops out. As each one tries to stay cool and watches for signs of alarm in the others, the room fills up with smoke. Under these circumstances, the noxious cloud was reported far less frequently. Taking their cues from one another, they built a shared illusion that nothing was amiss even when the smoke started to make them rub their eyes, cough, and choke. These groups of men elaborated on their interpretation by offering what they thought might be plausible explanations to one another. "Chemistry lab in the building," said one. "Truth gas," said another. No one suggested that it might be a fire.[157]

LET SOMEONE ELSE TAKE CARE OF IT

The sheer number of bystanders also affects the chance that a person in need will receive help because as group size increases, each individual feels less responsibility for offering to assist. Even if you notice the event, and interpret it as a possible call for aid, you still might ignore it because you figure someone else will step in to take care of the problem. Of course, everyone will be thinking about the same thing so no one acts.

John Darley and Bibb Latané demonstrated this by manipulating the assumptions people were making about the presence of others during a simulated emergency. They invited students to participate in a group discussion on problems of urban life in which each person would sit alone in a separate cubicle, talking to the others over an intercom system,

---

[157] Latané, B., and Darley, J. (1970). *The unresponsive bystander: Why doesn't he help?* New York: Appleton-Century-Crofts.

rather than in a face-to-face group. In fact, there was only one real subject in each "group," and one confederate who, unbeknownst to the subject, would soon have an emergency in his cubicle. Each subject was led to believe different things about the size of the group. Some thought it was just the two of them. Others were told there were three people in the group, and still others thought they were in a group of six. They couldn't see the others, of course, but this was how Darley and Latané planted a sense of group size in their heads without letting them see one another.

During the early part of the discussion the confederate casually mentioned over the intercom that he had epilepsy and city life seemed to be making him more prone to seizures. This set the stage for the sounds that came later: choking, gasping, crying, and then ... total silence. When that critical moment came, guess which subjects were most likely to run to assist? Every single one of the people who thought they were the only one around to render aid came to the rescue. But that willingness to assist faded when the subjects thought someone else was around, and more than a third just ignored the incident when they thought there were several others who could take care of it.[158]

The subjects who failed to help were not misinterpreting the seriousness of the event because they were taking misleading cues from others. There were no cues to take, no facial expressions to see. Instead, the number effect was due to the way responsibility for action gets spread a little thin when more people are around. Just as people feel less personally responsible for destructive acts when they are in a large group, they also feel less responsible to help another person. It seems we are almost calculating the amount of responsibility and dividing it by the number of people present.

NUMBERS ON THE NET

The Internet is a big place with millions of users. That global village is jam-packed now, and you might conclude that any call for assistance would be completely lost in the numbers phenomenon I just described. Yet pleas for help are often not ignored because the "number of people present" plays out rather differently depending on where you are on the net. In some psychological spaces, crowd size is relatively easy to guess.

[158] Darley, J., and Latané, B. (1968). Bystander intervention in emergencies: Diffusion of responsibility. *Journal of Personality and Social Psychology, 8,* 377–383.

In others, it is not obvious at all, and you may wildly misjudge that number. Like those subjects sitting in the isolated cubicles who thought they were in groups of different sizes, we can hear calls for help but we can also be misled about how many others are hearing it.

On one end of the spectrum is the simple email with the distribution list in the header. You may not know whether the sender also included a few people in the "blind carbon copy" line, but at least you can see the email addresses of everyone else. Once we start entering other Internet niches, however, judgments about group size can get a little fuzzy. The synchronous chat rooms, for example, provide a clear impression of how many others are in the "room" with you because you can see all the nicknames in a little window. However, some of those nicknames might not be real people sitting at their keyboards at all. They might be bots – those computer programs that perform a variety of tasks on the net, one of which is to assume the guise of actual participants. Their nicknames appear on the list just like actual people. Simple ones might just sit in the room and respond to requests for help files or channel rules. More complicated ones might serve coffee, hurl insults at the real participants, or make philosophical comments at opportune moments.

Group size is also elusive in the chat rooms because you have no idea who is actually attending to the action. Some might be afk (away from keyboard) and others might have joined several chat rooms simultaneously, trying to split their attention among them. Quite a few are probably in private chats with a friend or two who are also on the Internet but who may or may not be in the same room. Because of the lag, it is not at all uncommon for people to successfully divide their time between several synchronous conversations at once. At some point, of course, they enter that eerie state when they overextend their attention span and typing speed, and their fellow chatters may notice. In a face-to-face setting, you could just glance around the room to see who is reading, sleeping, or whispering to their neighbors but in the chat rooms you can't.

On MUDs you can usually find out how many people are in the virtual space with you using a "look" command. On Lambda, for example, when you "look" you see a description of the room you're in and the names of the characters, sorted by gender. On the graphical metaworlds, you can actually see the avatars of the characters on your screen so you know about how many people are "present," though some worlds allow players to travel around as invisible ghosts. As in the chat rooms, the metaworlds also have bots that look and act like regular players, and occasionally it isn't easy to tell the difference. These NPCs (nonplayer characters) wander the towns and badlands, operating the pawnshops, arresting villains, and serving vittles to tavern patrons. One especially annoying one hangs out in the Kesmai town square begging for money to buy ale. Any real player who mistakes him for a live participant and generously tosses a coin is publicly insulted as a cheapskate.

The asynchronous communication environments, such as mailing lists, newsgroups, and Web discussion forums, leave much to the imagination with respect to the number of people "present," so misperceptions are even more likely. On mailing lists, for example, you can usually find out how many people are subscribed by sending a command to the listserver software, but many people don't do this because they aren't aware of the feature. Over time, you will get some impression of the size of the group from the number of different people who submit messages, but mailing lists generally have a large and silent lurker contingent. As I mentioned in another chapter, they may just be deleting the messages without reading them, or they may be quite attentive to the goings-on. You just don't know. On newsgroups, group size is also extremely hazy, especially because of the large number of crosspostings to more than one group. Again, the inferences people make about the number of people present are likely to be influenced by the number of people who post frequently, rather than the actual number of readers.

Moving to the Web, the numbers become more difficult to perceive. It is difficult to predict how many people will visit a Web site; placing a call for assistance there is a little like erecting a billboard on a highway, or taking out an ad in a newspaper. People may wander onto your site for other reasons and then respond to your request for help. Or you might let people know about your site through the discussion forums and encourage them to visit. A growing trend, for example, is for researchers to post their survey questionnaires on the Web, and then send messages to likely discussion forums asking people to visit the site and answer the questions as volunteer respondents.

If people see your request for help, and they are certainly more likely to see it in some Internet environments, will they come to your aid? In face-to-face situations, they don't. They first want to interpret the request, and they typically watch the other bystanders to see what they're doing. Here is another ingredient that is very different on the net, one that might make a subtle contribution to the high levels of altruism online. At least initially, you and your fellow Internet users, all sharing the same virtual space, are more like the subject in the cubicle using an intercom. You cannot rely on the reactions of the others present because you can't see them and have no idea what the others are thinking, doing, or feeling. You wouldn't see anyone roll their eyes, for example, to show that they thought the request wasn't worthy of a response. Until someone else speaks up, the reader of your request for help is unable to draw any conclusions about what others think about it.

The diffusion of responsibility could work both ways on the net because group size can be ambiguous. When you know or guess that a large number of people read a call for assistance, you will surely feel less responsibility to assist. However, on a newsgroup or mailing list you might easily underestimate the size of the actual group so you could feel somewhat more responsible than you would otherwise.

This numbers phenomenon that has such an important effect on our willingness to help in real-life situations seems to be playing its role on the net in complex ways. The actual number of people "present" is often elusive, but in most interactive settings in which people are communicating with one another, we are not standing in that giant global village with many millions of others crowding into the square. We are in small groups, and some features of the environment may make our group seem even smaller than it actually is. Also, the inability to rely on others to provide guidance leaves us free to make our own judgments, so the tendency to stay cool and engage in a shared illusion is probably weaker as well. Though the effects are subtle and complex, they may work to the advantage of the net, making helping a bit more common than it might otherwise be.

WHO HELPS WHOM?

What kind of people are most likely to provide assistance, and who is most likely to receive help when they need it? Much of the research on helping addresses this issue, and though the results are mixed, they also seem to lead to a tentative conclusion that the net, in terms of the ability of this environment to support and promote helping, can be quite effective.

First, let's consider the issue of gender. Much of the early research on this topic showed that men helped more often than women did, particularly in the kinds of situations that involved bystander intervention in an emergency. For example, men are more likely than women to help a person who falls on subway stairs, or who has a flat tire by the side of the road. Inspired by the Kitty Genovese incident, this line of research investigated many similar kinds of situations in which a bystander is offered the opportunity to render aid to a stranger in distress. Often, helping the stranger might involve some danger to the bystander. The vast majority of the research showed that men would help more often in cases like these.

Later research, however, found that women are more likely to help in other kinds of situations, especially those that require emotional assistance or nurturance.[159] It seems that the willingness to help is partly dependent on culturally established gender roles, so men tend to leap into the fray in an emergency in which physical action and superior strength are a plus, but women tend to help more when nurturing and emotional support are called for. John Dovidio, for example, did a study in a laundromat and found different helping patterns in men and women. His confederates approached customers and asked them to either help carry the laundry basket, or help fold the clothes. The male customers were more likely to volunteer their assistance to carry the basket, but the women customers helped fold more than the men did.[160] There are many subtleties to this gender phenomenon, of course, and people who do not adhere very closely to traditional gender roles – the androgynous people – behave somewhat differently. More androgynous women, for instance, are less likely to provide assistance on traditionally female helping tasks, but more likely to help in ways that men do. The gender of the person who needs help also influences whether someone will help them. Men are more likely to help women, particularly attractive ones, while women tend to help men and other women about equally. Women also ask for more help than men do.

On the Internet, gender differences in helping style seem to parallel the results from the research on real-life helping. As I described, men help more than women do in situations that involve traditional male behaviors, and though flat tires or emergencies of the Kitty Genovese kind are unlikely on the Internet, situations that call for characteristics traditionally associated with a male role are quite common. One example is technical expertise, something people on the net need in abundance. Men are more likely to provide this kind of assistance and many

[159] Otten, C. A., Penner, L. A., and Waugh, G. (1988). That's what friends are for: The determinants of psychological helping. *Journal of Social and Clinical Psychology, 7*, 34–41.

[160] Dovidio, J. F. (1993, October). Androgyny, sex roles, and helping. Paper presented at the convention of the Society of Experimental Social Psychology, Santa Barbara, CA. Cited in Schroeder, D. A., Penner, L. A., Dovidio, J. F., and Pilliavin, J. A. (1995). *The psychology of helping and altruism.* New York: McGraw-Hill.

formalize it by staffing the help channels and discussion groups in their free time. For example, judging by the nicknames and email addresses, the #dalnethelp channel on IRC is overhelmingly male. These are not paid positions – the staffers who assist IRC users with answers to questions about the network and software are volunteers. Requests for technical assistance are some of the most common kinds of help calls on the net, and most are answered by males.

The tendency for men to help women more often than they help men also shows up clearly in some Internet niches. For example, I mentioned in another chapter that male game players are often very willing to help new female characters get started, but not as willing to help the characters with male names. This pattern of altruism is what leads to that gender-swapping, as more male players log in with female names so they can get a head start.

The situations in which women may be more likely to help on the Internet are not so much found on the technical discussions or the competitive adventure games, but in the support groups in which people are sharing personal problems. A shining example was the late Glenna Tallman, who founded several online self-help support groups. As she herself was dying of AIDS, she participated in these groups very actively, sharing her own fears and experiences, and trying to help others with theirs.

PEOPLE LIKE US

People are more willing to help others they think are like themselves in terms of race, culture, attitudes, age, or other characteristics. On the Internet, where many of the demographic features of the person asking for assistance might be obscured, similarity judgments rely heavily on a convergence of attitudes and interests. People can often ascertain something about your attitudes just by the name of the Internet locale in which you meet. For example, subscribers to a mailing list on cancer know they all have something in common, just by being on the list. The newsgroup hierarchy that begins with soc.culture and includes a large number of forums sorted by country or culture, such as soc.culture.malaysia, soc.culture.tibet, also gathers people with similar interests.

As I mentioned in a previous chapter, the obscurity of some of the Internet niches allows people with very arcane interests to find one another, regardless of geographic distance. This is especially true for people who suffer from uncommon medical or psychological disorders. One example is Tourette's Syndrome, whose symptoms include excessive nervousness, hyperactivity, tics, quick reflexes, impulsiveness, and explosive cursing. Not very much is known about the disorder, and some people with mild cases are ambivalent about taking any medication for it because it slows them down. One man, for example, experienced violent tics since childhood and had difficulty holding down a job. His condition, however, actually helped him become a jazz drummer of some repute because of his wild improvisations and musical creativity. People who suffer from an unusual disorder like Tourette's, or who have relatives who do, can easily find one another on the Internet, as you can see from this short exchange between distant strangers on the alt.society. mental-health newsgroup:

```
Subject: Tourette, my child and me
From: <name>
Date: 1998/01/18
Message-ID:
<19980118235501.SAA26406@ladder01.news.aol.com>
Newsgroups: alt.society.mental-health
I live in France. My son, 11 years old has Tourette
syndrome, quite severe.
I'd like to meet someone on the net with the same
problem, and to exchange news and ideas!
Thanks a lot if you answer me.
<name>

Hi <name>:
I hope you get this message and it helps. The link leads to
a forum for people with your interest in Tourette Syndrom.
http://forums.sympatico.ca/WebX/WebX.cgi?13@^1373
8@.ee99e1a
Good Luck,
<name>
```

ASKING FOR HELP ON THE NET

Unlike a face-to-face situation, a person on the Internet who needs assistance must speak up in some way so the request will actually be noticed, just as the woman in France did on the mental health newsgroup. You can't see a fellow participant in a forum struggling with a problem like addiction, cancer, or a complicated software program, so you will not know there is any call for help unless the person says something, usually using the keyboard. Are people willing to speak up on the Internet?

Indeed they are, and often about very personal problems. You may recall from the last chapter how well the net seems to support and encourage self-disclosure and the hyperpersonal communication that can lead to strong attachments and intimacies. The same characteristics of the net make it also a great place to reveal things about yourself as you ask for help, especially in the support forums. It seems to free us to say things we might not want to say out loud to someone in the same room whose facial expressions and reactions are so close at hand.

Researchers find ample evidence for this phenomenon when they examine the way people describe their emotional and behavioral problems, either to a person, or to a computer. For example, patients at an alcohol treatment center who were interviewed by computer tended to report 30% higher levels of alcohol consumption compared to the patients interviewed in person. Patients are also more likely to reveal details about sexual problems to a computer than to a psychiatrist.[161]

Our willingness to reveal more intimate details about our problems to a nonjudgmental computer led Patricia J. Fleming to develop some early therapeutic software called *Listener*.[162] The program greets the user with a friendly, "Hello, I'm glad you could come by. What would you like to be called today?" and then gently calls the user by his or her name throughout the session. An example of a typical session with someone who chose to be called Human goes like this:

```
Human:      I feel so cut off from other people.
Software:   Have you always felt so cut off from other
people?
Human:      No.
Software:   There's more to it than that, isn't there?
Human:      Well, I sort of felt cut off from other people
            in school, too.
```

[161] Lucas, R. W., Mullins, P. J., Luna, C. B., and McInroy, D. C. (1977). Psychiatrists and a computer as interrogators of patients with alcohol-related illness: A comparison. *British Journal of Psychiatry, 131,* 160–167. Greist, J. H., and Klein, M. H. (1980). Computer programs for patients, clinicians, and researchers in psychiatry. In J. D. Didowsky, J. H. Johnson, and T. A. Williams (Eds.). *Technology in mental health care delivery systems.* Norwood, NJ: Ablex.

[162] Fleming, P. J. (1990). Software and sympathy: Therapeutic interaction with the computer. In G. Gumpert and S. L. Fish (Eds.) *Talking to strangers: Mediated therapeutic communication* (pp. 170–183). Norwood, NJ: Ablex. A software program called *Eliza* that uses a style somewhat similar to the *Listener* has been around for many years in different incarnations, and you can probably find it on the Internet, free for the downloading. *Eliza* has amused psychology students for years with its Rogerian response style and its deft changes of subject when the program can't parse your input.

```
Software:     As we were talking earlier you said that you
              sometimes don't like anybody very much. What's
              the connection?
Human:        I should try to like people more.
Software:     "Should"? sometimes it helps to think "could"
              instead of "should."
Human:        I see you have all the answers.
Software:     Human, who else besides me would you like to
              say that to?
```

Another program called Sexpert is used to provide therapy to couples with sexual dysfunctions, and the willingness of people to share intimate problems with a computer is a key ingredient in its effectiveness. This program does not try to simulate a conversation, but simply asks the couple to answer a series of multiple choice questions about their relationship, analyzes the results, and then presents feedback in a conversational manner. Empirical studies show that couples find Sexpert better than other sources of self-help, such as books or videos, but they rate time with a live therapist the highest.[163]

We are willing to talk more openly with a computer, but are we also willing to reveal intimate details to strangers online, knowing that other people are on the other side of the screen? Again, it appears that many people are. Laurel Hillerstein studied an electronic advice column called "Ask Aunt Dee," in place at a U.S. university, and found that the immensely popular service contained a surprising amount of self-disclosure.[164] Many of the problems people took to Aunt Dee involved relationships, and intimate details were not uncommon. One key ingredient appears to be the same thing that facilitates self-disclosure in radio talk shows and newspaper advice columns: anonymity.

Though the practice is controversial and still evolving, psychologists and other mental health providers have begun offering counseling via the Internet – through email, scheduled online chats, and other methods. For example, people can send in a question and receive a paragraph or two response from a mental health practitioner within a day or two. Some of these free or fee-based services are new and others are extensions of existing practices that now include an online delivery compo-

---

[163] Binik, Y. M., Cantor, J., Ochs, E., and Meana, M. (1997). From the couch to the keyboard; Psychotherapy in cyberspace. In S. Kiesler (Ed.), *Culture of the Internet* (pp. 71–100). Mahwah, NJ: Lawrence Erlbaum Associates, Publishers.
[164] Hellerstein, L. (1990). Electronic advice columns: Humanizing the machine. In G. Gumpert and S. L. Fish (Eds.). *Talking to strangers: mediated therapeutic communication* (pp. 112–127). Norwood, NJ: Ablex Publishing Corporation.

nent. For example, the free UK-based suicide prevention hotline called The Samaritans has been around since the 1940s. It began helping people via the Internet in the mid-1990s. One advantage to such services is that people will have access to a far greater range of specialties because physical distance is not an issue. The heightened tendency to self-disclose online may also be beneficial in this context. Nevertheless, much research is needed to assess the effectiveness of these services, develop guidelines, and find ways to protect consumers from online scams.

THE INTERNET'S SUPPORT NETWORKS

You need only visit one of the many support-oriented newsgroups to see how often people will share even very serious and stressful problems with an unknown and unseen audience, reaching out for caring and comfort. One man on the Usenet newsgroup alt.support.cancer, for example, shared his anguish about a woman who rejected him:

What she said hurt me very much. She asked questions like "Is it contagious?", "Don't all cancer's reocurr?", "You can't have children if you have cancer can you?" and "I don't want my children to have cancer." I was upset. I know that partners have to go through some grieving but I could tell by her questions that this was a major concern for her. Soon after that the relationship ended. She wanted to be "just friends" What hurt me so much is that she made the decision solely on one thing. My health history.[165]

Several replies followed, including this one:

How lucky for you that this woman is no longer in your life. You said she was intelligent, but any intelligent person knows that cancer is not contagious and often does not recur.
You will find the right woman, but it will help if you have the confidence that you have so many good qualities to offer – you will shine! Someone will grab you up – you'll see![166]

It is difficult to tell how much people are really helped by these groups, but testimonials from their members abound. Just being able to find someone with similar problems may be an important factor, especially if the problem is an obscure one. Yitzchak M. Binik and colleagues

---

[165] From a post to alt.support.cancer, *Relationships and cancer*, 5/7/98.
[166] From a post to alt.support.cancer, *Relationships and cancer*, 5/22/98.

at McGill University, the developers of Sexpert, suggest that there is much reason to believe people can be helped just by the mere act of writing out their problems and posting them to such a group.[167] We know, for example, that people who write diaries describing traumatic events in their lives show lower levels of stress and anxiety, and also better physical health. The exercise seems to help people work through their own thoughts and perhaps bring them to put troubling experiences behind them.

SUPPORT FOR STIGMATIZED GROUPS

The Internet plays a very special role for people who need support from caring others because they suffer from an affliction or identity that society stigmatizes. The relative anonymity of the net offers people a chance to talk about their problems to others who share them, without all the complications of face-to-face relationships. If you have a problem or concern that your family or close friends might not view very favorably, it is much easier – and perhaps safer – to discuss it with participants in an Internet support group. The research suggests that people who are members of stigmatized groups are particularly attracted to and helped by their virtual groupmates.

Kristin D. Mickelson of the Harvard Medical School and University of Michigan studied both electronic and face-to-face support groups for parents of children with special needs, and found the people who sought each of those environments out were rather different.[168] The parents who turned to the online world for help reported more stress, and also believed that having a special needs child – such as a baby with Down's syndrome – was more stigmatizing. They were either not seeking or not getting much support from their real life friends and families, and they found much comfort through the Internet's support networks. Men, in particular, seem attracted to this anonymous environment. Almost half the people in the electronic groups were fathers, but almost no fathers participated in the face-to-face counterpart. Perhaps men find it easier to ask for help and break out of traditional gender roles online.

---

[167] Binik, Y. M., Cantor, J., Ochs, E., and Meana, M. (1997). From the couch to the keyboard; Psychotherapy in cyberspace. In S. Kiesler (Ed.), *Culture of the Internet* (pp. 71–100). Mahwah, NJ: Lawrence Erlbaum Associates, Publishers.
[168] Mickelson, K. D. (1997). Seeking social support: Parents in electronic support groups. In S. Kiesler (Ed.), *Culture of the Internet* (pp. 157–178). Mahwah, NJ: Lawrence Erlbaum Associates, Publishers.

The anonymous Internet environment is especially well-suited for Internet support groups involving stigmas that are easy to hide, and that could be highly embarrassing if they came to light. Examples include people with hidden drug addictions, unusual sexual preferences, or non-mainstream political beliefs. These are somewhat different from notice-able stigmas like obesity or stuttering, because people can hide them, even from close family members. Katelyn McKenna and John A. Bargh studied the activity in a variety of newsgroups that centered around these concealable stigmas, especially to learn more about how the groups might be helping their participants come to terms with their marginalized identity in real life.[169]

In their study, the newsgroups designed for people with concealable stigmas focused on discussions of drug addiction, bondage, homosexuality, and erotic spanking, while the visible stigma groups dealt with obesity, stuttering, cerebral-palsy, and baldness. Judging from the amount of active participation by each member, it seemed that the newsgroups dealing with concealable stigmas were considerably more important to the lives of their members. A plausible explanation for this is that people with concealable stigmas are far less likely to find others in real life with the same stigma to talk with, especially if they have not "come out" about their problem. On the Internet, however, they can quite easily find others like themselves and their virtual groupmates may be the only ones with whom they *can* talk.

McKenna and Bargh surveyed many of the participants in these groups and discovered another intriguing way in which the groups were benefiting the people with concealable stigmas. As a direct result of their newsgroup participation, their feelings of self-acceptance grew and many of them eventually chose to "come out" about their secret identity to their families and friends. It seemed that the opportunity to find others like themselves, share their concerns, and discuss their fears, helped these people come to terms with their identity rather than hide it.

HOW MAY I HELP YOU?

John Grohol, who I mentioned at the beginning of this chapter, set up Psych Central on the Web to help people find the right Internet place to

---

[169] McKenna, K. Y. A., and Bargh, J. A. (1998). Coming out in the age of the Internet: Identity "demarginalization" through virtual group participation. *Journal of Personality and Social Psychology, 75(3),* 681–694.

ask for assistance about different psychological issues. He is far from the only one who created a Web presence for altruistic reasons. Quite a number use the free disk space that comes with their Internet accounts to provide some service to others, not just show off their dog's pictures and their unpublished poems. Some of them spend hundreds of hours creating an Internet spot they hope will help someone out there. Jeff Hartung, for example, brought up the Adoptee's Mailing List Home Page in his personal account to provide reams of information to people who want to search for their biological parents. Noodles constructed the Panic-Anxiety Page to point people with panic and anxiety disorders to useful resources.

Psychologists debate over whether altruism is primarily selfish behavior in which the helper obtains rewards for helping, in the form of higher self-esteem, praise from others, a warm glow inside, or simply relief from the distress they feel as they watch someone else suffer. Some argue that truly empathic altruism really exists, although it may not be the main reason why people help one another. We know a great deal about why people behave very altruistically in some settings and much less so in others and, fortunately for all of us, the net seems to provide a context for human interaction that sometimes pushes us toward more helpfulness.

11

GENDER ISSUES ON THE NET

On the Internet, people want to know whether you're male or female. Gender has not vaporized in cyberspace, and problems related to gender roles and conflicts have, in some ways, been exacerbated as we migrated to the online environment in large numbers. Unlike skin color, age, or other visual features that trigger stereotypes, gender is often apparent on the Internet because of the person's signature, nickname, or use of pronouns. It is true that you could take measures to conceal gender as you participate in discussion forums or create a Web site, but the effort becomes awkward after a while and many people are rather uncomfortable dealing with someone whose gender is unknown. They can be unnerved if they think you are deliberately veiling or lying about your gender.

I have touched on some gender issues in previous chapters as they related to impression formation, aggression, helping, and other aspects of the psychology of the Internet. To understand why gender is relevant to our online behavior, and why this environment appears to magnify certain conflicts, we first need to look closely at the stereotypes people often hold about men and women, particularly where they come from and how they affect our behavior in real life.

MALE AND FEMALE: NOT OPPOSITE SEXES

Calling men and women "opposite" sexes has probably biased our thinking about gender roles. The truth is that there are far more similarities than differences, and even when statistical differences are found on some measure the variation *within* each group is almost always extremely high. If, for example, a study finds that the mean score for men on a test designed to measure spatial abilities comes out higher than the mean score for women, the finding is often reported with the headline, "Research confirms that men have better spatial abilities than women." The underlying data would have shown considerable overlap, with many women outscoring men, but that is not the way it appears in the press. We like things simple, and it is just easier to slap labels on people than to struggle with the complexity underlying any kind of human behavior.

Consider, for example, a multinational study by John Williams and Deborah Best.[170] They described two different people to their subjects around the world. The first is adventurous, coarse, dominant, forceful, independent, and strong, while the second is affectionate, dependent, dreamy, emotional, submissive, and weak. In country after country, the subjects came to the same conclusion: the first one is a man and the second one is a woman. The adjectives we tend to associate with each gender seem quite opposite, even though the reality underlying them is far more complicated.

Research on behavioral differences between demographic groups is often controversial because results are so easily misreported, misinterpreted, and potentially misused. They are also quite slippery, and differences that appear in one study can easily vanish in the next. Yet, news stories about differences in achievement test scores, personality measures, brain functioning, or whatever can be blown out of proportion and used to perpetuate stereotypes and discrimination, especially when the details are lost in the fine print. But politics and oversimplifications aside, researchers have certainly found differences between men and women on a variety of behaviors. Sometimes these are negligible and never appear again in later studies. Sometimes they are larger and more stable, though there is always that overlap.

Some of the differences match the stereotypes, while others counteract them. On personality tests, for example, men – especially young men – often do, on average, come out higher on aggressiveness, competitiveness, dominance, and task orientation. Women tend to show more orientation toward connectedness and relationships, more empathy, and more sensitivity to the emotions and feelings of others. Judith Hall, for example, reviewed a large body of research on the way people interpret nonverbal cues that provide information about a person's emotional

---

[170] Williams, J. E., and Best, D. L. (1990). *Measuring sex stereotypes: A multination study*. Newbury Park, CA: Sage.

state.[171] She found that women tend to be better at deciphering these cues; they can "read" the unspoken emotional message better than men can. When they watch a short silent film showing the face of a woman who is clearly upset, for example, on the average they have less difficulty, compared to men, judging whether the person is criticizing someone or discussing a painful divorce. Women's emotional antennae seem to be a bit more sensitive in social settings.

GENDER AND LANGUAGE

You can't see people's faces on the net, so women are not able to use that particular ability. What you can see is their words, so the relationship between language use and gender is more important.[172] People use words differently for many reasons, and each of us can quickly adapt our style of speaking – those registers I described in the first chapter – to the social context and the audience. To a friend, I might say, "How about lunch tomorrow?" To a professional colleague, I might say instead, "Are you available for a lunch meeting tomorrow?" thereby embedding a hint that I would like to discuss professional issues. To my daughter, "Let's grab some Chinese food," would be appropriate. Though the context is probably the main ingredient that determines the kind of language all of us use, gender may play some role. The research is not consistent, but a few small differences seem to reappear in many of the studies.

For example, in some contexts men generally talk longer than women do, and women tend to use more verbal fillers – relatively meaningless words or phrases to fill a silence, such as *you know*. Women tend to use more intensifiers, as well, with words such as *so, awfully, quite,* or *really*. Hedges and qualifiers that soften the statement in some way are also somewhat more common in women's speech. Phrases like, "It seems to me that..." or, "Perhaps it is..." are more reluctant and less definitive compared to, "It is the case that..." or, "Obviously..."[173]

Women ask more questions in conversation and show more agreement with the partner than men generally do. Women also tend to use

---

[171] Hall, J. A. (1984). *Nonverbal sex differences: Communication accuracy and expressive style*. Baltimore: Johns Hopkins University Press (pp. 198–200).

[172] This controversial research area mushroomed after the 1975 publication of R. Lakoff (1975). *Language and woman's place*. New York: Harper and Row.

[173] In some cases, these sex-differentiated softeners are built into the grammatical structures of the language itself. Japanese, for example, has certain forms that are only used by women. The particle *wa* appears at the end of some sentences used by women, and its role is formally called a softener.

more justifiers in their speech, in which they make a statement and then follow it up with a reason. Compare "We should do it this way," to "We should do it this way because I think it is the fairest approach." The overall impression from these differences is that in some circumstances women may be using speech in more submissive and hesitant ways, and also in styles that emphasize the relational aspects of the social environment rather than a task-oriented approach.

A study that involved face-to-face conversations between same-sex or mixed-sex pairs illustrates both that there appear to be slight differences in speech patterns, but also that people adapt, depending on who they are talking to.[174] Each of the conversational pairs were given five minutes to discuss a burning issue about their university's financial crisis, while their conversations were videotaped. The tapes were transcribed and coded for various speech events, and the data were analyzed according to the genders of the subject and the conversational partner.

Regardless of who they were talking with, the women used more justifiers and intensifiers than the men, and they also expressed more agreement with their partners. Men used more vocalized pauses such as *ahhhh, errrr,* or *ummmm.* Interruptions and conversational overlaps showed some interesting differences, depending on whether the pairs were same or mixed-sex. An interruption was defined as simultaneous speech in which a listener speaks at a point that was not a possible completion point in the speaker's utterance, while an overlap is simultaneous speech that occurs at a point that is more likely to be a transition or ending point. Both of these were higher in the mixed-sex pairs, perhaps because the partners were somewhat more involved in the discussion.

LANGUAGE AND POWER

Differences in language use may have more to do with power than with gender. For instance, some studies have shown that women who have more power adopt more "male-like" speech patterns. Joseph Scudder and Patricia Andrews manipulated the power equation between pairs of people artificially through a rigged scenario in which one person tries to sell a car to the other.[175] The seller always had a backup position – an

---

[174] Turner, L. H., Dindia, K., and Pearson, J. C. (1995). An investigation of female/male verbal behaviors in same-sex and mixed-sex conversations. *Communication Reports, 8,* 86–96.

[175] Scudder, J. N., and Andrews, P. H. (1995). A comparison of two alternative models of powerful speech: The impact of power and gender upon the use of threats. *Communication Research Reports, 12,* 25–33.

offer from a dealer – so the seller could always refuse the buyer's offer. In different scenarios, however, the dealer's offer was higher than others. The sellers with the higher backup option would, in principle, have more power in the negotiation with the private buyer and would not need to compromise as much to make a good profit. The sellers whose dealer offered the bare minimum had far less power.

These researchers analyzed the conversations between the sellers and buyers, watching especially for the use of direct or implied threats. The use of threats is certainly a power-oriented verbal strategy; people with little power are not likely to use that technique unless they are extremely good bluffers. In a bargaining situation like this one, a threat could surface as a statement like, "Unless you improve your offer, there is no deal." A less obvious example might be, "I have a good offer for the car now." The telling feature is that the person is threatening to wield power.

Their results support the notion that the power may be more important than gender when people choose their words. Both gender and power differences affected the use of threats, but power was more important. Women who were in positions of power used threats just about as often as the men did, and men who were in low power positions used fewer threats. Gender, though, was a key element in the kind of threats the people in the higher power positions used. The men were more likely to use direct and explicit threats, while the women seemed to prefer a bit more subtlety.

This study is especially intriguing because it highlights the situation and its effects on how humans behave in different settings, regardless of gender. It is always problematic to state that x, y, and z differences exist between the sexes when all of us are so influenced by the environment in which we are behaving.

INTERACTION STYLES

Gender differences in interaction styles also have appeared in some studies. On average, women seem to place greater emphasis on the socioemotional role that words play to maintain cohesion and cooperation within a group, while men are more likely to take a task-oriented tack with their speech. For example, I mentioned earlier that women are more likely to indicate agreement than men are, while men are more task-oriented. A simple speech act of agreement, such as "Yeah, good idea," tends to build cohesiveness in a group. This remark can make women seem friendlier in group settings and more willing to engage in behavior that has less to do with their own power and prestige and more to do with the maintenance of the group as a team. The greater task orientation that men show creates a stronger "getting down to business" atmosphere.

Sarah Hutson-Comeaux and Janice Kelly demonstrated that the different styles can each lead to productive group work, but not necessarily for the same kind of work.[176] They asked same-sex groups of three to work on a task such as "identifying the personal characteristics likely to make someone a successful person." Some of the groups were told to approach the task more as a brainstorming session, and to come up with as many solutions as possible to the problem. Quantity would be the yardstick of success, not quality or consensus. Others, however, were instructed to come up with the single best solution and to prepare an essay to justify their conclusions. The two sets of instructions required the people in the groups to relate to one another in two different ways. In the brainstorming session, group members could be extremely task-oriented because there was no need for any group consensus. However, the "best-solution" approach required some group rapport and cooperation to even accomplish the task.

The groups got down to work while the researchers videotaped them. Afterward, group-member comments were categorized according to their function. For example, when someone offered a suggestion or an opinion about the task, the comment was lumped into the "active task" category. Passive task remarks were similarly task-oriented, but instead of *giving* suggestions or opinions, the participant was *asking* for them. The positive socioemotional category included statements that showed friendliness and agreement, while remarks that showed tension, unfriendliness, criticism, or disagreements were coded into the negative socioemotional category.

In all the groups, task-oriented remarks formed the lion's share of the conversation – well over half the total remarks for both men and women. The active task-oriented remarks were most common in the male groups (63% for men vs. 59% for women), while positive socioemotional remarks were slightly more common in the female groups (26% for women vs. 23% for men). Notice that although the differences are there, they are small. As I said, men and women are not exactly

---

[176] Hutson-Comeaux, S. L., and Kelly, J. R. (1996). Sex differences in interaction style and group task performance: The process-performance relationship. In R. Crandall (Ed.), *Handbook of gender research* [Special issue]. *Journal of Social Behavior and Personality, 11,* 255–275.

opposite sexes, and there is considerable commonality in the way the genders approach a group effort. We are not separate and alien species from Mars and Venus.

When the researchers compared the quality of the solutions, they found that the women did a better job on the task requiring consensus, while the men did better on the brainstorming sessions by generating more ideas. Again, the differences weren't large but they suggest that the interaction styles of men and women can affect group productivity in ways that depend on what the group is trying to do.

Jennifer Coates also examined interaction styles in same-sex groups, but in more natural settings outside the laboratory.[177] She took great care to transcribe the conversations and then used a special notation system to indicate pauses, unintelligible material, nonverbal components of speech (such as laughter or sighs), and overlaps and interruptions. These transcriptions visually highlight the "conversational floor" and how men and women use it a bit differently. For men engaged in an informal chat there is little or no overlap in their speech. Each man speaks his piece, or takes over the floor, in his turn. Among women, however, a more collaborative floor often emerges in which people speak at the same time, finish each others' sentences, or add a supportive point smack in the middle of another's remark. Men were taking turns on the floor, while it looked like the women were dancing together on it, or holding a musical jam session. One of the fallouts from these conversational styles is that the two genders might interpret overlap and interruption differently. Men might perceive it as a rude power play to grab the floor, while women could see it as a contribution to a shared narrative. I can't help but wonder whether women feel more at home in the crazy world of synchronous chat where the conversational floor is a little more like that jam session. Men may be more comfortable in the asynchronous forums where they can speak (type) their thoughts and no one interrupts.

THE LEAP TO CYBERSPACE: ARE WE TYPING IN PINK AND BLUE?

When men and women show up in cyberspace, can you tell which is which by what they say and how they say it? Some people have sug-

---

[177] Coates, J. (1997). One-at-a-time: The organization of men's talk. In S. Johnson and U. H. Meinhof (Eds.), *Language and masculinity*. Oxford, UK: Blackwell Publishers Ltd.

gested this, but given how subtle and fleeting the differences often are, I find that assertion highly unlikely. Also, we have a whole new set of registers with different social contexts, and while some of the same differences are appearing, others are not.

You might expect, for example, that women's tendency to inject a bit more emotion into their language might lead to more of those smiley faces in their online messages. Diane Witmer and Sandra Lee Katzman scoured 3,000 newsgroup posts for such graphic accents and found that women did indeed include more of them in their posts than the men did.[178] However, they were not all that widely used by anyone. Only 13.2% of the posts contained them. A shocker from the same study was that the women were sending more flames and challenges than the men. There weren't many posts from women – just 16.4% of the total – but they did contain proportionally more zingers than the ones from males.

Susan C. Herring at the University of Texas, Arlington, looked at interaction sytles on the Internet and also found a few surprises.[179] One involved the way men and women were using the Internet. Given their socioemotional orientation, one might suppose women use the net mainly to promote and maintain interpersonal relationships, while the task-oriented men use it to share information. Things are just not that simple.

To get at this issue in a more systematic way, Herring examined the structure of the posts made to two mailing lists that include both men and women, looking first at the way posters organized their messages, and second at the content. One was LINGUIST, a discussion forum for academics involved in the study of linguistics, and the other was WMST, another academic list for people interested in women's studies. Both forums have many thousands of subscribers and are quite active, but WMST is mainly women, while LINGUIST is mainly men. The LINGUIST discussion under the microscope whirled around the term *cognitive linguistics,* a controversial one to linguists, while the WMST discussion was about sex differences in the brain.

---

[178] Witmer, D. F., and Katzman, S. L. (1997, March). On-line smiles: Does gender make a difference in the use of graphic accents? *Journal of Computer-Mediated Communication* [Online], 2(4). Available: http://jcmc.mscc.huji.ac.il/vol2/issue4/witmer1.html [1998, May 20].

[179] Herring, S. C. (1996). Two variants of an electronic message schema. In S. C. Herring (Ed.), *Computer-mediated communication: Linguistic, social, and cross-cultural perspectives* (pp. 81–108). Amsterdam/Philadelphia: John Benjamins Publishing Company.

Herring first identified five sets of macrosegments that commonly appeared in the messages. Two were epistolary conventions: a salutation at the beginning (such as "To Joe:") and a signature file or other kind of formal closing at the end. Within the messages, a common macrosegment was an introduction that might serve various purposes, such as making some link to the content of a previous post. The body of the message might do different things as well: express the author's views, request or provide information, express feelings, or suggest a solution. Many messages also contained some closing remark. These were rarely formal closings, but they wound down the message and made a more casual exit with an appeal to hear others' views, an apology for long-windedness, or even a snide remark that berated the other participants.

This microscopic analysis of the message structures was intriguing, first because it demonstrated that certain elements were quite common on both lists. Obviously, norms had developed and the posters tended to ape one another. Very few, for example, included any salutation (such as Dear List Members:), and a majority began their posts by linking to some previous message. Most also included a signature file, though almost none include any kind of complimentary close or postscript.

Analyzing the frequencies of the different kinds of macrosegments in the mostly male and mostly female lists, Herring found considerable similarity. For example, the most common elements on both lists were an expression of views and information sharing. Clearly, both men and women participate on these Internet forums for similar reasons – to share information and viewpoints. Surprisingly, and belying the stereotype that men are more concerned with the exchange of information than women are, requesting and providing information were more common on WMST than on LINGUIST. In the male-dominated LINGUIST discussion, most posters were expressing opinions, not sharing hard facts. You may recall from chapter 1 that study on the electronic language register and how it resembles the public interview, or the spontaneous speech. Given the demographics at the time, most of that material probably came from men.

Another gender difference on these lists seemed to support stereotypes about the competitive, aggressive male, and the supportive, relationship-oriented female. Herring identified two different variants of the basic message that begins with a link to someone else's post and then goes on to expand it in some way. The first is the "aligned variant," in which the author is supporting the person who contributed the original point, while the second is the "opposed variant," in which the writer takes a critical and opposing stance, sometimes quite aggressively. An example of the former might open with, "I completely agree with S.T. and want to also point out that..." Contrast that with, "J.K.'s remark took me by surprise because it is so completely without data to back it." Those opposed variants would be reasonably polite on professional forums like these, but they can burn a hole in your screen on others.

In these discussions, the percentage of aligned variants was much higher on the WMST list than the LINGUIST list. More than four times as many messages began with an aligned style opening on WMST compared to LINGUIST. The appearance of opposed variants was even more telling. They were almost nonexistent on the WMST discussion, but were extremely common in LINGUIST. Since WMST posts come mainly from women and LINGUIST posts come mainly from men, the tempting conclusion is that interaction styles show quite a large gender difference on these lists. Herring nailed this down further by looking at individual posts and linking them to the gender of the sender, regardless of list. The data were very clear: the vast majority of the aligned variants came from women, while remarkably few came from men. For the opposed variant, the results were opposite.

ADAPTING TO THE MALE MAJORITY

One other result from Herring's study is especially fascinating. Women on the LINGUIST list posted more opposed variants compared to women on WMST. One possible explanation might be that women linguists are just more irascible and argumentative than women involved in women's studies programs. Another, though, and one that may be more plausible, is that women – as the minority gender on LINGUIST – are adapting their posts to the dominant male style. When they are in the majority, the dominant male style that favors the expression of views through disagreement is not particularly in evidence, and norms evolve that favor a more supportive discussion environment. I'm tempted to conclude that those pioneering female Internet users I mentioned in an earlier chapter, who were doing more flaming in the newsgroups were adapting to the male-dominated online world, and going them one better.

Herring points out also that the minority gender on WMST – the men – may also have modified their style. One male poster, for example, sent in an opposed variant to WMST, arguing that a biological basis for certain sex differences should be considered, but he was rather indirect about it and included lots of hedges such as "it seems to me" and "perhaps." Recall that these hedges are slightly more common in women's speech compared to men's.

Victor Savicki, Dawn Lingenfelter, and Merle Kelley[180] confirmed that the gender composition of online groups is significant, and it affects how we act. They analyzed 2,692 messages sent by 1,208 different people to 27 different newsgroups, looking for signs of gender differences in style, and comparing these to the proportion of women in the groups. Unlike the mailing lists, where you can obtain a list of all the subscribers and get some notion of gender ratios and size of the group, these discussion forums were wide open with no subscription needed. No doubt they had many lurkers whose gender remains unknown. The gender ratios in these groups are based only on those who actually posted a message.

First, and to the surprise of these researchers, *all* of the groups had more men than women, and almost 75% of the posts came from men. Of the remaining posts, about 13% came from women and the others were from people whose gender could not be identified. Even though women were always in the minority, the pattern of interaction styles differed depending on the size of that minority. For example, groups with a higher proportion of males contained more messages with language in which the author made opinionated statements disguised as facts, linguistically speaking. An example was, "The government is loaded with freeloaders," leaving out the "I think" at the beginning. The groups with more men also contained posts with more calls to action. Groups with a higher percentage of women had posts with more self-disclosure in them, and also more attempts at tension prevention and reduction.

As you can see, we are affected by the characteristics of the group around us, and some of the subtle gender differences we see online may diminish as the gender ratio evens out. The proportion of women online shot up from 31% to 38% between 1997 and 1998, and for the 10- to 18-year-olds, the sex ratio is even closer to even (46% to 54%).[181]

STEREOTYPES AND PERCEPTIONS

Although differences in online behavior are often small or nonexistent, our stereotypes about gender loom large. Because gender is one of those few characteristics that is usually apparent online, it may dominate the

---

[180] Savicki, V., Lingenfelter, D., and Kelley, M. (1996, December). Gender language style and group composition in Internet discussion groups. *Journal of Computer-Mediated Communication* [Online], *2*(3). Available: http://www.usc.edu/dept/annenberg/vol2/issue3/savicki.html [1998, May 30].

[181] GVU's WWW Survey Team, Graphics, Visualization, and Usability Center, Georgia Institute of Technology (1997). *GVU's 8th WWW User Survey* [Online]. Available: http://www.gvu.gatech.edu/user_surveys/ [1998, May 30].

impression more than it might in real life. Even though people can conceal it, they usually don't. In all of these studies of messages posted to the Internet, for example, there are always some people whose gender can't be deciphered from the content, but that number is rarely more than 10% or 15%, and often it is much lower.

What happens when you know very little about another person other than gender? Kimberly Matheson at McGill University conducted an ingenious study that isolated those stereotypes, making sure the behavior of the partner had nothing whatever to do with the way the subject was reacting.[182] She created a programmed negotiator for her subjects to bargain with on a series of financial contracts in which each person's objective was to acquire as much money as possible without turning the partner into an enemy. Then she led her subjects to believe the "person" at the other end of the computer-mediated bargaining table was male, female, or of unknown gender. The programmed opponent was designed to be "firm but fair" in the sense that it was reasonably tolerant when the real subject failed to make concessions, but it refused to come to agreement until equity was achieved in the deal. She gathered data about each subject's impressions of their partner before the negotiations started, and then several times during the course of the bargaining session.

Stereotypes about males and females appeared, and both men and women showed them. Women who were told their partner was female expected "her" to be fair and cooperative. In contrast, men who thought their partner was male expected less fairness and cooperation from "him." As the negotiations wore on, and even though the programmed negotiator was doing the same thing regardless of what the subject had been told about its gender, the "female" partner was still viewed as more cooperative and less exploitative by the women subjects; the men thought their "male" counterparts were tougher competitors. Another interesting finding came from the men and women who were told nothing about the gender of their negotiating partner. They tended to rate the partner the same way the subjects were rating the imaginary male partner, as though the male stereotype is the "default."

THE NEW BATTLEFIELD FOR THE WAR BETWEEN THE SEXES

Conflicts between men and women happen online, just as they do in real life, and one thing that seems to trigger them is when women break

---

[182] Matheson, K. (1991). Social cues in computer-mediated negotiations: Gender makes a difference. *Computers in Human Behavior, 7,* 137–145.

out of the stereotype. Without thinking much about it, one man participated in a discussion group using his wife's Internet account and was
astounded when he received harsh criticism from some of the men in
the group. They definitely did not like that dominant and assertive posting style from a putative female, but his wife enjoyed watching him
learn a lesson in gender stereotypes. Susan Herring and her colleagues
studied two examples of gender conflicts that occurred on professional
mailing lists, analyzing their causes and the strategies the men and
women used to debate and discuss, especially as things became tense.[183]
One discussion occurred on MBU, Megabyte University, a forum for the
discussion of computers and the teaching of English composition, and
the other occurred on LINGUIST. At the time of the study, men were in
the majority on both lists, but not overwhelmingly so.

The trouble on MBU started when one of the men posted a message
saying he intended to develop a new course on men's literature. He
planned to examine works by Robert Bly, Ernest Hemingway, and others
from the point of view of the men's movement. Other group members
obligingly sent in some ideas for readings, but one woman voiced concern about the legitimacy of the course itself, arguing that male viewpoints already dominate literature courses anyway. Eventually, the group
split along gender lines and the discussion became so contentious that
one member threatened to unsubscribe in a huff.

For LINGUIST, the conflict began when a woman described a billboard in Salt Lake City that showed a Corvette, with the caption, "If
your date's a dog, get a vet." The car dealer had received criticism about
it, but he insisted it was not sexist and *dog* could be either male or
female. The poster asked LINGUIST participants for usage examples of
the word *dog* to bolster her argument that the sign was sexist and
demeaning to women. In this discussion, too, women began participating at a much higher rate than usual and the debate split along gender
lines, just as it did on MBU.

Herring and her colleagues suggest that the men, who typically domi-
nated the discussion in these groups, employed some very subtle tactics
to regain control when the participation from women grew to unusually
high levels. The first tactic was avoidance; on MBU, none of the men

[183] Herring, S., Johnson, D. A., and DiBenedetto, T. (1995). "This discussion is going
too far!" Male resistance to female participation on the Internet. In K. Hall and
M. Bucholtz (Eds.), *Gender articulated: Language and the socially constructed self*
(pp. 67–96). New York: Routledge.

responded to the women's concerns about the men's lit course for more than two weeks. Finally, a woman remarked about this tactic:

I am fascinated that my thoughtful […] response on the
"men's lit" thread was met with silence. [M]y own
fledgling analysis of MBU discourse from last summer
suggests that there is a real pattern of male response to
males and lack of response to females in "important"
topics on MBU (Here I mean socially important.) When
threads initiated by women die from lack of response
that's silencing; when women do not respond on threads
initiated by men for reasons to do with fear (and the
fear may be fear of verbal or other reprisal, ridicule,
whatever) - that's silencing.

Another tactic involved diverting attention away from the message the women were trying to express, often by focusing on a tangential piece of the message but not its real intent. In one of her posts, a woman made an analogy between men's lit courses and King Claudius in Hamlet, and a man who responded chose to discuss how Shakespeare is taught rather than the concern the women were voicing. A woman replied:

It's like ellen and many of us are trying to make some
points about why this men's lit issue is going to the
core and eating away, and the come back is not dealing
with the issue but with the text used to make the
example; it's frustrating, are you (in general) listening
to what's being communicated?

As the conflicts in these groups heated up, the proportion of messages and words contributed by women reached far higher levels than usual. Typically, their contributions were proportionally much smaller, both in terms of number of messages and number of words. On LINGUIST, for example, the women, who comprised 36% of the subscribers, posted only 20% of the total messages, and a mere 12% of the words (because their messages were shorter). For a few days on both lists – at the height of the conflicts – these proportions shifted and women contributed slightly more than the men. This was the point at which anger surfaced and men thought the discussion was "going too far!" In MBU, men started complaining about being silenced by the women's voices, and one threatened to unsubscribe. The quantitative analysis, however, shows that men actually contributed 70% of the words overall to the discussion, suggesting that "silencing" is a subjective matter. After the discussions ended, women on both lists dropped down to their usual low contribution level.

Many of the conflicts in which the debaters split along gender lines seem to revolve around gender issues themselves, as these two discussions did. They can get surprisingly vitriolic on the Internet, even in professional groups. That group polarization phenomenon seems to operate very quickly as men move to one side of the battlefield and women the other, marching further and further apart and out to the extremes. The tendency toward more disinhibited behavior exacerbates the tension, because people may start saying things they regret later. The man who threatened to quit, for example, apologized after he cooled off. Because gender is such a salient feature of your online persona and stereotyping is so easy to do, this problem may not completely disappear when the ratio becomes more balanced unless we better understand why these conflicts occur online, and what we can do to defuse them.

WOMEN-ONLY AND MEN-ONLY GROUPS

A balanced gender ratio would be in the neighborhood of 50/50, and a skewed one would include a far smaller percentage of the minority gender. What happens in the groups in which no "tokens" are present at all? Are the online discussions and group activities of men and women very different when there are no members of the opposite sex present?

Victor Savicki and his colleagues looked at what happens when all-male, all-female, or mixed groups use email to discuss the morality of the actions of fictional characters in a weird story called "Lovers."[184] To synopsize, Portland, Oregon-based Lance is in love with Susanna, who lives on the Olympic Peninsula. An earthquake rocks the U.S. Northwest, and Lance is desperate to confirm that Susanna is alive and safe in her wilderness cabin. The roads are impassable, but Lance turns to Portia, who has an airplane, for help. Portia agrees on the condition that Lance sleep with her, but he refuses and goes to his friend Ralph to talk over the problem. Ralph doesn't want to get involved; he's watching a football game on TV. Lance decides he must get to Susanna, and sleeps with Portia to secure her help. They fly to Susanna, who decides she

---

[184] Savicki, V., Kelley, M., and Lingenfelter, D. (1996). Gender and group composition in small task groups using computer-mediated communication. *Computers in Human Behavior, 12,* 209–224.

never wants to see the unfaithful Lance again. Lance returns home, turns to his friend Pat, who becomes infuriated with Susanna's actions and sends her some poisoned hemlock tea. Susanna is hospitalized, and the curtain closes as Lance laughs at the poetic justice. After three weeks of email discussion, the groups submitted their consensus rankings of the actions of each character.

One reason the researchers used this bizarre story as the means to stimulate discussion was that previous research had used activities that were probably more appealing to men than to women. A common example is the Lost on the Moon scenario, a very task-oriented exercise in which the participants play astronaut roles. They crash in a crater and together must rank fifteen items on the basis of their importance for survival and rescue. Everyone agrees they need oxygen, of course, but group members get into interesting battles when they start ranking matches, foodstuffs, and other items. NASA has an answer to this puzzle, so researchers can score a group's submission for accuracy. Men tend to dominate discussions like this, so Savicki and his colleagues wanted to try another topic to see if women would participate more. Presumably, women would be more involved in a discussion about the intricate relationships and moral judgments, or at least our gender stereotypes would lead us to think so.

The largest differences occurred between the female-only and the male-only groups, with the mixed-sex groups usually falling in the middle somewhere. The male-only groups were least satisfied with the whole process, and the female-only groups were most satisfied. The men in the male-only groups were less likely than the women in the women-only groups to change their initial positions after group discussion, as though the conversation among men was more of a debate with unsuccessful attempts to change one another's views. Women used more individually oriented pronouns (such as I, me, or my) in their computer-mediated conversations, suggesting they were using language to express personal views and relate their own experiences as they pertained to the discussion. There was little flaming or argumentativeness, though what coarse language appeared was generally confined to the male-only groups.

On the Internet, there are innumerable male-only environments, though I know of none that actually prohibit women from joining, at least formally. They are male-only because of demographics and interests, and perhaps because their tone eventually drives women away. Groups formed specifically for women so they could discuss women's concerns are often populated mainly by men. Usenet's soc.women, for example, typically has more posts from men than women.

There are a few women-only groups that have sprung up as electronic havens, and one example is Systers. A mailing list for women in computer science and related disciplines, the forum provides that "port of call" feeling for women involved in an overwhelmingly male career. L. Jean Camp describes her experiences in it, showing how a supportive environment and that "aligned" style of interaction is so important to her:

> *Systers has given me comfort when I needed it, reminding me every day that I am not alone. The feeling is small, but constant. As Systers has filtered into my being over time, it has become a tremendous positive force in my life. ... The very strength that Systers offers can make it a sanctuary on a hostile net.*[185]

GENDER IDS IN THE GAMES

In the more lighthearted spaces on the net, people can play with gender identities in unusual and fanciful ways. MUDs, for example, often allow wide latitude in the choice of a gender, and might include many besides male and female. The choice affects the pronouns that are used as the MUD reports your actions and words. For example, a character named Bellows who chooses the "Spivak" gender would be assigned e/em rather than he/him or she/her, and someone who chose a plural gender (swarm of bees?) would be assigned they/them.

Even though MUDs allow these fantastical gender choices, not many people use them, emphasizing again how important gender is and how prominent it may be as part of our online personas. For example, GammaMOO had 8,541 characters in 1994; 21% were female, and 23% were neuter. The latter were mostly guests who had not yet learned how to set their gender, since neuter is the default. Of the remaining 56% almost all were male. Even when people try to maintain a gender-neutral or gender-deviant persona, they are usually questioned relentlessly about their true gender and often reveal it.

On some of the graphical metaworlds, latitude about fantasy genders vanished almost entirely. In WorldsAway, for example, you choose a character that must be either male or female. Admittedly, you can create a head for your character that represents an animal or inanimate object, and many people go around without heads at all – generally because they foolishly removed it and the head was stolen by bandits. But your avatar's body is decidedly male or female.

[185] Camp, L. J. (1996). We are geeks, and we are not guys: The Systers mailing list. In L. Cherny and E. R. Weise (Eds.), *Wired_Women: Gender and new realities in cyberspace* (pp. 114–125). Seattle, WA: Seal Press.

Eddie Geoghegan, an Irish player who migrated from the online chats known as CB (for citizen's band) into the graphical WorldsAway, expressed his delight that he could now use his favorite nickname, Madra Rua, despite its feminine sound, because gender is graphically displayed:

```
Madra Rua has been a citizen of Phantasus since November
1995. I came to WorldsAway from CB which I was starting
to find a somewhat hostile environment. Madra Rua is, in
fact, the Irish phrase for "Fox", literally meaning "red
haired dog". It had been my CB/handle for a while, but
without the benefit of graphics, people seemed to assume
that I was female, so I gave up on it. I was delighted to
be able to use it again when I discovered WA.[186]
```

Another graphical gaming world called Britannia lets players choose between just the two genders as well, though it also offers a nod to one other aspect of physical appearance by allowing characters to adjust their skin tone. Unfortunately, the tones vary from a muddled gray to an unnatural pink, so the attempt to accommodate diversity in skin color is more humorous than meaningful.

A HOSTILE WORLD FOR WOMEN

I have been talking mainly about the subtleties of gender interactions on the net, focusing especially on how women in relatively tame Internet environments are faring as they confront stereotypes and find ways to interact in their own styles. The Internet, however, is home to more hostile environments, and some of them make women particularly vulnerable and uncomfortable.

The MUDs, for example, are populated mainly by males, especially younger ones. The evolved culture emerges as the combined effect of the MUD programming and the MUD's demographics. I described in a previous chapter how MUDs can encourage achievers, socializers, explorers, and killers. In her research on MUDs, Lori Kendall finds that the environment can still be very enticing for women, and some make their marks as strong, independent, and savvy players. But the worlds can be discouraging to others. As happens often on the net, particularly in the less settled psychological spaces, women wind up in the category of newbie.[187] They are usually the target of more attention, and they fre-

---

[186] Eddie Geoghegan's Web World (1998). WorldsAway Page [Online]. Available: http://homepage.tinet.ie/~eddiegeo/page2.html [1998, May 20].

quently get more assistance from the male players. This trend fits well into the gender stereotype of men as the knowledgeable experts and females as the dependent newcomers.

The conversation on MUDs ranges all over the boards. Given the interests and demographics of many of the players, it is not surprising that some highly technical conversations occur, and these will omit more women than men. They can also be bawdy and overtly sexual in ways that objectify women. Kendall describes the *objoke* as one example of how a ritualized convention that might offend women arose in a MUD. Objokes are puns based on word endings such as "er" and the ending is converted to "her" for a little word play:

```
Stem4 says "Pendants are sticklers for correct spelling."
Elflock .o O (you brought 'er, you stickler)

Ronald Ann just gets her cable through the heater vent
from the apartment downstairs … no choices
henri says "HEATER VENT"
Mender says "heat 'er vent? I hardly know 'er"
```

Women also can be targets for online sexual harassment in some net environments, especially those in which anonymity and nicknames flourish, and social interaction is the main focus. Women who use nicknames that suggest the female gender might receive some unwelcome attention in the synchronous chat rooms, for example. Sometimes the harassment goes much further, as it did for Stephanie Brail, who became, as she describes it, the Poster Queen for the online harassment issue in 1993.[188] The incident began when she was participating in a Usenet group called alt.zines about homegrown, underground publications and one woman in the group requested some discussion about Riot Grrls zines. Riot Grrls is a political movement of young punk postfeminists who stress "girl power," sisterhood, pride, self-respect, and outspokenness. The movement was inspired by all-female bands such as Bikini Kill and the Breeders, and it often elicits intense reactions from males. That certainly happened on this newsgroup when men started posting vehement objections laced with obscenities. Brail was incensed at the reaction and jumped in. "I didn't

---

[187] Kendall, L. (1996). MUDder? I hardly know 'er! Adventures of a feminist MUDder. In L. Cherny and E. R. Weise (Eds.), *Wired_Women: Gender and new realities in cyberspace* (pp. 207–223). Seattle, WA: Seal Press.

[188] Brail, S. (1996). The price of admission: Harassment and free speech in the wild, wild west. In L. Cherny and E. R. Weise (Eds.), *Wired_Women: Gender and new realities in cyberspace* (pp. 141–157). Seattle, WA: Seal Press.

think I was doing anything wrong. I felt I had to speak up, largely because a few men were telling us women to sit down, shut up and go away."

The harassment began in earnest as anonymous emails began appearing in Brail's electronic mailbox. The assault escalated as reams of pornographic text were delivered, and the anonymous harasser – who called himself "Mike" – rambled on about his motives and intentions. He faked some posts to other groups to make it look as though Brail had written them, and he sent her email address to people on alt.sex.bondage so they would start contacting her. Meanwhile, Brail was having a difficult time coping:

> *I was incredibly paranoid. I made sure the doors to our bungalow were always locked; I practiced self-defense. When a male friend called us and left a prank message, I thought Mike had found our number and I panicked.*

Eventually, Mike's finesse with anonymous email messages failed him and Brail identified his true Internet address. She forwarded one of his messages to him without comment and the harassment suddenly stopped. Although shaken by the experience, Brail did not leave the net in disgust. She said, "That's when I decided I wanted to get more women on the Internet, to even things out." Soon after, she founded her own Web consulting business whose purpose is to support and promote women who strive for success.[189]

The fallout from this kind of harassment is that women are not entirely comfortable in some online environments, even in a relatively innocuous place like alt.zines. Of course, anyone can be harassed, and men, women, and children can all be either victim or victimizer, so this is certainly not exclusively a problem for women. In an environment in which contention can flare up so quickly, where it is so easy to misinterpret people's remarks, where anonymity and physical distance provide protection from counterattack, online harassment is more likely. It is also much harder to track down, given the ease with which people can veil their identities on the net.

LEGAL ASPECTS OF ONLINE HARASSMENT AND THREATS

Defining harassment and threats in legal terms is difficult enough in real-life settings, and an even greater challenge in cyberspace because of its global reach and uncertain jurisdictions. In the United States, the First

---

[189] Gornstein, L. (1998). The digital Amazon. *Utne Reader,* July–August, p. 22.

Amendment grants citizens considerable leeway about what they can say, write, or depict, but it does not protect everything. With respect to threats, federal legislation reads, "Whoever transmits in interstate or foreign commerce any communication containing any threat to kidnap any person or any threat to injure the person of another, shall be fined under this title or imprisoned not more than five years, or both." In other words, certain kinds of threats are not protected by the First Amendment. Some courts have been extremely cautious about prosecution, however. In *The People vs. B.F. Jones,* the ruling stated, "It is not the policy of the law to punish those unsuccessful threats which it is not presumed would terrify ordinary persons excessively; and there is so much opportunity for magnifying undefined menaces that probably as much mischief would be caused by letting them be prosecuted as by refraining from it."[190]

Though many anecdotal cases of online harassment and threats have been reported, few have gone all the way through the U.S. legal process so that a judicial ruling becomes part of case law. One notable exception was the explosive case of Jake Baker, who earned considerably more than his 15 minutes of fame in the Internet world. As a University of Michigan student, Baker posted a story to the newsgroup alt.sex.stories in which he graphically described the torture, rape, and murder of a woman who was identified, in the story, as a classmate of Baker's. University officials learned of it – oddly enough, through an attorney in Moscow – and they suspended Baker and began contemplating legal actions.

The U.S. government investigated Baker and found much more than just the story posted to the Usenet group. Dozens of emails had been exchanged between him and a person in Canada known as Arthur Gonda, in which the two discussed their shared interests in torture and appeared to be planning violent acts that would be carried out in real life, not just as online fantasies. Ultimately, the U.S. officials decided to base their case of harassment against Baker on the contents of the private email rather than the public Usenet posting. Attempting to show a "true threat" as it is defined in the law, government attorneys cited examples from the emails. In one message to Gonda, for instance, Baker writes:

I've been trying to think of secluded spots. but my knowledge of Ann Arbor is mostly limited to the campus. I don't want any blood in my room, though I have come upon

[190] Hodges, M. W., and Worona, S. L. (1997). The first amendment in cyberspace. *Cause/Effect* [Online]. Available: http://www.cause.org/information-resources/ir-library/html/cem9732.html [1998, May 20].

an excellent method to abduct a bitch - As I said before,
my room is right across from the girl's bathroom. Wiat
until late at night. grab her when she goes to unlock the
dorr. Knock her unconscious. and put her into one of
those portable lockers (forget the word for it). or even
a duffle bag. Then hurry her out to the car and take her
away … What do you think?[191]

The incident sparked considerable controversy at the university, and
the debate spread through the lightning-fast Internet mailing lists and
newsgroups. On one mailing list called PTISSUES, populated mainly by
faculty and students in English and rhetoric, the participants raised concerns about free speech, confusing jurisdictions, lack of due process,
women's rights, sexual harassment, and privacy. One poster thoughtfully expressed the painful ambivalence many felt about Baker's case:

Ultimately, I am willing to endorse the idea of language
as symbolic action, and think that this story probably
should constitute a very public threat to the woman named
within, but I'm not sure I want to give 100% endorsement
to state or federal organizations who may use these types
of situations to begin/continue policing the Net.[192]

The case was debated fiercely in less academic circles as well, and a
newsgroup called alt.jake-baker was even created to discuss it. Free
speech is one of those issues about which most Internet users can
become extremely adamant, but this case put a very bright spotlight on
the down side of that position. The debate became even more contentious and troubling when the news reported that Baker's original
name was not the all-American *Jake Baker,* but Al-Khabaz.

Ultimately, the District Court threw the case out and concluded that
the evidence did not constitute true threats. One judge remarked that
the language used by Baker "was only a rather savage and tasteless piece
of fiction," and the U.S. Attorney's office was admonished for pursuing
the charges in the first place. While applauding their sincerity of purpose, the briefing ends with "I am not sure that sincerity of purpose is

---

[191] *United States of America, Plaintiff, v. Jake Baker and Arthur Gonda,* Defendants (1995,
June 21). [Online]. Available: http://www.vcilp.org/chron/news/jakebake.htm
[1998, May 30].

[192] Brooke, C. (1995, Feb 5). Posting to PTISSUES [Online]. Available:
http://www.uta.edu/english/V/JBaker1.html [1998, May 20].

either synonymous with a good case under the law, or even the exercise of good judgment."[193]

We learned more from the Jake Baker case than just the way the courts would be defining "threats" as they unfold in cyberspace. The debates shed light on our own values, and our ambivalence about reprehensible online activities. Clinging passionately to our long-standing and fervent belief about the need to protect free speech around the globe, we also recognize that there are sometimes very significant costs, as they were for the Jane Doe who was the victim in Baker's stories.

THE MR.BUNGLE AFFAIR

The ambivalence and conflict threading through the debates about Jake Baker emerged in another, earlier, incident, though this case was "tried," more or less, in an Internet court, within the virtual community in which it occurred – not by any government panel or judge.[194] The case involved a MUD character named *Mr.Bungle* on LambdaMOO, and the crime was cyberrape. *Mr.Bungle*, a male-presenting clown-like character whose description was laced with obscene and repugnant epithets toward women, was in the crowded Living Room on the MUD one evening with several other players. Around 10 P.M. *Mr.Bungle* used a programmatic device called a voodoo doll to make it appear as though *legba*, one of his victims, was performing sexual acts for his pleasure in front of the others. On their computer screens, the players in the Living Room saw statements scrolling up their screens describing legba's performance, and the voodoo doll made it appear as though legba were voluntarily typing in these actions herself. *Mr.Bungle* left the room but continued his assault from another location in the Lambda mansion, using his programmatic magic trick to make it appear as though another player, *Starsinger*, was engaging in sexual activities with the others who were still in the room. Eventually a player silenced *Mr.Bungle* with another techie device: a gun with special powers that could envelop its target in a cage that could prevent the use of such voodoo dolls.

---

[193] *United States of America, Plaintiff, v. Jake Baker and Arthur Gonda,* Defendants (1995, June 21). [Online]. Available: http://www.vcilp.org/chron/news/jakebake.htm [1998, May 30].

[194] Dibbell, J. (1993). A rape in cyberspace or how an evil clown, a Haitian trickster spirit, two wizards, and a cast of dozens turned a database into a society [Online]. Available: ftp://ftp.lambda.moo.mud.org/pub/MOO/papers/VillageVoice.txt [1998, April 1]. The article originally appeared in *The Village Voice*, December 21, 1993, 36–42.

The real human beings whose onscreen characters were legba and Starsinger felt violated, and were furious and distraught. The next day legba, who in real life was a graduate student working on her doctorate, denounced Mr. Bungle publicly in the MOO social-issues mailing list, demanding retribution for his vile actions. She called for his "toading" – the MOO equivalent of a death sentence for his character.

Most players were outraged and sympathetic, and a large group gathered on the MOO to discuss what actions to take. The discussion drifted to many related topics about virtuality, freedom of speech, sexual violence, and due process. Though the group unanimously condemned *Mr.Bungle,* a substantial number were reluctant to endorse toading because of its implications for free speech and due process. The participants eventually wandered off, back to their real worlds, and no consensus was reached, no action plan endorsed. One of the wizards, however, decided to take things into his own hands and later that night permanently banished *Mr.Bungle* from the MOO database. Although most understood why he did it, they were incensed that the wizards had gone back on their word to stay out of social disputes. As I discussed in chapter 6, Pavel Curtis had just announced that the wizards were going out of the judge business. Though he changed the plan later, at the time he promised that wizards would no longer make the final judgments in player battles – that the role should be assumed by the "community" at large.

If all of this sounds surreal and weird to you, and too virtual and detached to have any real effect on these players, you are underestimating how powerful involvement in virtual communities can be. Julian Dibbell, the journalist who first documented the case in the *Village Voice* and who, as a newbie, happened to be present at the MOO gathering in which the case was discussed, writes, "Where before I'd found it hard to take virtual rape seriously, I now was finding it difficult to remember how I could ever *not* have taken it seriously."

The two victims of the Mr.Bungle affair experienced some retribution in this case, but the entire event and its aftermath left the community feeling confused and angry. The passion with which we, as Internet users, embrace free speech – even in a place like Lambda where no legal grounds exist – can sometimes put us in an awkward and uncomfortable position. The cost of our beliefs can be high. Hate groups can promote their views online and cults can recruit members. In the context of this chapter, another price we pay for our online freedom is a more hostile environment for women.

GENDER ISSUES ON THE FRONTIER

I've often heard the Internet compared to America's wild west, and I use that analogy myself. The men and a few very adventurous women went out there first – to claim the land and seek fortune and glory. There were few people, fewer laws, and almost no one to enforce them anyway. Very dangerous for the pioneers, but the adventure and rewards lured them. Women were in the minority, but as they moved west their presence brought order and conduct control, and more flowered curtains on the cabin windows. The Internet started out as a lawless and male-dominated place and even now, after the towns, cities, and shopping malls were built, some of its characteristics remind us of that frontier.

Like most analogies, this one breaks down quickly when you carry it beyond the superficial. Cyberspace is not physically dangerous and superior writing, typing, and technical skill mean more than superior strength. When you see www.pizzahut.com on a billboard you know civilization has arrived. Yet some elements of that frontier may linger a bit longer than others, and more rigid gender stereotyping is probably one of them. This applies not just to women, whose more assertive contributions to the Internet discussions can be met with anger and annoyance, but to men who are expected to play out that masculine stereotype online. A male colleague of mine confided that he would love to use more emotional expressiveness in his email and his online submissions to some forums, add a few emoticons, a <smile> here and there. But he said, "I know I sound pretty cold online, but I just can't do that. They'll think I'm a woman."

Women are entering cyberspace in vastly increasing numbers now, and as the gender ratio becomes more equal, some of the psychological phenomena I described in this chapter should certainly change. In a forum with just one or two women in it, the male participants react to them as people react to any token minority. Their views, for example, will be seen as representative of their gender, rather than those of an individual with separate experiences. For their part, women will act like token minorities often do – acutely aware that their contributions are perceived as coming from the "woman" participant, not just "a" participant. Yet some of the factors that make the Internet a place in which gender stereotypes are more persistent will not go away so easily.

NURTURING LIFE ON THE INTERNET

The net is so vast and is growing so rapidly that each person's experience with it can only be a tiny sample of the whole. This is one reason it is so enchanting: you just never know what you will find when you click the mouse and explore a new location. It may also contribute to the diversity of opinions about the net's value in our lives and to society in general. Each of us partakes of different Internet niches, and our experiences can leave us with markedly different views.

Some early net pioneers, like the astronomer turned hacker-tracker Clifford Stoll, finds little worthwhile in the Internet's virtual life. In *Silicon Snake Oil*, Stoll writes:

> It's an unreal universe, a soluble tissue of nothingness. While the Internet beckons brightly, seductively flashing an icon of knowledge-as-power, this nonplace lures us to surrender our time on earth. A poor substitute it is, this virtual reality where frustration is legion and where – in the holy names of Education and Progress – important aspects of human interactions are relentlessly devalued.[195]

Stoll's sample of Internet activity is probably larger than most, and I have some sympathy with his point – especially because certain features of the Internet have some alarming psychological effects. As I mentioned, some research suggests greater Internet use is associated with increased loneliness, and the net does take away time from other kinds of social activity. "It is a hollow world, devoid of warmth and human kindness," Stoll writes, and recommends we all stop overpromoting this network and get a life – a real one.

[195] Stoll, C. (1995). *Silicon snake oil*. New York: Anchor Books.

However, the research suggests that other features, and other Internet environments, seem to do just the opposite. Anyone in need of help who drops into one of the online support groups is likely to find an astonishing amount of warmth and human kindness from total strangers. Though we might question how "real" their compassionate feelings are, they are forming commitments and attachments that clearly mean a great deal to them, and that they might not have otherwise. Paradoxically, some aspects of the net draw out our warmth and openness and lead the shy out of their shells.

TECHNOLOGICAL DETERMINISM REVISITED

If there is worthwhile life on the net, then we are part of that life and we may be in a position to guide this technology and what happens inside of it. Yet, how much can ordinary Internet users really influence the direction of a technological juggernaut like the Internet? Historians have debated questions like this for many years in the context of technological determinism. How much do inventions, like the Internet, drive social history once they take hold? For example, Karl Marx's comment about how the hand-mill gave us the feudal lord, and the steam-mill gave us the industrial capitalist, suggests we would all still be living as serfs or nobles if those particular inventions had never happened. They did happen, of course, and the social changes that followed were very dramatic. Once technology was around that could support large-scale production in a centralized location, the economics of power and survival changed and our social structures changed with them. Our values and beliefs can also be profoundly affected by technological innovations. For example, the introduction of the machine gun during World War I shook our views about what it means to be a soldier to the core.

On the other end of the debate is the social construction position that technological innovations are more *effect* than cause. Social and cultural forces build up and set the stage for a technological breakthrough, perhaps by directing human energy and capital toward solutions for existing problems. On the TV show *Jeopardy,* a popular "answer" in search of the correct question goes something like this: "In 1895, his invention of the radio ushered in a new era of wireless communication." "Who is Guglielmo Marconi?" would earn the point, but think of all the technologies out there whose inventors we can't remember. That is partly because no single person is responsible; social forces attracted many people to think about the problem and come up with solutions. The more people who work on a technical problem, the more likely someone will "invent" a solution. Sometimes this is crystal clear, as when the conflict between the United States and the Soviet Union led to enormous outlays of money in the 1960s on the space race – and many new space-related technological advances in both countries. Sometimes the underlying social forces are not so obvious, but they may still be there, and they are clearly entwined in any widespread adoption of a new technology.

Technological innovations, however, can be both cause *and* effect of social change, and certain aspects of them may affect how they slide back and forth between the two. Economist Robert L. Heilbroner, whom I mentioned in the first chapter, suggests that there is much more determinism in the free-wheeling capitalist environment compared to the socialist one because there are no organized societal agencies to control or guide an emerging technology.

Thomas Hughes coined the term *technological momentum* to clarify why some technologies – at certain points in their life cycles – have tremendous power to drive social change:

> A technological system can be both a cause and an effect; it can shape or be shaped by society. As they grow larger and more complex, systems tend to be more shaping of a society and less shaped by it. ... The social constructivists have a key to understanding the behavior of young systems; technical determinists come into their own with the mature ones.[196]

Somewhere between the poles of technological determinism and social construction lies the Internet. Its roots were in academia and research organizations, but now it has gone well beyond those early foundations and become embedded in almost every kind of human activity. Though some concerns linger, socialistic paternalism toward Internet content and activities has been rejected by most of the Internet community who believe that governments should stay out of the content regulation business. As for its age, the net is a mixed bag, psychologically speaking. Some spaces – like email – are out of their adolescence, while others are still neonates. Overall, though, it is far from a mature technology and what seems to be a high tech Web site today may appear, a decade from now, as quaint as the black and white Ed Sullivan Show. These factors add up to a still malleable Internet, one that is not

---

[196] Hughes, T. P. (1994). Technological momentum. In M. R. Smith and L. Marx (Eds.), *Does technology drive history?* (pp. 101–114). Cambridge, MA: The MIT Press.

yet a technological armored tank, immune to social forces. In other words, the timing is good and the political environment auspicious for our own role in the Internet's development.

A PERFECT PLACE FOR CONSPIRACIES

When most writers use the term *empowerment* in connection with the Internet, they are referring to the technology's potential to spread around power. For example, Esther Dyson, one of the movers and shakers in the Electronic Frontier Foundation, writes:

> It's worth stressing that although the Net can be used for good and bad (like most powerful tools), it is asymmetrical in the way it gives power to the powerless. That is, it undermines central authorities whether they are good or bad, and it helps dispersed forces to act together, whether they are good or bad. In other words, it's a feeble tool for propaganda, but it's perfect for conspiracy.[197]

All of us Internet users are part of those "dispersed forces" and "conspiracies," and if we want to promote the good and discourage the bad we would do well to start with our own behavior. I have drawn on a considerable body of research to show the many ways in which the peculiar features of the Internet can bring out our best, our worst, our boring sides, and our most illuminating. We don't mutate into a new species when we connect to cyberspace, but the psychological factors that affect our behavior in real life play out differently online because the environments we enter are different. The more we know about these environments and their effects on all of us, the better chance we have to use our own contributions to them to shape them into something better.

I have no bulleted list of "10 ways to make the Internet a better place for human habitation" in this book. Human behavior is far too complex for such a distillation, and the range of experiences you might have as you touch down in different corners of the Internet is much too great. Yet, throughout this book you have seen research showing how we are affected by the net, and how our own behavior can have positive or negative consequences on our net companions. Certain themes are especially important for Internet users because of their empowerment potential. The first is the discussion about discussion, aka:

[197] Dyson, E. (1997). *Release 2.0: A design for living in the digital age.* New York: Broadway Books.

THE METADISCUSSION

Imagine that you subscribed to a mailing list on alternative medicine, eager to hear people's experiences with glucosamine as a treatment for backaches. You read a few unrelated messages and then send in your first contribution, mentioning a brand name, source, and price in the text, and asking the group if they've ever tried it. The next day, one participant publicly criticizes you for making such a thinly disguised sales pitch, pointing out that spam is unacceptable in this forum. Another poster humorously bemoans all the Internet newbies who never read the discussion group rules. A third sends you a private message introducing himself and telling you his own experiences with the glucosamine he took to treat arthritis. At the end of his message, he adds a postscript: "BTW, better not mention brand names in this group because it can look like free advertising. They might think you're a dealer or something."

You unwittingly violated the group norms by mentioning a brand name. The three people who reacted to the offense used distinct strategies, each with different psychological effects. The first used an aggressive ad hominem attack, one that could very easily trigger a sarcastic rebuttle from you. You would feel unjustly accused and it would be hard to resist the temptation to fight back in the public forum. If you were too shy to do that, and if this had been the only reply you received, you would probably just leave the group with a bad taste in your mouth about how mean-spirited all those Internet users are. It doesn't take many experiences like that to form a negative impression; you might conclude that yes, you found life on the net, but it seemed rather nasty, brutish and arrogant. The second person aimed a gentle jibe at *all* newcomers, but still criticized you indirectly. The psychological subtext of a message like that is to underscore and solidify the sender's status as a patient but superior Internet veteran, a strategy that boosts the sender's ego at the cost of the recipient's.

The third person answered your inquiry directly, thereby showing respect for your question and a shared interest in the subject – two very potent social rewards. He also wisely chose to remind you of the rules privately rather than publicly. Knowing how humiliating and provocative such public criticism can be, especially for a new person in a group, he avoided doing it. He assumed the best about you, that you were not a cunning dealer and that you just made a mistake, and he made a friend. With his support, you might stay in the group and just laugh together in your email backchannel about how some of those people in the alternative medicine forum have an attitude. You two might – conspiratorially – think up some appropriate herbs for them to take. A little virtual chamomile, perhaps.

A surprising amount of human interaction on the Internet consists of the metadiscussion in which people step back from the subject at hand and mull over the nature of the discussion itself. All three of those replies to your alternative medicine query contained elements of a metadiscussion because they referred to rules and conventions of the interactions – what is and what isn't appropriate for this group discussion. This happens less in real-life settings because the norms and expectations are usually more stable and better understood, but it happens frequently on the Internet.

From the standpoint of this book, it is worthwhile to spend a few moments in a "meta-metadiscussion." This may sound like psychobabble, but I simply mean that the tone and style of those metadiscussions can have an important psychological impact. The three different reproaches in that alternative medicine thread, for example, show clearly that the way people handle a metadiscussion can have dramatically different effects.

Other examples of metadiscussions come from those arguments from the WMST-L mailing lists about the men's literature course, discussed in a previous chapter. One woman remarked, "There is a real pattern of male response to males and lack of response to females." Here again, people are not talking about the subject, but about the style people are using to talk about the subject. The women were pointing out how the discussion style itself revealed discrimination.

Another common theme for metadiscussions involves judgments about what people consider off-topic. I have seen these go on for many days and some harmless posts can trigger considerable tension in the group. One example that started such a metadiscussion simply mentioned the weather in Seattle, Washington. A slightly irritated reply came back about "flooding the list with off-topic and irrelevant messages." The debate continued as another poster said, "A little friendly banter doesn't hurt anyone." The next one got more personal, referring to "the curmudgeon who thinks pressing the delete key is too strenuous an exercise."

We need to be careful about how we conduct metadiscussions on the Internet, especially when they are public and contain critical remarks, because they so often escalate into bitterness. On the positive side, metadiscussions are important to the Internet because we can use them to develop consensus on group norms. Also, since much of what happens on the net is documented, we can sometimes analyze communication patterns quantitatively to help push aside our stereotypical biases. It is an easy matter, for example, to actually count the number of replies the posts from men and women are getting, to confirm or disconfirm a perception that the men are ignoring the women, or vice versa.

On the negative side, the metadiscussion can create tensions that might lead to disharmony and group breakdown. The group polarization phenomenon will apply just as well to the metadiscussion as to the discussion. In that debate about whether it was or was not appropriate to describe Seattle's weather on the forum, people began to take one side or the other and it was many days before the group could put it aside and get back to talking about their subject. Metadiscussions are needed, but because the Internet strips away certain communication channels that can soften the hard edge of your message, they can sometimes sound as patronizing as, "Don't talk with your mouth full," or as aggressive as, "I didn't like the way you said that, buddy. Shut up and sit down."

ANONYMITY AND ACCOUNTABILITY

Weaving through those environments on the Internet and mediating their effects on us is the degree of anonymity and accountability we feel when we are in them. People can act in very uninhibited ways when they think no one can find out who they really are. In the environments that offer this, or at least offer some measure of it, people tend to let loose in both positive and negative ways.

Leaving criminals aside for a moment, why would we want anonymity online? On the positive side, we know that self-disclosure occurs more readily in anonymous environments, a feature particularly helpful for online therapy and support groups. Psychologist John Grohol, who manages the extensive Mental Health Net Web site, states this clearly in the site's policy page:

We respect the rights of anonymity online and will make no effort to verify anybody's real life identity, ever. … We believe every individual has the right to remain anonymous if he or she chooses. We will uphold that individual's right while visiting our Web community to the greatest extent technically and morally possible.[198]

[198] Grohol, J. M. (1997). Anonymity online: Mental Health Net's policies. [Online]. Mental Health Net. Available: http://www.cmhc.com/archives/editor26.htm [1997, December 1].

People might also want to remain anonymous to voice their complaints, test out bizarre ideas and identities, ask questions that might reveal their stupidity, or engage in behavior they prefer others would not know about. In the political arena, anonymity has always been a treasured commodity because governments have so much more power than individuals. We vote anonymously, for example, and people in repressive countries might find any loss of online anonymity life-threatening. A celebrity might want to use a nickname and an anonymous email address to participate in the Internet forums without causing riots. Maybe that character on the MUD with you or in one of the online support groups is actually a famous politician wearing sunglasses and a wig, Internet-style. A conference convened by the American Association for the Advancement of Science in 1997 addressed the issue of online anonymity, and the participants generally concluded that it is not inherently bad and that governments should not attempt to restrict or eliminate it. However, no one denies that online anonymity has its down side and can bring out some very troubling behavior.

On the San Francisco-based online service called the WELL, for example, one group of subscribers wanted to have an anonymous conference where identities would not be known, and the results were startling. Perhaps starting out as games, the participants began telling tales about each other, attacking one another, and eventually pretending to *be* one another in vicious ways. Strangely, attacks and counterattacks were perfectly acceptable in the nonanonymous conferences, but they were not at all acceptable when they appeared as unsigned or forged notes. Subscribers asked the management to close the conference after just 2 weeks because the behavior that it unleashed was just too destructive. WELL founding father Stewart Brand said, "trust was the casualty. It was easy to destroy; hard to rebuild."[199]

How much anonymity do people actually have when they log on? This varies in the different Internet environments, and it keeps changing as more software tools are developed to track traffic and addresses on the Internet. A banker told me he liked to submit articles to some of the wilder Usenet newsgroups when he was younger but stopped instantly when he learned that Usenet newsgroups were being archived and search engines were available to find posts by keywords. One keyword you can use is the author's email address. This means that anyone –

[199] Brand, Stewart, in an email to Esther Dyson, quoted in Dyson, E. (1997). *Release 2.0: A design for living in the digital age.* New York: Broadway Books.

including his employer or clients – might be able to read his outlandish remarks if they knew where to look. He was careful not to use his business email address at the time, but he also didn't take special precautions to keep his personal email address a secret from people he knew in real life. It was just a nickname, but many people knew about it.

Tools like the Usenet search engines push people toward the desire for more anonymity because their online words have become part of an easily searchable database, forever available to posterity. At first, the banker thought of the newsgroups as lively and heated conversations with strangers in which everyone's words would vanish as soon as the system administrators needed more disk space. Linguistically, newsgroups seem like this, but the transcripts are stored on the Internet, and anyone can search them for as long as they remain there.[200]

Ironically, much of this online anonymity is based on our trust in whatever holding organization has the information that could link a nickname with something more concrete and identifiable, such as a real email address or real name. These "organizations" might be giant Internet Service Providers, or just a few college students who run a MUD on their home PC. Sometimes they can be pushed into difficult legal and moral corners when problems arise. For example, the operator of one of the anonymous email services received an alarming fax from the Austrian federal police asking him to turn over the identity of one of the service's users who was distributing Nazi propaganda. They believed the perpetrator was living in Austria, where that activity was considered illegal, but the service resided in the United States. Lance Cotrell, the operator of the email service, replied that he would only open his books with a U.S. court order. Wary of such legal entanglements, he kept no records to turn over anyway.[201]

From a psychological perspective, online anonymity is a two-edged sword and many people are adamantly opposed to its use in any corner of the Internet. I understand the concerns, yet I also see that anonymity is the "default setting" in some of our other communication media, such as snail mail and the telephone. You don't have to sign your name or say who you are. Efforts to change that, such as through caller ID, have met

---

[200] This became a fascinating treasure hunt after the Heaven's Gate mass suicide, for example. Usenet users searched the archives for posts that seemed to be from cult members and found a few that looked like online recruitment.

[201] McCullagh, D. (1997). Anonymity at any cost. *The Netly News*. [Online]. Available: http://cgi.pathfinder.com/netly/opinion/),1042,1594,00.html [1997, November 24].

with demands to be able to block the technology if the caller chooses. Although related, anonymity is not the same as privacy, and the latter has always been one of the chief concerns of Internet users. A hypothesis is that people who answer those surveys mix the two together conceptually; they are really indicating that they want control over what others can learn about them. Sometimes they want their communications to be anonymous, for any of those reasons I mentioned earlier. And they also want information they consider confidential, such as email between two people or their personal records, to be private.

If we recognize how anonymity can affect our behavior, as we've discussed in many examples throughout this book, we have an excellent chance to ameliorate its negative effects and still take advantage of the positive aspects. We can also spot its influence when an anonymous person begins mixing with nonanonymous participants in a discussion forum. At that point, we might want to begin a thoughtful metadiscussion to explore the pros and cons of anonymity with the group, raising that critical issue of trust in online communities.

THE TRAGEDY OF THE ELECTRONIC COMMONS

Trust winds its way through another aspect of online behavior – the social dilemma called the tragedy of the commons. A social dilemma exists when the choices people make are rewarding to the individual but collectively, if everyone makes the same choices, they lead to disaster. You may have heard of the prisoner's dilemma, for example, in which two guilty crime suspects are arrested and interrogated separately by the police. Each is given the same choice: confess and rat on the partner, or deny all charges. The dilemma emerges because the outcome for each prisoner is affected by the choice of the other. If only one confesses, the confessor will get immunity and the one who tried to stand firm will get the maximum sentence. If both confess, they will get moderate sentences. If they stick together and both deny the charges, trusting one another to do the same, they will receive light sentences. Unfortunately, trust is usually in short supply in these games, and most people rat on their partner because that choice is best for the individual. Mathematically, it would have been better for both if they had a little trust, but they usually don't.

Ecologist Garrett Hardin pointed out a related social dilemma that occurs in large groups, one that is especially relevant to the psychology

[202] Hardin, G. (1968). The tragedy of the commons. *Science, 162,* 1243–1248.

of the Internet.[202] In old English towns a centrally located pasture called the *commons* was available for farmers to graze their livestock, as a kind of adjunct to their own land. If each showed restraint and used the resource sparingly, the grass replenished and the commons flourished. But if one family started to let its cows overgraze and others followed suit, the commons was destroyed. The individual family might think that a few extra days for their cows on that commons couldn't hurt and they would probably be right. The dilemma arises because all families reason the same way. The tragedy of the commons can occur to any limited resource shared by a large group of people – oceans, air quality, heating oil, or food. It also is a hazard for the Internet.

The Internet's limited bandwidth is one of those resources, and many people, equipped with flat-rate unlimited access, are making choices about its use that are individually rewarding but collectively disastrous. People are downloading or transmitting enormous files of graphics, music, videos, and software at peak times, as they themselves go out to dinner and just leave their modems humming. The illegal exchange of copyrighted music in digital format became a major bandwidth hog when software to capture music from CDs on your hard drive was distributed. Now you can just plop a CD into your CD-ROM drive, run software to convert it, and then jump into a chat channel to make trades. And the *warez* sites are loaded with cracked and pirated software that people who know where to look can download for free. The term *bloatware* applies to much modern software in terms of file sizes, and any transmission over Internet pipes can take many hours. The potential for a commons tragedy won't go away entirely as high bandwidth services become more widely available, or Internet 2 emerges. The pipes will be bigger, but the applications we want to transmit through them will also grow. There will be movies, interactive video, high-resolution graphics, and of course, bigger and bigger software programs, always pushing the envelope of the bandwidth we have to transmit them. The frustration of long waits may persist for some time, at least under flat-rate pricing models."

The Internet is vulnerable to another kind of tragedy of the commons, one that is less obvious, but psychologically even more hazardous. This one involves trust, and the individual choices people make to deceive others in the online world. I am not talking about the role plays in which everyone acknowledges that a play is going on and all are playing a part. That consensual masquerade is quite different, psychologically, from an online deception in which one party trusts and the other deceives.

You may recall the psychiatrist who pretended to be a disabled woman online and established intimate relationships with many other women who fell for his charade. Individually, people who engage in these deceptions might justify them as highly valuable for self-exploration and learning. And no doubt they often are. It can be quite instructive for people to feel firsthand how others react to them when they change their persona's gender, race, age, or any other characteristic. Yet the classic social dilemma exists because the more people make that individually rewarding choice, the more we damage the online trust that is so essential to the establishment of vital virtual communities. It does not take too many experiences as a dupe to make you forever skeptical of anyone you meet online.

TRUST AND GRASSROOTS E-COMMERCE

Even conservative analysts predict an explosion in electronic commerce over the Internet, but we still have much to learn about how to develop that critical ingredient of trust between buyers and sellers. Online shopping and ordering offer tremendous potential for many reasons, not the least of which is the ability to extend services to a global market 24 hours a day. However, even before the corporations began building elaborate Web sites with shopping carts and searchable catalogs, grassroots e-commerce between people who meet one another in forums and chat rooms was booming. While we have legal means to address problems that arise from online transactions between a corporation and a customer, we are more vulnerable to scams in these grassroots transactions. In a case in 1998, a high school student masquerading online as the 27-year old proprietor of a small CB radio business was murdered by a man he conned in one such transaction. After failing to ship the promised equipment, the student received a box in the mail that contained a bomb.[203]

The strategies that are evolving to deal with the trust issue in this context are fascinating, and so far, none of them have been completely successful. For example, the online auction house called eBay that I mentioned in a previous chapter is eager to evolve systems that will support the "self-policing" aspect of the community. To help build trust, they developed an electronic feedback database to help buyers and sellers evaluate a potential partner's integrity and reputation. Any registered

[203] Kirsner, S. (1998). Murder by Internet. *Wired,* December, 210–216ff.

user can post a positive, neutral, or negative comment about any other user and a person who is contemplating a transaction can check the files to see if other eBay users thought highly of that individual. This system is not perfect, of course, and users might flood the database with positive comments for their friends to inflate their reputations. However, the company recently tweaked the software so that negative comments must be associated with a particular transaction number, so using that kind of flooding as a means to damage someone's reputation is more difficult.

The company management clearly recognizes how important trust is to the success of this kind of grassroots, Internet-based commerce. They list "We believe that people are basically good" as the first of their community values.

ENCOURAGING CRITICAL THINKING

The enormous collection of materials on the net varies considerably in quality and accuracy, and we should use, and encourage in others, critical thinking about the nature of the sources. A few years ago, for example, educators were enthusiastically helping students get online to do research; now, many are concerned that students are submitting term papers whose bibliographies list nothing *but* Internet resources, and many of the sources they cite are questionable. Universities are rapidly revising their curricula to promote the critical thinking aspect of information literacy, not just the earlier wholesale promotion of online information searches.

Consider, for example, a person looking for material on a disorder known as agoraphobia, which is an intense fear of open spaces, perhaps to write a school paper, an article for a newspaper, or because someone close is experiencing symptoms. Using one search engine, I turned up a number of Web sites created by reputable mental health organizations that I recognized, and that I would trust to contain reliable material. However, another search engine returned many hits of private sites, often with no authors and no organizational sponsorship, but still loaded with statistics, definitions, and treatment suggestions. Many people would not know how to evaluate the quality of the information on such pages, or have enough experience and knowledge to separate the wheat from the chaff.

The race to include long lists of links to "other resources" on Web sites devoted to particular topics can compound the problem, because most of these links remain unevaluated. Webmasters eager to increase the number of visitors to their sites conduct "link campaigns" in which they find related sites, and then propose a reciprocal linking arrangement: you include a link to my site, and I'll add a link to yours. It is very easy for the unwary net surfer to be confused by the wealth of material and unable to assess the value of the information. Also, because of the nature of hyperlinks, you may not be quite sure where you are and whether the material you are reading was endorsed or filtered by some trustworthy source.

Certainly, information quality varies considerably in other media, as well, but we all have far more experience making distinctions in those contexts. For a term paper, students would generally know better than to cite the *National Enquirer* in the same way they would cite an article from a respected, peer-reviewed, academic journal. We also have some long-standing filtering mechanisms to sort out the material even before we find it. At a college library, for example, I can put some trust in the librarians who select the journals and books. On the Internet, we have few of these critical evaluation measures in place yet, so we must use more caution and critical thinking, and encourage others to do the same.

PROVIDING GUIDANCE

Many of the concerns surrounding the Internet involve children and adolescents. Within just a few years, an immensely powerful technology arose that opened up easy access to the best and the worst that humankind has to offer, and everything mediocre, amusing, or peculiar that lies between. In many families, it is the child who introduces the technology into the home, who maintains it, and who tries to explain the new developments to the parents. Also, it is often the youngsters who become the Internet adventurers, exploring new corners and novel capabilities while the parents rarely log in, or remain content with a little email and a few favorite web sites. The knowledge the children gain during their Internet explorations is transmitted quickly to one another, but few parents may tune in. The pattern is typical, even in other primates. I am reminded of some classic research on the way new knowledge spread through a troop of Japan's snow monkeys.[204] When a lower ranking individual came up with a useful innovation, such as rinsing the sand out of wheat by dropping the stalks in the water, the technique was

---

[204] Kawai, M. (1965). Newly acquired pre-cultural behavior of the natural troop of Japanese monkeys on Koshima Islet. Primates, 6, 1-30.

quickly picked up by the younger troop members. The older and more dominant members were always conservative and reluctant to try something so novel.

Our genuine belief in the Internet's educational value, and also our hope that technology can solve thorny educational problems, may have led some to ignore the Internet's multidimensional nature. It is far more than a public library on a desktop, and young people need guidance and direction when they explore-more than they need in a school library. Unfortunately, wise and technically savvy guides are in short supply because adults are not very comfortable with the technology yet either. We know we are responsible for guiding children away from trouble spots and danger zones on the net, but many may not feel particularly competent in this role.

The issue of pornography was discussed in a previous chapter and for many parents, the triple X-rated Web sites are at the top of the danger zone list. The use of filtering software and Web site rating services will certainly help parents and teachers with their roles. However, automated tools won't replace sound judgment and guidance, particularly because the Internet moves so quickly and pornography is just one type of material on the net that would be inappropriate for children. Other examples are the hate sites that vilify specific groups, the discussion forums on violence and weapons, or the hacker sites that promote illegal access. Young people differ from one another, as well, and an Internet activity that would be harmless to one might be far less so to another. This is why judgment is so critical.

Reactions to the horrifying events in Littleton, Colorado, in April, 1999, illustrate some of the ambivalence adults feel about the Internet and their role as parents and teachers in connection with this technology. Two Columbine high school seniors carrying guns and bombs murdered a dozen fellow students and a teacher during a rampage at the school, and then took their own lives. One of the shooters had built a Web site filled with messages of hate and rage, and also instructions on bomb building. A quote from one of his pages essentially informed the world of his plans: "I will rig up explosives all over a town and detonate each one of them at will after I mow down a whole [expletive] area full of you snotty ass rich [expletive] high strung god-like attitude having worthless pieces of [expletive] whores."[205]

[205] Russakoff, D., Goldstein, A., and Achenbach, J. (1999, May 2). In Littleton, neighbors ponder what went wrong. The Washington Post, Al, A30.

Immediately after the tragedy, the media carried stories that attempted to assign blame and the Internet was mentioned frequently as a root cause. As more was learned about the two students and their behavioral problems, the tendency to blame the Internet subsided. Their Internet access may have played some role; if they were visiting other hate sites, for example, they may have experienced some corroboration and support for their extreme views, as I described in the chapter on group dynamics and polarization. Nevertheless, it soon became clear that the two students had a history of problems and the Internet appeared to be an outlet for their rage rather than a cause. That instant public reaction to blame the Internet, however, points to a kind of love-hate relationship we have with this technology. We are struggling to understand it and its effects on children; whenever it appears as part of an event like this, it may take center stage.

A recent survey conducted by Joseph Turow of the Annenberg Public Policy Center at the University of Pennsylvania found evidence of these ambivalent feelings about the Internet's role in the family. In this study, 78% expressed concern about Internet dangers for children, and almost two out of three indicated that the Internet might cause their children to become isolated. Large numbers also thought the Internet might interfere with parents' ability to teach values and beliefs, or cause antisocial behavior. At the same time, however, the respondents expressed considerable optimism about the technology's value in some contexts. For example, 59% thought children without Internet access were at a disadvantage, and about three out of four thought that the Internet was useful for homework and a fascinating place for their children to explore. Intuitively, the respondents recognized that the Internet can be a force for good or ill and that its effects depend to a large extent on our own choices.[206]

As parents and teachers, adults bear the responsibility for guiding children as they explore the online world, and that points directly to the need for people to become better acquainted with what is out there, how it is evolving, what our children are doing, and what effects their experiences have on their development. We need a more balanced approach to the Internet's positives and negatives with respect to the technology's role in the family and we should not abrogate this responsibility because the technology is still awkward to work with.

---

[206] Turow, J. (1999, May 4). The Internet and the family: The view from the family, the view from the press. The Annenberg Public Policy Center of the University of Pennsylvania [Online]. Available: http://appcpenn.org/intemet/ [23 May, 1999].

REWARDS ON THE INTERNET

One of the most powerful tools we have to shape the behavior of other people is the reward, and on the net we have several to hand out. Indeed, an important feature of our empowerment is control over those sought-after rewards, but we need to understand what they are to use them wisely. A major one is simply attention. We are in an age when attention is a commodity in short supply but very great demand. The commercial vendors are not the only ones clamoring for it with their usual advertising, free giveaways, contests, and promotions. Ordinary people are hungry for a little attention from their fellow net users, too. They create home pages, politely and prominently including, "Thanks for visiting my site!" and, "Please check back often!"

They are also bringing up some of the wackiest Web sites you could imagine, and that ardent desire for attention is a key reason. There is Kevin Greggain's "Rude Things in My Fridge" site, on which he posts photos and descriptions of rancid food from his Kenmore, and then there is Matthew J. Collins's "Squashed Bug Zoo," complete with details of how the critters met their two-dimensional fates. Pope Rich, creator of "The Church of the Bunny" Web site, offers words of wisdom to other net users who might want to add something weird to the Web: "Go for it! If there's something you have to say, or something you want to do, get your sorry butt on the Web and let everyone know! You'll be amazed at the response!"[207]

Bucking the trend toward wild animations, bizarre photos, and infuriatingly long download times, Bjorn Borud of Norway created a minimalist home page in Courier type and lowercase – "like one of those Calvin Klein models." He gives more advice to others who want to attract attention:

man pointing to pointing man
some times when I visit other people's pages the only
thing I find is a collection of paths to go somewhere
else. it's like they're saying <<nothing to see here,
move along>>, and maybe they're right. maybe these people
are so boring that you'd rather not know more about them
than what direction they'd like to cart you off in.[208]

---

[207] Duderstadt, H. (1996). *The world's wackiest Web pages and the people who create them*. San Francisco: No Starch Press.

[208] Borud, B. (1998). *Link pages considered harmful* [Online]. Available: http://www.init.no/~borud/links.html [1998, Mar 10].

Attention is such a powerful reward that even negative remarks and flames can be reinforcing to people. Just like children who deliberately misbehave to get attention from parents and teachers who might otherwise ignore them, net users may find *any* reply better than *no* reply to their post, even if it is a criticism or insult. However, we can differentially use positive reinforcement and punishment to encourage the kind of online behavior we want to promote. Simply responding to a person's Web site or post in a discussion forum is a powerful reward, and praising or agreeing with it is even better. Even if you have little to add to the person's point, a simple "I agree" is very rewarding – much like the nod people use in face-to-face discussions. Those aligned variants I discussed in a previous chapter are very effective tools to mold and shape the behavior of other people. When you want to disagree or debate some point on the net a "praise–criticism–praise" sandwich can be an effective strategy. It shows respect for the other person's views, but still gets your point across.

Discouraging certain kinds of behavior on the net – such as flaming – is extraordinarily difficult but the principles of operant conditioning are probably still our best bet. If the group is reasonably cohesive, you will usually be more effective if you simply ignore flames from a single participant. One good strategy is to continue discussion with the others on different topics, denying the flamers the attention they seek. The problem, though, is that such people probably have a history of partial reinforcement for disrupting one group after another, and they may well persist, escalating the insults to get a rise out of someone. Any behavior on one of those variable ratio reinforcement schedules is notoriously difficult to extinguish. If a flamer gets nasty enough, sooner or later someone will give in and hand out the reward of attention by responding.

The total gag could be applied by the moderator if there is one, but most moderators believe in free speech and are quite reluctant to use this extreme form of behavioral control. Individuals in the group might decide to put the person's email address in the kill file list, but this is not all that effective as a means of discouraging the behavior, and in fact, some people brag about how many kill files they are on. The person could also just switch email accounts, or keep up the vitriolic debate with the rest of the group. In any case, even if you are eventually successful at shoving the person out of *your* group, you haven't done much toward improving the net's human climate.

Another, more difficult strategy is to watch for opportunities to use differential reinforcement by rewarding any rational and meaningful posts the person makes with lavish attention, but ignoring the flames.

For a single post, you might snip out the insulting remarks and just respond in a relaxed manner to valid points. Shaping, which involves rewarding successive approximations of the desired response, might also be partly effective. If you would like the person to come around, you might try responding to only the least contentious post. Then before you respond again, wait until the flamer sends something that comes closer to the desired tone.

Behaviorism as a comprehensive theory of human behavior has limitations, and the influence of this perspective in psychological research circles has waned. Human behavior is richer and more complex than the early behaviorists suggested, and the consequences of behavior – those rewards and punishments – are just one ingredient in the mix. Nevertheless, they are powerful tools and too few people use them to promote the kind of behavior that we want to see flourish on the net, and discourage the kind that poisons the virtual environment. Just as in real life, we often inadvertently reward the wrong things with attention and ignore the positive behavior.

PSYCHOLOGY OF THE INTERNET: THE NEXT GENERATION

In this tour through the psychological spaces of the Internet I have focused mostly on today's technology and the way we are acting and interacting inside the existing niches. Email, the World Wide Web, the asynchronous discussion forums, and the synchronous chats, MUDs and metaworlds, are all available now. Internet-based interactive video and voice are not widely dispersed, and often people in those spaces spend more time adjusting configurations or cursing dropped connections than they do interacting with one another. Yet, they, too, are out there, and people are using them to reach out to one another. So, what's next?

Another aspect of empowerment is our ability to influence what technological features are added to the online world, how the virtual living spaces we already have can be improved, and what new ones we might want. Based on what we know about human behavior online and how people are working and playing on the Internet, what new features would we ask for? What would we pay for? How will any new features change the psychology of the Internet as we understand it today?

Lee Sproull of the Boston University School of Management and Samer Faraj of the Robert H. Smith School of Business at University at Maryland, College Park, point out that that much of the net evolved as an information storehouse rather than a social technology, so the software tools developed for it stressed information storing, searching, and gathering.[209] We now have unbelievably powerful database technology, browsers, search engines, and reporting tools, and the content to rummage through is expanding rapidly. But the software and services we need to use the net for human interaction are far less developed. Our online groups flourished despite this benign neglect, however, which says something about how important this aspect of the net is to us. We struggle with arcane commands, buggy shareware, and dozens of different user interfaces to participate, and we certainly need improvements here. For many, it is still a badge of technical prowess to even be *on* a mailing list, and nontechies who have leaped the hurdles to try out groupware or enter a MUD are rightfully proud.

As these social software tools develop and become more standardized, we should see a shift away from the traditional social hierarchy on the Internet in which the technically savvy sit on top. We are also seeing a much wider range of people in the different psychological spaces, both in terms of demographic characteristics and interests. In chat rooms, for example, you can find people of all ages discussing religion in Russian or skiing in French. The dominance of the young-white-male-high-tech-American is fading rapidly in most corners of the net although our stereotypes about who we meet out there may not follow along as quickly. For instance, when the question of geographic location comes up, an American might say Cincinnati but a Korean would probably say Korea. Each is assuming something about the other based on lingering stereotypes of Internet demographics. The American assumes they are mostly Americans out there and they would know where Cincinnati is. The Korean guesses the conversational partner is not from Korea, so would not know where Pusan is, even though the city is the second largest in Korea, with a far more people than Cincinnati.

Widespread installation of that eyeball camera attached to your monitor with a suction cup is another advance that will significantly affect the Internet's environments. The net, as the all-purpose status equalizer and stereotype neutralizer, will change dramatically. For some people, the technology will add much improvement, but for others, it will mean an end to their ability to interact on a more level playing field, free from the heavy weight attached to physical appearance. Initially, the camera will

---

[209] Sproull, L., and Faraj, S. (1997). Atheism, sex, and databases: The net as a social technology. In S. Kiesler (Ed.), *Culture of the Internet* (pp. 35–51). Mahwah, NJ: Lawrence Erlbaum Associates, Publishers.

be an option and you will be able to choose whether you want to transmit a live picture. However, as time goes on and most people have one, your choice to turn it on or off will be part of the impression you make.

Consider, for example, a chat room for a distance education class in which all members appear as small talking heads on your screen. What will people think if you refuse their requests to turn on your camera? Are you so hideous that no one would talk to you if they saw your face? If and when interactive video becomes the norm on the Internet, all the stereotypes associated with physical appearance will rush back into the dynamics of social interaction. These are extremely powerful, as I explained in an earlier chapter, and the Internet's ability to eliminate most of them is – at the moment – one of its most important psychological features. The technology to enable Internet-based interactive video is sloppy right now, but it will get better quickly. Even if people in some Internet niches prefer to live without that cue, their voices may be drowned in a wave of technological determinism.

A simple feature in that interactive video software is the ability to flash your own image up on the screen, along with the moving pictures of your virtual groupmates. Technically, this is a no-brainer and will probably be the default in most software. Psychologically, however, it is dynamite. You will constantly glance back to your own image, checking your posture, adjusting your self-presentation, worried about how you appear to others. In a face-to-face conversation, you don't usually have a mirror handy to check out your appearance, and even if one were nearby you would seem exceedingly vain if you kept looking at it. Now, however, you will be able to watch yourself constantly without anyone knowing about it. Psychologists often use a mirror to increase people's self-awareness in experiments, and we know the simple act of watching yourself creates a wave of self-consciousness, turning a person's thoughts inward. I expect this barely noticed feature of interactive video software will drastically increase self-awareness and lead to significant changes in group dynamics on the net. The most confident among us will eventually decide to turn it off so we can participate more naturally and spontaneously in group discussions.

Virtual reality is another technology destined to tweak the psychological impact of many spaces in the net. The term means many things at the moment, from a simple screen display you can rotate or explore with your mouse, to elaborate headsets, gloves, computer-controlled chairs and body suits that stimulate many more sensory systems than just vision. Some of them cause motion sickness now, but they will improve.

Down the road, these "virtual" experiences will simulate "real" experience more and more closely. From a psychophysiological perspective, we don't experience the world directly anyway; we just use our sensory receptors to translate environmental energy into information our brains can process and interpret – neural impulses. Electromagnetic radiation strikes our retinas and the chemical reactions cause our rods and cones to generate neural signals that travel to the brain. Sound waves set our eardrums in motion and sensory cells in the cochlea convert the fluid vibrations into neural signals, headed for the auditory cortex.

It will be safer for our children to learn to drive in virtual reality simulators, and lots of fun to try virtual skydiving in our eighties. Therapists look forward to using virtual reality in desensitization programs, especially for people with phobias. Virtual reality experiences with spiders can be controlled with fine precision so the arachnophobe can become desensitized in tiny, progressive steps. But what would it be like to hold your family reunion in a virtual reality space? Or walk into a virtual party and actually smell the popcorn, or feel the sofa's cushion move when someone – outfitted in a holographic custom-designed avatar – sits next to you? I mentioned that the graphical metaworlds are a different environment compared to the MUDs, even though the themes are often similar. Many think the text-based MUDs are actually better for the imagination and social interaction because the graphical worlds are so clumsy and the multimedia elements so primitive and distracting. Click on "laugh," for example, and everyone hears the same guffaw, regardless of who did the clicking. Advances in virtual reality may make these spaces more appealing or just kill them off with an overdose of reality.

What will we choose for our Internet and what will we reject? Or will we just let Microsoft decide? Despite their vast power in the software business, they have had many early headaches and missteps with the Internet, and at first ignored it altogether. They figured out it was important, but then they initially failed to grasp its force as a social technology that turns power over to the people. Microsoft released NetMeeting, a business-oriented groupware product that allows people around the world to chat, exchange files, and work on one another's documents over the Internet. Soon after its debut, Microsoft's directory of NetMeeting users filled up with people eager to engage in casual flirtations and sexual exchanges with these innovative collaborative tools, bringing a new meaning to the term "groupware." Business users doing a software test drive were not impressed that Microsoft inadvertently moved the Internet a bit closer to Howard Rheingold's virtual reality vision of intimacy.[210]

We have many questions about the psychology of the Internet and few solid answers, but we do have much research on human behavior to guide us. Even though the Internet as a technology is a moving target, we humans behave predictably when dropped into certain kinds of environments, and social science research about the effects of the Internet's environments, in particular, is mounting. Some aspects of our virtual world bring out our best, others our worst, but if we understand why that happens we can do something about it – in ourselves and in the people we interact with online. And we have both the power and the responsibility to influence what happens on our global commons. Those vital virtual communities about which we have heard so much are built one brick at a time from a psychological perspective, and we can all contribute to them by remembering that they are made up of people with all the usual human frailties.

Jokes, legends, and hoaxes float around the Internet, catapulted from one list to the next and back again, over and over, until you have the same eerie feeling you get when you watch your socks going round and round in the dryer. Comedian Dave Barry tells of the time he wrote a column about how the Oregon State Highway Division used half a ton of dynamite to blow up a dead whale that had washed up on the beach, on the theory it would be easier to cart off many small parts rather one extremely large and smelly one. Someone posted the piece on the Internet without citing the source, and years later people continue to send him his own column, suggesting that he should write a column about it.[211]

Another widely disseminated bit of Internet humor of uncertain origin went something like this:

You have all heard that the laws of probability predict that a million monkeys typing away for millions of years on a million typewriters will eventually produce all the works of Shakespeare. Thanks to the Internet, we now know this is not true.

Shakespeare already did that, and we millions of Internet users have other work to do anyway.

---

[210] Rheingold, H. (1991). *Virtual reality.* New York: Simon & Schuster.
[211] Barry, D. (1996). *Dave Barry in cyberspace* (pp. 164–165). New York: Crown Publishers.

INDEX

Achievers, in Internet games, 96
Adamse, Michael, 154
Addiction, Internet, 178–181
  games and, 99
  life at the Palace example,
    185–186
  naming the affliction, 188–189
  as newbie disease, 186–188
  synchronous psychological
    spaces and, 182–185
Adolescents, 246–247
Adoptee's Mailing List Home Page,
  207
Age, impression formation and,
  21–22
Aggression. *See also* Flaming
  anonymity and, 124–126
  cathartic release of, 129–130
  causes of, 111–112
  frustration and, 112–113
  hair-trigger responses, 116–117
  Internet style and, 130–132
  over-retaliation, 123–124
  retaliation and, 117–119
  software and, 127–128
Aliens Online, 91, 93
Alpha World, 23–24
Altruism, 109–207. *See also* Helping
alt.support.depression, 191
American Civil Liberties Union, 106

America Online, 7
Angry.org, 129–130
Anonymity, 8, 239–242
  physical distance and, 124–126
Aronson, Eliott, 146
Asch, Solomon, 15, 59
Asynchronous discussion forums,
  5–6. *See also* Mailing lists;
  Newsgroups
Attention, need for, 249–251
Attraction, interpersonal, 136–138
  attitudes and ideas and, 141–142
  complementary relationships
    and, 143–144
  humor and, 147–150
  I like you- you like me spiral,
    144–145
  Internet and, 138–139
  Law of Attraction, 141–142
  power of gain and, 145–147
  self-disclosure and, 150–151
Attribution, 37
Auctions, online, 177–178
Authority, presence or absence of,
  9
Availability, heuristic, 158

Bargh, John A., 206
Barry, Dave, 253
Bartle, Richard, 96–99

Baym, Nancy, 148–149
Behavior moderation, 69–73
Belmore, Nancy, 11
Berkowitz, Leonard, 116
Best, Deborah, 209
Binik, Yitzchak M., 204
Bishop, George, 75–76
Blue Ribbon Campaign for online
    freedom, 106
Brail, Stephanie, 226–227
Brand, Stewart, 240
Brenner, Victor, 180
Brewer, Marilynn, 21
Britannia, 93–94, 225
Bruckman, Amy, 95

Cancelbot software, 132
Candid Camera, 59
Category priming, 25–26
Channel wars and takeovers, 132
Chat rooms, 6–7
    group size in, 196
    lag on, 115
    language usage in, 10–11
    operant conditioning and,
        184–185
    role play on, 42–44
Child Online Protection Act, The,
    167
Children, 246–247
Coates, Jennifer, 214
Cognitive miser, 19
Cold impressions, 15
Collot, Milena, 11
Colubine high school, 247–248
Communications Decency Act, 106
Confirmation bias, 26
Conflict and cooperation
    intergroup rivalries on Internet
        games. *See* Games, Internet
    intergroup tensions, 99–101
    Robber's Cave experiments, 89–90
Conformity, 59–61
    Leviathan and, 69–71

on the net, 62–64
reproaches and, 66–69
Conformity Game, 104–105
Connolly, Terry, 84
Conspiracies, 236
Copyright infringement, 243
Counseling on Internet, 203–204
Critical thinking, encouraging,
    245–246
Curtis, Pavel, 22, 29, 68, 71–73, 95,
    105
Curtis, Rebecca, 144
Cybersex, 152–155

Dabbs, James, 192
Danielson, Peter, 64
Darley, Jon, 194–195
Davis, Keith, 124
Deception
    detecting on Internet, 50–51
    in identity experiments, 49–50
    partners in, 51–53
    varieties of, 39
Deleters, 35
Demographics, and Internet addic-
    tion, 180–181
Deuel, Nancy, 53, 153
Dialectizer, The, 9
Dibbell, Julian, 231
Dick List, The, 131
Digital Citizens, 103
Discussion groups, 35. *See also*
    Workgroups
    language usage in, 11–12
Donnerstein, Edward, 164–165
Dovidio, John, 199
Dyson, Esther, 236

eBay, 26, 177, 178
E-commerce, 244–245
Electronic brainstorming, in online
    workgroups, 83–84
Electronic Frontier Foundation,
    106, 167

Electronic Privacy Information
    Center, 106
Elitist ingroups, 101–103
Elkind, David, 34
Email, 5
    addresses and impressions, 20–21
    anonymous or disguised, 126
    corporate, 86
    Internet conformity and, 62–64
    socioemotional expressiveness in,
        18–19
Emoticons, 18
Empowerment, 12–13
Expert-ism, 101–103
Explorers, in Internet games, 97
Eyeball cameras, 250

Family, Internet's role in, 248
Faraj, Samer, 251
Festinger, Leon, 123
First impressions, 15
Fiske, Susan, 19
Flaming. *See also* Aggression
    attention and, 250
    defining, 119–120
    flame wars, 118–119
    lab and field studies of, 120–122
    reproaches and, 122–123
Fleming, Patricia J., 202
Floyd, Kory, 134, 150
Forwarding frenzy, 86
Framing, 127–128
France, Anatole, 39
Frequently asked questions (FAQs),
    65
Friendships, online, 155–156. *See
    also* Romantic relationships
    involvement in, 134–135
    nature of, 135–136
    physical attractiveness and,
        136–138
    proximity and, 139–141
Frustration
    aggression and, 112–113

in Internet environment,
    113–116
Fuller, Rodney, 16
Fundamental attribution error, 37

Games, Internet
    gender identification in,
        224–225
    helping in, 191
    Internet rivalries on, 91–96
    player types and motivations,
        96–99
GammaMOO, 224
Gender
    behavioral differences, 208–210
    composition and interaction
        styles, 217–218
    conflicts between, 219–222
    distinguishing on Internet,
        214–217
    help responsiveness and,
        199–200
    hostile environments and,
        225–227
    identification in games, 224–225
    impression formation and,
        22–24
    interaction styles, 212–214
    language and, 210–212
    ratio on the Internet, 218
    stereotypes and, 216–217,
        218–219
    swapping and role play, 44–47
    women and men-only groups,
        222–224
GeoCities, 32
Gibson, William, 178, 185
Giffin, Holly, 40
Gilboa, Netta, 103
Goffman, Erving, 28–29
Goldberg, Ivan, 187
Grohol, John, 191, 206, 239
Group decision support systems
    (GDSS), 80

Group dynamics. *See also* Conflict
and cooperation
conformity, 59–64
defining group, 57–59
emergence of, 55–56
group formation and, 79–80
moderating behavior, 69–71
polarization, 73–78
reproaches and, 66–69
rules of behavior, 64–66
virtual work groups. *See*
Workgroups, online
Group power, Internet, 105–109
Group support systems (GSS), 80
Groupware, 80
Growing Up Digital, 168
Guidance, providing, 246–248
Gurak, Laura, 106–107

Hacker community, 102–103
Hacker Quarterly, 102
Harassment, online, 227–230
Hardin, Garrett, 242
Hayano, David, 51
Heilbroner, Robert L., 13, 235
Helping
asking for help, 201–204
effect of numbers and, 192–194
feelings of responsibility and,
194–195
gender differences and,
199–200
Internet numbers and, 195–198
Kitty Genovese case, 191–192
random acts of kindness,
190–192
similarity judgments and,
200–201
stigmatized groups, 205–206
support networks, 204–205
who helps whom, 198–200
Herring, Susan, 215–217, 221
Hightower, Ross, 81

Hillerstein, Laurel, 203
Hobbes, Thomas, 11, 69
Hochman, Eric A., 57
HomeNet study, 169–170
Home pages
impression formation and,
31–34
self focus and, 34–36
typical, 33
Homesteading, 32
Hughes, Thomas, 235
Hultin, Geoffrey, 142
Humor, 147–150
Hutson-Comeaux, Sarah, 213
Hyperpersonal mediums, 151

Identity experiments, 47–49
deception in, 49–50
pros and cons of, 53–54
Illusion conservation rule, 40
Imaginary audience, 34–36
Impression formation
categories and stereotypes and,
21–24
home pages and, 31–34
keyboard use and, 36–37
on-line self-descriptions, 30–31
rhythms of, 26–28
shortcuts, 19–21
types of impressions, 15
Impression management, 28–31
Information sharing, gender and,
216
Information sources, 245–246
Ingroups, Internet, 99–101
Interaction styles, gender and,
212–214
Interactive video and voice, 8,
250–251
Internet addiction disorder, 188
Internet Censorship Bill, 106
Intersection frequency, 139–140
IRCarnage, 132

Jake Baker case, 228–230
Jarvenpaa, Sirkka, 85–86
Jones, Edward, 124

Katzman, Sandra Lee, 215
Kelley, Merle, 218
Kelly, Janice, 213
Kendall, Lori, 225
Kiesler, Sara, 77, 120–121, 125
Killers, in Internet games, 97
Korenman, Joan, 56–57, 99
Koster, Raph, 95
Kraut, Robert, 172

La Femme Nikita, 176
Lag, 114–115
LambdaMOO, 22, 31, 68–69, 71–73,
    95–96, 105, 230–231
Language
    gender and, 210–211
    Internet, 9–12
    power and, 211–212
Latané, Bibb, 192, 193, 194–195
Law of Attraction, 141–142
Leakage, Internet, 41–44
Legends of Kesmai, 67–68
Leviathan, 69–73
Life at the Palace program, 185–186
Linder, Darwyn, 146
Lingenfelter, Dawn, 218
LINGUIST, 215–217, 221–222
Linguistic softeners, 18
Listener, 202
Loceff, Michael, 176
Locus of control, 173–175
    exercising control and, 175–177
Lorenz, Konrad, 111–112
Lotus Marketplace case, 106–109
Lurkers, 35
Lying, patterns of, 39

Mabry, Edward, 128
Machrone, Bill, 71

MacKinnon, Richard C., 69
Mailing lists, 5
    audience and, 35–36
    automatic filers and, 35
    group size in, 197
    self-presentation on, 30
MAMA patterns, 47–48
Mandel, Tom, 46, 57
Marx, Karl, 13
Masks, online. *See* Role play
Masquerades, online. *See* Role play
Matheson, Kimberly, 219
McKenna, Katelyn, 206
McLaughlin, Margaret L., 66
McLeod, Poppy Lauretta, 82
McMurran, Mary, 187
Megabyte University (MBU),
    220–221
Mehta, Michael D., 160
Men-only groups, 222–224. *See also*
    Gender
Mergy, Jonathan, 130
Metadiscussions, 237–239
Metaworlds, 8. *See also* MUDs
Mickelson, Kristin D., 205
Microsoft, 86, 254
Miller, Kim, 144
Minimal group phenomenon, 92
Minority opinions, in online work-
    groups, 82–83
Minors, pornography and, 167–169
Motta, Sheree, 154
Mr.Bungle affair, 230–231
MUDs, 7–8
    aggression on, 131
    category priming in, 25
    conformity and, 68–69
    gender issues in, 22–24, 53,
        224–225
    gender-swapping and, 44–47
    group size in, 196–197
    hostile environments on,
        225–226

MUDs *(continued)*
    moderating behavior on, 71–73
    operant conditioning and,
        184–185
    self-presentations on, 30–31
    sexual encounters on, 153–154
    socioemotional expressiveness in,
        19
    underlying dynamics of, 97–99
Myers, David, 75–76
Myers Briggs Type Inventory
    (MBTI) personality test, 16

Nationality, 24
Navigation problems, 115–116
Netiquette, 65
NetMeeting, 254
Net splits, 115
Newbies, Internet addiction and,
    186–188
Newsgroups, 6
    stigma groups and, 206
    support oriented, 204
Nicknames (nicks), 29–30
Nonverbal communication
    research, 15–17

On Aggression, 112
Online persona, 14–37. *See also*
    Impression formation
Operant conditioning, 183–184
Osborn, Alex, 83
Over-retaliation, 123–124

Palalcoholics, 187
Parks, Malcolm, 134, 150
PernMUSH, 30
Personality tests, gender differences
    on, 209–210
Person types and categories, 21–24
Player-killing (pking), 94
Polarization
    group, 73–76

group formation and, 79–80
on the net, 76–78
virtual work groups. *See*
    Workgroups, online
Pornography
    aggressive and violent, 163–165
    availability of, 159–161
    commercial *vs.* noncommercial,
        160–161
    protecting minors, 167–169
    psychological aspects of, 161–163
    sensationalizing cyberporn,
        157–159
    unique aspects on Internet,
        165–167
Priming, 25
Production blocking, 83
Psych Central, 206
Psychology of Addictions, The, 187

Relationships, complementary,
    143–144. *See also* Attraction,
    interpersonal; Friendships,
    online
Remailer services, 126, 131–132
Reno, Janet, 106
Reproachable conduct, 66–69
Reproaches, flaming and, 122–123
Retaliation, 117–119
Rewards, Internet, 249–251
Rhythms, in impression formation,
    26–28
Risky shift, 74–75
Robber's Cave experiments, 89–90
Rodin, Judith, 193
Role play
    as danger areas, 44–47
    on the Internet, 41–44
    origins of, 40–41
Romantic relationships. *See also*
    Attraction, interpersonal;
    Friendships, online
    enhancing, 151–152

fragility of on Internet, 155–156
physical attraction and, 137–138
virtual passion, 152–155
Rotter, Julian, 173
Ruedenberg-Wright, Lucia, 42
*Rule of the Net: Online Operating
Instructions for Human Beings,*
46
Rules of behavior, communicating
on the Internet, 64–66

Samaritans, The, 204
Savicki, Victor, 218, 222
Sayeed, Lutfus, 81
Section 2 mailing list, 175–177
Seiler, Larry, 107
Seinhardt, Barry, 167
Self-disclosure, online, 30–31,
150–151, 202–204
Sexpert, 203
Sexual encounters, 152–155
Sexual harassment, 226–227. *See
also* Gender
legal aspects of online harass-
ment, 227–230
Shea, Virginia, 65
Sherif, Muzafer, 89
Silberman, Steve, 45, 47, 48, 50
Skinner, B.F., 182
Skinner box, 182
Smith, Mark Ethan, 46
Social comparison, 76
Socializers, in Internet games, 97
Socioemotional expressiveness,
18–19
Software
angry responses to, 127–128
pirated, 243
tools, 252
Southerly, Bill, 70
Spears, Russell, 77
Sproull, Lee, 251
Status cues, 99

Status equalization phenomenon,
100–101
Stereotypes, gender, 216–217
perceptions and, 218–219
Stigmatized groups, support for,
205–206
Stoll, Clifford, 233
Stoner, James, 74–75
Suler, John, 185
SwampFox, 31
Synchronous chats, 6–7. *See also*
Chat rooms
Synchronous psychological spaces,
6–7, 182–185

Tajfel, Henri, 92
Tapscott, Don, 168
Taylor, Shelley, 19
Technological determinism,
234–236
Technological momentum, 235
The People vs. B.F. Jones, 228
Threads, 5
Threats, online, 227–230
Time sink aspect of Internet,
171–172
addictive properties of, 178–181
compelling nature of, 181–182
life at the Palace example,
185–186
locus of control and, 173–175
online auctions and, 177–178
synchronous psychological
spaces and, 182–185
Toading, 69
Tragedy of the commons, 242–244
#trivbot, 92, 93
Trolling, 101
Trust
deception and, 243–244
grassroots e-commerce and,
244–245
in virtual teams, 84–87

Turow, Joseph, 248

Usenet groups, 6, 66
Usenet search engines, anonymity
    and, 240–241
User names, impression formation
    and, 20–21

Verbal aggression, 117
Virtual groups, 58
Virtual reality, 253–254
Virtual work groups. *See*
    Workgroups, online

Walther, Joseph, 27–28, 140–141,
    151
Wanzer, Melissa Bekelja, 147
Warm impressions, 15
WELL, 240
Werry, Christopher, 115
Williams, John, 209

Witmer, Diane, 215
WMST, 215–217
Women-only groups, 222–224. *See
    also* Gender
Workgroups, online, 80–81
    biased discussion in, 81–82
    developing trust in, 84–87
    electronic brainstorming and,
        83–84
    minority opinions in, 82–83
WorldsAway, 224–225
World Wide Web, 4–5
Wyatt, Nancy, 56–57, 99
Wynn, Eleanor, 33

X-Files, 176

Young, Kimberly, 179, 181–182,
    184, 186

Zajonc, Robert, 139